REVELATION AND THE QUEST FOR UNITY

Revelation and the Quest for Unity

BY
AVERY DULLES, S.J.

with a foreword by
ROBERT McAFEE BROWN

CORPUS BOOKS
Washington—Cleveland

Corpus Instrumentorum, Inc.
1330 Massachusetts Ave., N.W.
Washington, D.C. 20005

First Printing 1968

Library of Congress Catalog Card Number: 68–10450

PRINTED IN THE UNITED STATES OF AMERICA

Foreword

It was the original intention of both author and publisher that Fr. John Courtney Murray, S.J., should write the foreword to this book. There could scarcely have been a more appropriate choice. Although history will remember him particularly as the architect of the Vatican II declaration on Religious Liberty (*Dignitatis Humanae*), and as one who over the years helped to lay the groundwork on which such a document could be based, Father Murray had nevertheless devoted much of his professional life to the problem of revelation. His St. Thomas More lectures at Yale University, published as *The Problem of God* (Yale University Press, New Haven, 1964), represented a profound grappling with the issue of revelation, through a treatment of the biblical problem (the presence of God), the theological problem (the understanding of God), and the contemporary problem (the death of God). With disarming clarity, Father Murray led his readers through a labyrinth of complicated material, and I venture the prediction that his wise comments on "the godless man" will be of continuing benefit long after the "death of God" theologians have disappeared from the scene.

Father Murray was at least as fully involved with the other pole of Father Dulles' title, "the quest for unity." For years, along with his colleague Father Gustave Weigel, Father Murray represented just about the sum total of American ecumenical

5

initiative from the Roman Catholic side, and he took the lead in persuading Protestants who were then still sceptical, that it *really was* possible to be a Roman Catholic and still believe in freedom of religious expression for non-Catholics. Few issues were more ecumenically tense in pre-Vatican II America than this, and it is due in large part to what Father Murray said in private and public for many years, at great personal risk and cost, that Vatican II finally, only hours away from its closing moments, promulgated into the official teaching of the Roman Catholic Church the kinds of things Father Murray had previously been silenced for trying to say.

On all counts, therefore, Father Murray should be writing the foreword to this book. That a Protestant is chosen to fill the pages left blank by his death (a choice that entails a high order of spiritual apostolic succession) is perhaps an appropriate symbol of what has been happening theologically, due to the groundwork laid both by Father Murray and by Father Dulles; when the title of the book promises an examination of revelation in the context of "the search for unity," the appropriateness is even further enhanced.

It would not always have been so. Indeed, as some of Father Dulles' historical essays so ably document, the situation in which a concern for revelation could be coupled with a concern for unity is a phenomenon of relatively recent origin. Until even a few years ago, as Father Dulles elaborates in his chapter "Reflections on 'Sola Scriptura'," Protestant and Catholic approaches to revelation tended to divide them from one another in what seemed an irrevocable fashion. For centuries, Protestants had assiduously cultivated every square inch of a garden named *Sola Scriptura*, had tried to develop theologies based exclusively on what could be grown in that soil, and had insisted that anything harvested beyond such clearly delimited boundaries could only be barren fruit, or, more probably, poisoned produce. For their part, Catholics insisted that there must be two gardens, one named Scripture and the other named Tradition, which, if they partly overlapped, had nevertheless each its own unique growth, so that only when cross-pollination had taken place could the plant of true faith come to flower.

Each stance (to abandon the agronomical metaphor) persisted partly for polemical reasons. Woe to the Protestant who in his view of Scripture allowed the tiniest foothold to tradition, since the cloven hoof of Romanism, having trampled upon the *sola*, would inexorably proceed to destroy the *Scriptura* as well, as the faith once delivered to the saints was transformed into the man-made traditions that had subtly replaced the true gospel, thanks to the work of conniving Catholic theologians. And woe to the Catholic who even intimated the possibility of any kind of primacy or sufficiency to Scripture, for that would constitute an admission that the Reformers had really had the right of it on their side, and would jeopardize the authoritative status of infallibly defined dogmas whose clear basis in Scripture was, to say the least, less than immediately self-evident.

What has delivered us from this impasse? What has happened so that Father Dulles, instead of describing revelation as the thorny issue that makes unity impossible, can now argue that revelation furnishes one of the most hopeful paths in "the quest for unity"?

The miracle of Pope John is surely one part of the answer, even though the forces at work re-thinking the meaning of revelation were present before he appeared on the scene. It can be said, however, that he liberated Catholic ecumenical concerns of this sort, even if he did not initiate them. From the Protestant side it can be argued that the advent of Pope John made Protestants open to the possibility that new currents could emerge even with what at that time seemed to us the repressive atmosphere of official Roman Catholic thinking. We Protestants could thus take seriously the writings of Father Murray, even when it was clear that those writings were causing consternation within the Holy Office. The ethos created by Pope John began to persuade even us that the final arbiter of Catholic truth might someday turn out to be other than the Holy Office. A miracle, indeed.

But behind the phenomenon of Pope John lies a more fundamental fact, of which he was an exemplar, and of which the present writings of Father Dulles furnish additional evidence. This was the recognition, slowly developing in both Catholic and Protestant circles, that no institution, no theologian, no manual of dogmatic theology, no group of venerable cardinals sitting in Rome, either has, or ever can, put the truth about God in a final and perfect form. However the truth is expressed, it is in part at least conditioned by the time and place of its utterance, so that there is always another way in which it could be expressed, in principle at least as good and perhaps better than the old way, and possibly more appropriate for another time and place. The terms appropriate for one era may well be lacking in communicative and persuasive power for another era. Thus, while Jesus Christ is indeed the same yesterday, today, and forever, our attempts to illumine and convey and discuss that treasure are always contained in frail earthen vessels that may need to be shattered and re-shaped. Pope John himself made clear that while the substance of the Gospel does not change, the forms in which it is clothed not only can but must change—hence the Council, as an orderly means by which the updating necessary for our time could proceed.

The same point has been made by a Protestant theologian often quoted in the pages that follow, Paul Tillich. Tillich often spoke of "Catholic substance" and "Protestant principle." There is the on-going "Catholic substance," the *depositum fidei*, the givenness of what God has done for man. But this is always being corrupted by men, by theologians, even by churches, who claim too pure an understanding and possession of that substance so that they confuse their statements about ultimate reality with the reality itself. In this situation, we always need "the Protestant principle," the protest against any attempt to elevate a finite structure or system to the place where it is beyond criticism, where it becomes an idolatrous object of worship rather than a vehicle through which that which is more ultimate than itself can be conveyed.

Now there is a sense, of course, in which this is not a revolutionary idea at all, for surely few Protestant or Catholic theologians, if pressed, would have insisted that their particular way of putting things constituted an irrevocable final way of communicating the truth. But there have not until recently been many Catholic theologians who were willing to suggest that Catholic theology needed revamping, and that many former ways of putting things (such as the "two sources" theory of revelation referred to above) were not only archaic but positively misleading. Nor were Protestant theologians falling over themselves to acknowledge that Luther and Calvin had spawned certain aberrations—or at least if they were, it was not occurring to such theologians to look in the direction of Roman Catholic theology for corrective insights.

What has happened, in other words, is that both Protestants and Catholics have come to accept unambiguously the watchword that Protestants once thought was theirs alone, *ecclesia semper reformanda*, the Church always in process of being reformed. Since we can never exhaust or contain within our theologies the full meaning of God's revelation—that out of sheer grace he condescends to visit and transform us—we must always be exploring anew the implications of that blazing and unlikely and transforming fact.

It is this new spirit that one discovers breathing through all of Father Dulles' essays. In saying this I do not mean to imply that he is a kind of crypto-Protestant, but, conversely and precisely, to insist that he is a true Catholic, that he realizes that because God had bequeathed to his Church the task of ongoing reflection about his truth, the Church can never cease from that task of ongoing reflection. But it must be "ongoing"—it cannot and must not become static. Theology can never be only repetition of human and ecclesiastical speech from another era; it must be continuing reflection upon the primal fact and reality which elicited human and ecclesiastical speech in the first place. All honor, of course, to the Church Fathers who have gone before—and the Catholic theologian undoubtedly pays them much greater honor than his Protestant counterpart can yet muster up, and the Protestant will still have more difficulty than Father Dulles has in saying *vox Ecclesiae est vox Dei*. But the honor to be accorded them is not the honor of repeating their words mechanically; it is rather the honor of reflecting with them about the reality to which their words, and ours, continue to try to point.

Father Dulles' book sets a pattern in another way for the new theological "style" that must come to characterize the era of ecumenical theology into which we are now moving. In the past, we were accustomed to tilling our own soil, whether Protestant or Catholic, without much regard for one another, save to uncover materials useful in controversy. Protestants would quote Catholic theologians on grace in order to show how they had reduced grace to an impersonal "substance," and thus destroyed the biblical notion (so obvious to those reading Holy Scripture free from Catholic bias) that grace is relational rather than abstract. Catholics would quote Protestants on everything under the sun to demonstrate that Protestants made appeal only (in the notorious phrase) to "the right of private judgment," and that sheer religious anarchy was the only possible outcome.

From this era of polemics we then moved to a time of warm if gingerly appraisal of one another, in which we began to discover that there were nice chaps over there even if they did believe strange things, and that it was now possible to talk and write about the fact that in talking and writing we still disagreed about certain fundamentals. But withal, it was a refreshing breakthrough to get it all out in the open.

That era of ecumenism, I believe, has just about run its course. We are now embarking upon an era in which ecumenism, at the level of fundamental theological investigation, will not have to restrict itself to the subject matter of ecumenism. Instead of thinking about ecumenism, we will be able to think ecumenically. Instead of working out procedures for listening and responding to one another, we will simply get on with the business of listening and responding. Instead of making self-conscious use of one another's materials, we will be able to dispense with the question, "Is the writer a Protestant or Catholic?" and simply ask, "What does he have to say?" We will not look for Protestant and Catholic treatments of revelation, but will simply look for the best available study on revelation, whether Protestant or Catholic, realizing that we can trust the author not to grind his own ecclesiological axe to such a degree that he distorts the evidence. (Looking around this fall for a book on the Church to use in an undergraduate course on theology, it struck me as not the least unusual that the one I finally chose was entitled *The Dimensions of the Church*, by Avery Dulles, S.J., nor was I surprised while reading it to discover that fully a fifth of it is devoted to the implications for an understanding of the Church in the theology of Dietrich Bonhoeffer.)

And the thing which most impresses the Protestant who reads *Revelation and the Quest for Unity* is that Father Dulles' concern with Protestant theologians is not centered on a desire to score points against them but to learn from them. Tillich, Cullmann, Barth, Bornkamm, and others appear in these pages primarily as the purveyors of insights and not simply (as would have been true in an era not long behind us) as perpetrators of spurious doctrine. Without false eirenicism, Father Dulles manages to say—even of the "death of God" theologians— "What are these people saying that is important, that we need to hear, that we may be overlooking?" and out of this kind of approach to create the fruitful insights conveyed in the present book.

It would be hard to overestimate the kind of gain this represents. And although some of Father Dulles' chapters deal specifically with Protestant thinkers as interpreted from a Catholic viewpoint, there are others where he is dealing with a basic theological problem—be it myth, symbol, revelation, hermeneutics, or authority—and dealing with it in such a way that the whole range of contemporary theological reflection, whether Protestant, Catholic, or Orthodox, is called upon. This surely represents the "style" of theology for the future—a recognition that with all our remaining differences (which Father Dulles never fuzzes over in an effort to be superficially genial, as Chapter 5 makes quite clear), we still share the same concern about the same problems, and that no one of us can any longer afford to explore those concerns and problems without entering into consultation with the others.

A few years ago this would have been quite unthinkable. A few years hence it will be taken quite for granted. And the publication of *Revelation and the Quest for Unity* represents a fulcrum by means of which that change of location is now taking place.

Robert McAfee Brown

Contents

Introduction

With reference to Catholic theology, the decade 1956–66 is remarkable for dramatic advances in two important fields—the theology of revelation and the theology of ecumenism. These twin developments are closely interconnected. Renewed contact with Protestant theology in the years following World War II stimulated Catholics in their efforts to elaborate their own theology of the word of God. It is difficult to imagine what our contemporary Catholic theology of revelation would be like, had it not been for the impact upon us of thinkers such as Karl Barth, Rudolf Bultmann, Paul Tillich, and Oscar Cullmann, whose names appear so often in the pages of this book. Without them we can scarcely see how we could have found our way beyond the jejune apologetics of the period following World War I.

The theology of revelation, so largely sparked by Protestant influences, itself became a powerful impetus toward further ecumenical rapprochement. We Catholics came to recognize more fully that the word of God, as it resounds outside the juridical limits of the Roman Catholic communion, can effectively awaken the response of faith, and that therefore a genuine community of faith exists among all believing Christians. Even when they are divided into separate ecclesiastical bodies, they are still intimately linked together inasmuch as they all listen to the word of God which comes to mankind, today as formerly, in Jesus Christ, the living and eternal Word.

The two theological developments just described were consecrated and crowned by two of the finest documents of Vatican Council II—the Constitution on Divine Revelation and the Decree on Ecumenism. These documents are closely connected in their doctrine as in their authorship. It is highly significant that Cardinal Augustin Bea, the president of the Secretariat for Promoting Christian Unity—and thus the man chiefly responsible for the Decree on Ecumenism—was one of the two co-presidents of the Mixed Commission which redrafted the Constitution on Divine Revelation. The revised schema, which was to win approval, explicitly recognized the ecumenical dimension of revelation. It stated that the word of God is "a powerful instrument in the mighty hand of God for attaining to that unity which the Saviour holds out to all men" (n. 21, 4).

Vatican II, while it sanctioned the theological advances of the preceding decade, by no means brought them to a halt. Rather, the Council may be expected to serve as the starting point of a new and more vigorous line of development, the precise directions of which have yet to emerge in clarity. Presumably, the several Christian traditions will be forced into a more fruitful, and less self-conscious, collaboration, as all together seek to respond to the challenges of an ebullient secularity which brashly proclaims, now triumphantly and now dejectedly, the death of the Christian God. All Christian theologians should feel the urgent need for a deeper and more realistic theology of revelation, better adapted to the particular needs and insights of the age in which we live.

Toward this development the present essays would hope to contribute. Written during the past decade, many of them reflect the concerns of a period in which the several Christian traditions—especially Protestantism and Roman Catholicism in Western Europe and America—were cautiously exploring their points of agreement and divergence. But the achievements of these years must not be minimized. A clear understanding of what has been accomplished is, I believe, the necessary condition of fruitful progress in the decade to come. For those who might wonder about the pre-history of the various papers in this volume, the following information may be of interest.

Chapter 1, "Myth, Symbol and the Biblical Revelation," originally appeared in *Theological Studies* 27 (1966) 1–26, and has been reprinted in *New Theology No. 4* (eds.) M. E. Marty and D. G. Peerman (New York, 1967).

Chapter 2, "The Theology of Revelation," was first published in *Theological Studies* 25 (1964) 43–58 as a review article of the French edition of Latourelle's book by that title. The article has been slightly revised to take account of the English translation of that work, printed in 1966.

Chapter 3, "Reflections on 'Sola Scriptura,'" here published for the first time, is in substance the text of a conference given in Baltimore to a Missouri Synod Lutheran Ministerial Association on Oct. 16, 1963.

Chapter 4, "The Constitution on Divine Revelation in Ecumenical Perspective," was delivered orally at the Paulist Fathers' "Institute for Religious Understanding" in Boston on Dec. 14, 1965. It was printed in the *American Ecclesiastical Review* 154 (1966) 217–31, and has been somewhat amplified at several points to take cognizance of conciliar documents and other literature not yet available when the lecture was given.

Chapters 5 and 6, "The Church and the Faith of Catholics" and "The Church and the Faith of Protestants," are based on two lectures given at the Boston College Centenary Theological Institute in June, 1963. They have not previously appeared in print.

Chapter 7, "The Protestant Preacher and the Prophetic Mission," appeared as an article in *Theological Studies* 21 (1960) 544–80. Some additions have been made to bring it into line with more recent theological literature.

Chapter 8, "The Orthodox Churches and the Ecumenical Movement," was an article in the *Downside Review* 75 (1957)

38–54. I have considerably expanded the article for inclusion here, to take account of the important developments since the Evanston Assembly of 1954.

Chapter 9, "The Ecumenical Perspectives of Popes John and Paul," was originally a lecture given at a Day of Ecumenism at Boston College, April 11, 1964. The section on Pope Paul VI was published in the *Catholic World* 200 (Oct. 1964) 15–21.

Chapter 10, "Ecumenical Dialogue and Apostolic Renewal," was composed for the Third Annual Study Week of the Christophers in New York City, July 19–23, 1965. First published in the *American Ecclesiastical Review* 103 (1965) 300–15, it was reprinted in the *Catholic Mind* 64 (March 1966) 43–53.

Chapter 11, "Paul Tillich and the Bible," originally appeared in *Theological Studies* 17 (1956) 345–67, and was reproduced in T. A. O'Meara, O.P. and C. D. Weisser, O.P. (eds.), *Paul Tillich in Catholic Thought* (Dubuque, 1964) 109–32.

Chapter 12, "Jesus as the Christ: Some Recent Protestant Positions," is based on a lecture given for the Christian Culture Series at the Paulist Information Center, Boston, March 27, 1963. It appeared in article form in *Thought* 39 (1964) 359–79.

All the material that appeared previously in the above journals is used with permission.

Chapter 13, "The Death-of-God Theologies: Symptom and Challenge," here printed for the first time, was originally given as a lecture at Purdue University, Nov. 2, 1966.

All of these talks and essays have been retouched, and in some cases notably supplemented, to bring them into line with the achievements of Vatican II, with my own current thinking, and with at least some of the recent literature. The fact that revisions have been necessary makes it obvious to the author that it would be futile, even now, to claim any definitive value for his statements. If our generation has one special lesson for the theologian it is perhaps this: that he must feel content, and indeed privileged, if it be given to him to˙speak to his own time, and thereby to hasten the obsolescence of his own achievement. By accepting this situation, theology will be better equipped to fulfill its servant role.

PART ONE

REVELATION AND ECUMENISM

1

Myth, Symbol, and the Biblical Revelation

If revelation were a collection of eternal and necessary truths concerning God, the soul, and immortality—as some rationalists contended—the proper style of theological speech would not differ from that of philosophy. If the stuff of revelation were common historical facts—as some positivists seemed inclined to think—theology could speak the language of ordinary history. But revelation has to do with the hidden God and the ways in which He calls man into union with Himself. Its doctrine is, therefore, sacred doctrine; its history, sacred history. At every point the subject matter of theology touches on mystery. And how can mystery be expressed? Unlike historical or abstract truth, mystery cannot be described or positively defined. It can only be evoked. Religious language must contrive to point beyond itself and to summon up, in some fashion, the gracious experience of the mystery with which it deals.[1]

The Bible employs a great variety of literary forms. It is a small library containing historical records, poetic effusions, theological meditations, dramatic dialogues, hortatory epistles, etc. But in practically every biblical book we find exceptionally vivid and imaginative speech. The inspired imagery of the Bible may surely be reckoned as one of the main sources of its spiritual power. The biblical images astonish our expectations, grip our attention, challenge our receptivity, haunt our memory, stir our affections, and transform our attitudes. While the Bible is not lacking in doctrine, its language suggests far more about God and His ways with man than it conveys by express concepts. From the crude anthropomorphisms of Genesis to the luxuriant visions of the Apocalypse, the Bible proves itself a treasure house of vivid and majestic symbolism.

This very wealth of symbolism, however, is sometimes considered to be a stumbling block for modern man. Some are of the opinion that the "mythopoeic" idiom of the Bible has had its day, and that the educated man of the twentieth century must be given a religion in statements which he can clearly analyze and verify. Others maintain that while symbolism as such is a constant feature of religious communication, the symbols of the Bible are outmoded. The biblical imagery, emanating from a type of pastoral and patriarchal society which has vanished in most parts of the globe, is said to be beyond the grasp of modern man. Still others, more attached to what they revere as the divinely given sources, feel that the Bible has lost none of its power, provided it be properly studied and expounded. The main obstacles to Christian communication, according to these conservatives, come, not from the language of Scripture, but from the human philosophical categories into which the Christian message has all too often been transposed. A return to biblical language, it is contended, could spark a great revival of Christian faith and devotion.

In view of these difficult but urgent questions, considerable attention is currently focused on the question of symbol and myth in the Bible. What role does each of these actually play in the canonical writings? Are the biblical images themselves canonical—in the sense of pertaining to the substance of the revelation—or are they expendable? If they are expendable, should we try to devise new myths and symbols to take the place of those which are no longer appropriate? Or should we seek to "demythologize" the Bible by setting forth the Christian message in a language purged of mythical and symbolic elements? This essay, without claiming to solve these thorny problems, will perhaps throw light on a proper approach to them.

THE ROLE OF SYMBOL IN THE BIBLE

It would be tedious to begin with a long investigation of the exact nature of religious symbolism.[2] Very briefly, we may say that a symbol is a type of sign. It is a word, gesture, picture, statue, or some other type of reality which can be made present to the senses or the imagination, and which points to a reality behind itself. But this other reality is one which cannot be precisely described or defined; it is not knowable, at least with the same richness and power, except in and through the symbol. The symbol has power to evoke more than it can clearly represent because it addresses itself, not simply to the senses and the abstractive intelligence, but to the entire human psyche. It works on the imagination, the will, and the emotions, and thus elicits a response from the whole man. Symbols, therefore, have an existential power which is lacking to purely conventional or conceptual signs. Symbols are of vast importance, not simply for cognitive purposes, but also for the integration of the human personality, for the cohesion of human societies, and for the corporate life of religious groups. A religion without symbolism would be unthinkable.

Symbols may be found in the natural world, in the events of history, and in the inventions of art and literature. The Bible abounds in literary symbolism, thanks to its poetic and vivid style; but, more fundamentally, it is symbolic because it has to do with symbolic realities, especially with symbolic historical events.

The central theme of both Testaments is quite evidently the great series of mighty deeds by which God manifested His mercy, His loving power, and His enduring fidelity toward the people of His choice. These deeds may be called God's gestures in history, and, like human gestures, they are symbolic. The divine deed par excellence is the miracle. A miracle, according to the biblical conception, is a sign-event in which a properly attuned religious consciousness can recognize, so to speak, the handwriting of God. For those who have eyes to see and ears to hear, the miracles are eloquent. Like Caesar's wounds, they have tongues of their own.[3] They reveal, with compelling realism and vividness, what Paul calls the "philanthropy of God our Saviour" (Tit 3:5).

Quite apart from particular miracles—the true value of which has unfortunately been obscured by the opportunistic apologetics of a rationalistic age—the entire history of Israel constitutes, one may say, an immense continuing deed of God, and stands as an everlasting reminder of God's justice and mercy. The individual operations of God which punctuate this history—such as the crossing of the Red Sea, the manna in the desert, the entry into the Promised Land, and the return of the exiles from Babylon—are heavily charged with symbolic overtones, magnificently brought out by the figurative and hyperbolic language of the inspired accounts. Viewed in connection with their New Testament fulfilment, these events take on a fuller and more abiding significance.

In the New Testament the Incarnate Word is the absolute, unsurpassable earthly embodiment of God, and hence the supreme religious symbol. But for Christ to be effectively a symbol for us, He must be manifested for what He is. Jesus' mighty deeds, His symbolic actions (such as the cleansing of the Temple or the Eucharistic action at the Last Supper), His total self-oblation on Calvary, and God's acceptance of that sacrifice in the Resurrection and Ascension—all these events symbolically disclose various aspects of His person and mission. In Christ and the Church the religious symbolism of the Old Testament was "recapitulated"—in the rich sense given to the term by Irenaeus—and fulfilled beyond all expectation.

If we wish to fathom the true nature of symbol, we could not do better than to ponder a central Christian reality, such as the cross. Here, in a simple and easily imagined figure, we have a vast wealth of meaning that speaks straight to the human heart. The cross, as Susanne Langer has pointed out, evokes a whole gamut of related significances:

Many symbols—not only words, but other forms—may be said to be "charged" with meanings. They have many symbolic and signific functions, and these functions have been integrated into a complex so that they are all apt to be sympathetically invoked with any chosen one. The cross is such a "charged" symbol: the actual instrument of Christ's death, hence a symbol of suffering; first laid on his shoulders, an actual burden, as well as an actual product of human handiwork, and on both grounds a symbol of his accepted moral burden; also an ancient symbol of the four zodiac points, with a cosmic connotation; a "natural" symbol of cross-roads (we still use it on our highways as a warning before an intersection), and therefore of decision, crisis, choice; also of *being crossed*, i.e. of frustration, adversity, fate; and finally, to the artistic eye a cross is the figure of a man. All these and many other meanings lie dormant in that simple, familiar, significant shape. No wonder that it is a magical form! It is charged with meanings, all human and emotional and vaguely cosmic, so that they have become integrated into a connotation of the whole religious drama—sin, suffering, and redemption. . . .[4]

For reasons such as these, the cross performs in an eminent way what all symbolism tends to do: it binds up the shattered, alienated existence of individuals and gives meaning and direction where these previously seemed to be absent. It also serves to bring men together into solidarity with one another. Christians of all ages and nations are welded into a community by their common allegiance to the standard of the cross.

Thus far we have been speaking of the symbolic realities which form the substance of the biblical message. If we turn now to the language of Scripture, we immediately note that it is highly figurative and frequently poetic. The sacred writers quarry their images from many sources. Sometimes they build on the natural symbolic capacities of elemental realities such as fire, water, sun, bread, wine, and the like. Other images they take over from the social institutions of Israel. Thus, they speak of God as Father, King, Judge, Shepherd, Vine-dresser, and Spouse. And all these images, once they have imbedded themselves in the literature and thinking of Israel, begin to take on a history of their own, parallel to that of the people. As Austin Farrer has observed,[5] calamities

Myth, Symbol, and the Biblical Revelation 25

such as the collapse of the Davidic monarchy, the destruction of the Temple, and the Babylonian captivity providentially served to purify the images, to detach them from their terrestrial moorings, and in this way to give them a higher and more universal spiritual meaning. To give but one example: it was necessary for the Davidic monarchy to be irrevocably overthrown before the term "Son of David" could be an apt designation for the kind of Messiah Jesus was to be.

The literary imagery of the Old Testament was taken up with added power in the New. Christ described His own status in terms of the Old Testament figures. The parables which He preached are replete with Old Testament reminiscences. The Johannine Gospel, the most symbolic of the four, is built about dominant images such as the Good Shepherd, the True Vine, the Manna, the Living Water, and the Light of the World. Such symbols, as C. H. Dodd remarks, "retire behind the realities for which they stand, and derive their significance from the background of thought in which they had already served as symbols for religious conceptions."[6] The same is true in varying degrees of the other New Testament writings. The most highly figurative of all is, of course, the Apocalypse, which writes of heaven and things to come—that is, as Austin Farrer puts it, "of a realm which has no shape at all but that which the images give it."[7]

The abundance of symbolism in the Bible is not a matter of whim or accident. The language of everyday prose would be incapable of mediating the loving approach of the all-holy God with comparable warmth and efficacy. The inexhaustible riches which theologians and men of prayer have been able to find in the Bible would seem to be intimately bound up with its inspired symbolism; for every symbol, by reason of its concreteness and polyvalence, defies exhaustive translation into the abstract language of doctrinal discourse.[8]

The coexistence in Scripture of symbolic realities and symbolic language poses an obvious problem for the exegete. In many instances it is most difficult to ascertain whether the biblical writers intend to report an actually symbolic event or have supplied the symbolism in order to convey some theological insight. The infancy narratives of Matthew and Luke, because of their peculiarly literary genre (generally classified as midrashic), are a case in point. It may eventually be agreed that some of the incidents in these narratives are not, in the modern sense, historical events; but one cannot lay it down as a general principle that symbolism in a narrative is evidence against its historical realism. On the contrary, the central mysteries of the Christian faith derive much of their symbolic value from their historical reality. The cross, for example, is a compelling symbol of our redemption precisely because the Son of God was truly crucified. And the Resurrection is a symbol of our new life in Christ because it vividly declares what God has actually done for us. Some modern interpreters, especially outside the Catholic Church, are too ready to let the symbolism of language do service for the symbolism of actual deeds. Such an attitude is ultimately at odds with the realism of the Incarnation; it is more congenial to ancient Gnosticism than to normative Christianity.

MYTH: ITS NATURE

As a form of symbolic thought and expression, myth plays a central role in many, if not all, religions. Our consideration of Christian symbolism, therefore, raises inevitably the problem of Christian mythology. Can it be admitted that myth has a function in revelation, in the inspired Scriptures, in the Christian religion? These questions are large and divisive. In order to approach them fruitfully, we must form some approximate idea of what the term "myth" means or should mean in such contexts. The very meaning of the term is much disputed, and the diversity of opinion on the questions just posed is largely due to this variety of definitions.

   For some writers, practically any numinous symbol may be characterized as myth. If myth is whatever points up the permanent spiritual dimension of events, thus linking them with their divine ground, it is obvious that any religion, including Christianity, must have its mythology. John Knox, working with a very wide concept of myth, says that if modern man cannot accept myth, religion is no longer a possibility.[9]

But the problem of myth is more acutely posed if one defines myth, as most do, in a narrower sense. Brevard S. Childs, in an important study,[10] distinguishes among several current meanings. First, there is the view of the so-called "mythical school" of Old Testament critics (Eichhorn, Gabler, and G. L. Bauer), for whom myth is a primitive form of thinking in which unexplainable events are attributed to the direct intervention of deities. Second, there is the Form-Critical definition, held by the two Grimm brothers, W. Wundt, and H. Gunkel, who look on myth as any story in which the active persons are gods. But neither of these two definitions is satisfactory. The first rests upon the unspoken rationalistic assumption that only a primitive mind could attribute anything to an interposition of divine power. The second definition is too exclusively literary, and fails to do justice to the numinous and cultic dimensions normally associated with myth. A fanciful story told merely to entertain the imagination, even if some of its characters were deities, would not appear to deserve the name of myth.

It seems best, therefore, to arrive at our definition of myth— as Prof. Childs proposes—by a phenomenological method, taking advantage of the findings of modern ethnology and the history of religions. John L. McKenzie, in a recently reprinted article,[11] gives a very helpful synthesis, lining up some of the principal characteristics of myth, at least as found in the religious literature of the ancient Near East. Relying on studies such as this, one may list the following traits as characteristically mythical:

(1) Myth is a communal possession. In most cases myths have their origin in a very distant past, and are folk creations. If a modern author deliberately constructs a myth, this can be only an imitation of the ancient anonymous myths which have been handed down in tradition. And it will not really obtain

currency as myth unless it is accepted by a community as a symbol and carrier of its concrete form of life. It must be, as Wellek and Warren put it, endorsed by the "consent of the faithful."[12]

(2) Like other symbols, a myth is a figurative representation of a reality which eludes precise description or definition, but in contrast to the rather sophisticated symbolism of parable and allegory, mythical symbolism involves a minimum of critical reflection. The myth-maker thinks and speaks quite naively, without any effort to determine the extent to which his story corresponds to, and falls short of, the reality to which it points.

(3) Myth deals with a numinous order of reality behind the appearances of the phenomenal world. If there is an animistic stage of religious evolution, in which men divinize the objects of nature themselves, this stage deserves to be called premythical. The properly mythical phase presupposes that man has learned to make some distinction between nature and its transcendent ground.[13] Only when this insight has been achieved does man look to the actions of the gods as offering an explanation of what is experienced in the world.

(4) The numinous presence which myth discerns behind the world of phenomena is portrayed in personal terms. This does not mean that the god or gods are clearly recognized as being persons. Myth, being essentially vague, and closely bound to imaginative thought, would be incapable of conveying a definite judgment about whether the transcendent is ultimately personal, but the forces behind the world are at least depicted as if they were persons.

In a wider sense, the concept of myth can be extended to include impersonal agencies, provided these are hypostatized. In this looser usage, one may speak of the myth of inevitable progress, or the myth of democracy, but since the personal reference is lacking, we do not have myth in the strict sense. If a force such as progress is portrayed as a god or goddess, this can be only by the merest artifice.[14]

(5) The transcendent figures of the mythical world are represented as taking part in activities on a cosmic scale, which

exert a permanent causal influence on earthly happenings. Each particular myth aims to account for a whole series of recurring phenomena, such as the rhythm of the seasons, the variations of weather, the alternation of night and day. To all such events one may apply what McKenzie says of the fertility gods: "The gods of fertility are not merely symbols of natural forces; the succession of phenomena depends on the perpetual life-death cycle on a cosmic scale, and these gods make the cycle."[15]

(6) The cosmic event is expressed in the form of a story, a drama which unfolds in a dimension of duration quite removed from time as we experience it. As Eliade says, "mythic or sacred time is qualitatively different from profane time, from the continuous and irreversible time of our profane existence. . . . The myth takes man out of his own time—his individual, chrono-logical, 'historic' time—and projects him, symbolically at least, into the Great Time, into a paradoxical instant which cannot be measured because it does not consist of duration."[16] Through cultic action the mythical events are brought to bear upon particular earthly situations.

The time dimension proper to myth is of great impor-tance in distinguishing myth, not only from static types of symbolism (such as a skull or a flag), but also from legends, tales, and sacred history. Legends or sagas are imaginary, divinatory amplifications of events which are located in history. Tales take place in an indefinite time, "once upon a time," but not in a distinct species of time which causally underlies the time we experience on earth. Sacred history, as we shall see, unfolds in the dimension of irreversible, earthly time, and is, therefore, not mythical.

(7) The stories of myth are not told for their own sake. As we have already indicated, they deal with matters of intense concern to man. Thanks to mythical symbolism, as Eliade says, "man does not feel himself 'isolated' in the cosmos. . . . He 'opens out' into a world which, thanks to a symbol, proves 'familiar.'"[17] This existential import gives myths their religious value and their holding power, but myths vary in the immediacy with which they are connected with the present concerns of man. This will appear

from any of the standard classifications of myth by reason of their content. Following Tillich,[18] we may break down myths into categories such as (*a*) theogonic, (*b*) cosmogonic and cosmological, (*c*) anthropological, (*d*) soteriological, and (*e*) eschatological. All these areas are capable of being treated mythically insofar as realities within them are attributed to actions of the gods described in the form of symbolic narrative.

A final question about the nature of myth may now be raised. Is it necessarily polytheistic, or does the notion of myth prescind from the alternatives of polytheism and monotheism? Of itself, myth is not a doctrine, but a mode of thinking and expression. It might seem, then, that a man could think mythically about one god as well as about many, but the content of myth cannot surpass the capacities of mythical representation. Since the rhythms of nature are apparently manifold and mutually opposed, myth can hardly look upon the divine ground as being other than multiple. For the same reason, this ground will be viewed as closely involved with the forces of nature, and as having some kind of successive duration, ambiguously related to time as we know it. Of itself, myth cannot criticize or rise above these limitations in its own mode of representation.

In summary, then, we may conclude that myth, at least in the sense in which we shall use the term, is a particular type of symbol. It is a symbolic narrative which deals with events attributed to super-human, personalized agencies. These events, unfolding in a time above that of our experience, are conceived as having a profound influence on the typical occurrences familiar to us. Through the recital and cultic re-enactment of the myths which it accepts, a community feels itself delivered from the grip of cosmic forces, and, on occasion, brought into union with the divine. Not all these elements, of course, will be equally prominent in every instance. There are borderline cases which it is hard to classify as myth or legend or simple tale. Some authors may wish to give a wider or narrower meaning to the term "myth" than ours, but the description given in the preceding paragraphs is not arbitrary; it has a solid basis in the usage of many acknowledged authorities, and commends itself by its relative clarity.

THE ABIDING VALUE OF MYTH

From the Enlightenment until the twentieth century, myth was generally characterized as a primitive mode of thought, practically devoid of value as an approach to truth. This point of view is reflected in the definition in the Oxford English Dictionary: "A purely fictitious narrative usually involving supernatural persons, actions, or events, and embodying some popular idea concerning natural or historical phenomena." The assumption behind all such definitions is that while primitive, prelogical men may have taken myths seriously, modern man goes to them only for entertainment or relaxation. The myth in itself says something false. If it contains a hidden grain of truth, this can and should be restated in strictly rational terms.

Modern studies in fields such as depth psychology and the history of religions have brought about a far-reaching rehabilitation of myth. It is rather commonly regarded today as a distinct mode of knowledge which can never be adequately reduced to rational discourse. Some contemporary thinkers, under the influence of a Kantian epistemology, stress chiefly the value of myth in the subjective order. Cassirer, for instance, considers that it registers states of soul which cannot be otherwise expressed.[19] For Jung, the study of myths affords new insights into the structure of the human psyche, inasmuch as myths have their source in the archetypes of the collective unconscious, and never cease to emerge from it, at least in the forms of dreams and fantasies.[20]

A second group of modern thinkers who defend the permanent validity of myth are known as "symbolico-realists." They prefer to stress the transsubjective content revealed by mythical symbols. Eliade, for instance, has explained at length how the myths of polarity and reintegration in many religious traditions—for example, the myth of androgyny—disclose the structure of the divine as *coincidentia oppositorum*, thus lending support to the whole tradition of Christian negative theology from Pseudo-Dionysius to Nicholas of Cusa.[21] Tillich, building on the religious philosophy of Schelling, agrees that myths, as a source of knowledge, have independent value. Symbols concerning divine figures and actions, he holds, are uniquely apt for relating man to the object of his ultimate concern, which is the proper domain of religious faith.[22]

While he looks on myth as an abiding religious category, which can never be simply left behind, Tillich acknowledges that, in a certain sense, we live in a postmythical age. Once critical thought has been applied to religious questions, mythical portrayals of the gods, as involved in the flux and multiplicity of natural phenomena, are seen to be inadequate. The divine is grasped as unconditionally transcendent; but in the postmythical period the myth survives, according to Tillich, as a symbol or pointer to the divine. It is no longer taken literally, but is understood to be, precisely, a myth. In being recognized as such, it is, in a certain sense, demythologized; it becomes what Tillich likes to call a "broken myth." Thereafter both myth and critical thinking coexist, Tillich affirms, in a state of correlation or dialectical tension. Neither succeeds in completely eliminating the other.

Many authors object that a myth, once it has been "elucidated into a symbol," no longer remains a myth in the true sense of the term.[23] Others maintain that it remains a myth properly so called, for it is still accepted as an element of community tradition which, in some mysterious way, answers to the deeper aspects of experience.[24] Tillich's term, "broken myth," seems to combine what is valid in both these approaches. While the application of critical thinking represents a real advance over the merely mythical mode of conception, it does not fully displace the latter. Even for modern Western man, Greek myths such as those of Prometheus, Oedipus, and Sisyphus, although clearly distinguished from historical events, have not lost their psychic power. They continue to speak to the depths of our existence, and help to reintegrate us with ourselves and our universe. If this be true even of pagan myths, we must consider seriously whether there cannot be such a thing as Judeo-Christian mythology.

The very term will seem shocking to those who look upon religion exclusively as revelation, and upon revelation as a collection of dogmas set forth in strict propositional language. But if religion is a dialogue between man and God, and if revelation is the whole process by which God draws near to man and manifests His presence, one must keep open, at least provisionally, the possibility that the divine presence might be apprehended and registered in mythical thought and expression. Without prejudice to the dogmatic content of revelation, which is certainly not mythical in the sense described above, it seems possible to hold that the doctrines are sometimes surrounded by a penumbra of thinking and speech that deserves to be called mythical. If myth is ever a bearer of revelation, we should expect to find that this is true in the Holy Scriptures.

MYTH IN THE BIBLE: A PRIORI CONSIDERATIONS

Catholics and conservative Protestants have often expressed the view that myth can have no place in revelation or in the Bible. Billot, for instance, wrote that since myth is a product of popular credulity or is invented by the learned to foster popular credulity, God could not inspire such a thing.[25] Benoit, in the French edition of his *La prophétie* (1947), after observing that it is not for us to decide antecedently what literary forms are or are not worthy of God, adds in a footnote: "There is nevertheless one type which must, a priori, be excluded from the Bible as unworthy of God: this is 'myth'—for it introduces error and fiction into the very essence of religious speculations about the divinity."[26]

As a partial explanation for these negative judgments, it may be pointed out that these authors, and the Church documents to which they appeal,[27] presuppose the "rationalistic" notion of myth which was popularized by the "mythical school" already mentioned. But it is also doubtless true that Catholic authors, until very recently, took it too much for granted that revelation occurred through objective historical events whose meaning was determinately given, prior to any intervention of the human mind. If we hold that God made Himself known, not simply through historical happenings "which impinge from above upon Israel, and to which she subsequently adds subjective reflection," but rather through "the total experience of Israel," the question of myth presents itself in an entirely new light.[28] Like other creative expressions of the Israelite spirit, myths might well serve as building blocks of the great temple that was to receive its capping stone in Christ. We believe, therefore, that myths cannot be excluded on principle from the Bible on the ground that they are "fabula religiosa falsa" (Nicolau, no. 188), but that the question should be resolved a posteriori. We should examine what is actually to be found in the biblical books, conducting this search in the light of the notion of myth we have derived from comparative religion and ethnology.

MYTH IN THE OLD TESTAMENT

At first sight it would seem that myth bulks large in the Old Testament. Competent scholars are practically unanimous in recognizing in many sections of the Old Testament, especially in Genesis, reminiscences of myths which can likewise be found in Sumerian, Accadian, and Canaanite literature.[29] The stories of the formation of the world, the Garden of Eden, the Flood, and the Tower of Babel—to cite several well-known examples— would seem to be adaptations of primitive myths such as we find in other cultures. But once we allow the presence of *mythical elements* in the Bible, the question still remains intact: Are they still *myths* as they appear on the pages of Scripture?

From the beginning of their existence as a people, the Israelites had an overriding conception of Yahweh that cannot be written off as myth. As McKenzie says, myth, when left to its own resources, remains imprisoned in the order of shifting phenomena; it merely retells the story of the phenomenal world on a larger scale, and is incapable of attaining the divine in its transcendence.[30] Since the time of Gunkel it has been a commonplace that Israel was not favorable soil for myths, since they link the divine with nature in a way contrary to that of the Bible, and are basically incapable of overcoming polytheism.[31] As distinct from all the mythical gods, Yahweh is constantly portrayed by the Israelites as unique, free, and totally sovereign over every other power in heaven and on earth.

Closely linked with the absolute sovereignty of Yahweh is the fact that the Bible disavows all nature religion. Barth is fundamentally right in holding that the Bible deals from first to last with God's historical action. Not everything in the Bible is history in the modern and technical understanding of the term; much of it is rather saga, i.e., a poetic and divinatory elaboration on history.[32] But saga, like history, claims to deal with unique and unrepeatable events, whereas myth does not intend to be, but merely pretends to be, history.[33] The creation account in Genesis, far from falling in the same category as the Babylonian cosmogonies, may be viewed as a polemic against them. According to Barth, it asserts precisely what myth cannot grasp, namely, the transcendent and creative act whereby God gave the universe an absolute beginning.[34]

The central faith of Israel undoubtedly rests, not upon mythological construction, but upon a privileged religious experience giving the people and its religious leaders a singularly vivid knowledge of Yahweh as Lord of the universe. This insight issued in firm doctrinal affirmations, in exclusive claims, and in a demand for total commitment—responses in no way required by myth, which can coexist quite contentedly beside its own contrary.[35]

Since their essential faith was nourished by something quite different from myth, it is not surprising that the Israelites produced no mythology of their own. They did, however, borrow from the mythologies of the surrounding peoples, and in some cases subjected these to a process of demythologizing which is, at best, relatively complete. For example, In various references to the creation, we find allusions to mighty struggles between Yahweh and mysterious monsters such as Leviathan and Rahab (e.g., Ps 73 [74], Ps 88 [89], Is 27, Job 9, Job 20).[36] What have we here if not a mythical representation—not false but not fully translated into doctrinal terms—of the ceaseless conflict between Yahweh and the powers of evil? In other passages, such as the mention of the sexual intercourse between the sons of God and the daughters of men (Gn 6.4 ff.), the myths seem to have been only lightly retouched, and to remain, as Childs points out, in partial tension with the fundamental faith of Israel.[37]

In the later portions of the Old Testament the mythological elements are subjected to stricter control. The prophets use mythological themes with considerable detachment and deliberation to suggest the quality of events which had not been revealed to them in detail. Especially is this true of the accounts of the creation and final consummation. Dodd gives a good explanation:

> These first and last things can be spoken of only in symbols. They lie, obviously, outside the order of time and space to which all factual statements refer. They are not events (as the historian knows events), but realities of a suprahistorical order. In referring to them the Biblical writers make free use of mythology.[38]

The entire process, which leads from the earliest traditions of Genesis to the latest contributions of the postexilic prophets, may be characterized as a continual process of demythologizing.[39] The primitive pagan myths, which gave concrete expression to man's longing for divine deliverance from the hostile powers, are gradually answered by divine revelation. As the answer is heard and assimilated, the myths are progressively purified, broken, and sublimated, but for the fulness of the answer, we must look beyond the Old Testament.

MYTH IN THE NEW TESTAMENT

The question of myth in the New Testament has been the subject of lively controversy in recent years, and requires some special treatment, even in so brief a survey as we are attempting. The New Testament itself uses the term "myth" in a definitely pejorative sense. On four occasions in the Pauline pastoral epistles, *mythos* is denounced as contrary to revealed truth and sound doctrine.[40] Moreover, 2 Peter vehemently declares that the Christian faith is founded on solidly attested facts, vouched for by eyewitnesses, and is therefore totally unlike "cunningly devised myths (*mythois*)" (2 Pt 1.16). The very fact that the New Testament writers, toward the close of the first century, are obliged to warn the faithful so insistently against following myths, and to remind them that the gospel itself is no myth, implies that there was enough similarity so that some Christians were confusing the two. If the gospel is so closely related to myth, we may well ask whether myth did not, in fact, gain some foothold in the New Testament.

Since the early nineteenth century, various scholars have argued that the New Testament is heavily infected with myth. To simplify a complex chapter in the history of modern theology, we may content ourselves with a brief sketch of three main "mythicizing" positions.

(1) The first great movement in this direction was influenced, on the one hand, by the rationalistic Old Testament critics (G. L. Bauer and others), and, on the other hand, by the idealistic philosophy of Hegel in particular. David Friedrich Strauss, the most eminent representative of this movement, maintained that the central truth of Christianity— namely, the idea of God-manhood—initially emerged in mythical form, which was the only way in which the men of the day were capable of accepting such a lofty idea. Strauss's conception of myth, substantially taken over from the "mythical school," included every kind of intrusion of religious ideas into historical narration. Adapting Christianity to the *Zeitgeist* of the modern age, as he understood it, Strauss systematically rejected miracles and supernatural revelation.[41] Some of his successors in the Hegelian school, outstripping even Strauss in their mythomania, went so far as to deny even the historical existence of Jesus.

(2) Early in the twentieth century, and especially in the 1920's, the history-of-religions school gave a new account of the

mythical elements in the New Testament.[42] They maintained that great numbers of the early Christians were converts from the Hellenistic mystery religions, which consequently exerted a decisive influence upon their understanding of their new faith. For many of these former pagans, the mystery god simply acquired a new name, Jesus of Nazareth. Thus, the Christian doctrine of the resurrection of Jesus owed much to the pagan myths of gods who died and rose; the Sacraments of Baptism and the Eucharist were Christian counterparts of what had previously been practiced in the worship of Attis, Serapis, and other deities.

(3) The most recent champion of the mythical view of the New Testament is Rudolf Bultmann. In a series of writings which go back to the 1920's—and especially in a controversial article published in 1941[43]—he has argued that the New Testament is thoroughly imbued with myth, notably in the three crucial areas of cosmology, eschatology, and Christology.

The cosmology, he maintains, is mythical, since the New Testament writers accept a three-decker view of the universe, in which the earthly realm is subject to constant incursions from numinous powers who inhabit the heavens above and the underworld below. The course of history is largely shaped by the incessant struggle between the spirits of light and darkness, who seek to wrest it to their own ends. In this supernatural dualism Bultmann finds traces of Iranian mythology.

As regards eschatology, the early Christians, according to Bultmann, took over the contemporary Jewish ideas concerning the coming drama of the end-time. This was to be ushered in by the advent of the Antichrist and a season of great tribulation. Then the Messiah would appear in glory, the dead would be recalled to bodily life, the nations would be judged, and the elect admitted to the heavenly banquet.

In the realm of Christology, Bultmann finds that the figure of Jesus was heavily overlaid with Jewish mythical expectations concerning the Messiah, the Son of Man, and the Suffering Servant. Even more significantly, the Christology of Paul and John, he holds, was influenced by the Gnostic myth of the primal man (*Urmensch*), which seems to have been Iranian in origin, but was widely current by that time in the Near East.

In developing his thesis, Bultmann contends that the New Testament ideas of the incarnation and virginal conception of Jesus, His miracles, His bodily resurrection and ascension, are all mythical. This mythology has become a grave obstacle to the preaching of the gospel, for modern man can no longer understand or accept it. Bultmann himself proposes a fascinating existential reinterpretation of Christianity. The Church, he maintains, must summon man to decision and authentic existence, but this summons can be issued without invoking those elements of the New Testament which Bultmann, in his existential reinterpretation, discards as mythical.

To attempt any general critique of Strauss, of the *religionsgeschichtliche Schule*, or of Bultmann would take us far beyond the scope of this essay. The only question which concerns us is whether they have shown that the New Testament is, to a great extent, shot through with myth.

In the first place, it may be noted that both Strauss and Bultmann use the term "myth" in a very wide sense, to include practically everything they themselves reject. For Strauss, it embraces all allegedly supernatural events, much that we should call legend, and even poetic passages. For Bultmann, every assertion that God is active in the physical world is forthwith dismissed as mythical; so, also, everything betraying a prescientific approach to physics, medicine, or astronomy. By bracketing under a single term such radically diverse materials, these authors have tended to confuse the discussion.

Proceeding from a carefully considered notion of myth, not unlike that adopted in this essay, Heinrich Schlier has written a very helpful article on myth in the New Testament.[44] He lists three possible sources from which such myths might conceivably have originated: (1) contemporary Jewish apocalyptic, which sometimes made use of symbolic schemata to depict the unfolding of celestial events; (2) the Gnostic myth of the primal man, the redeemed Redeemer, which may have been current in the Mediterranean world at this time; (3) the Hellenistic and

Oriental mystery religions with their dying and rising gods—although these are scarcely known to us except from post-Christian sources which afford no direct evidence for the period that concerns us.

As regards the apocalyptic elements, we may concede, with Schlier, that the New Testament borrows ideograms and terminology from the apocalyptic passages in Isaiah, Daniel, and other Old Testament prophets, as well as from the further development of these forms in intertestamental Jewish apocalyptic. The Synoptic Gospels, Paul, 2 Peter, and the Apocalypse, freely make use of such stereotyped imagery in referring to the eschatological events which will bring time to a close. When they speak of the days when the sun will lose its brightness, when the last trumpet will be sounded, when the elect, both living and dead, will be summoned to sit at the Messianic banquet, they are surely aware of the limitations of human language in dealing with such matters. They would, no doubt, be hard pressed to draw a precise line between their own doctrinal affirmations and the symbolic imagery in which these are clad, but are they using myth? The doctrinal context of these passages, their reference to a determinate future, and, above all, the conscious employment of sophisticated literary forms, differentiate these apocalyptic scenes from myths in the strict sense we have adopted. The mythical elements have been taken up into an expression of eschatological faith. To the extent that critical thought has not completely penetrated the primitive imagery, we may admit the existence of a certain "mythical residue" in these passages; but there are no grounds for dismissing the whole New Testament teaching concerning the end-time as myth.

The other two ostensible sources of myth are somewhat problematical. Part of the difficulty comes from our lack of knowledge as to the forms which Gnostic speculation and the Hellenistic mystery cults had assumed by the first century. It seems probable that there were myths about, not unlike those known to us from the second and third centuries. We cannot antecedently deny that such myths may have influenced the New Testament writers.

At least it is clear that the Gospel was not radically mythicized. Nowhere in the New Testament do we find a full-blown mythical tale; we find only fragments and suggestions of myth. The faith of the community is evidently built upon a particular historical person, His actual death at some moment of world history, and His actual resurrection, the nonoccurrence of which would reduce the Christian religion to an empty tale (cf. 1 Cor 15.14). The events and the interpretation which faith set upon them may be judged true or false, but they do not share in the radical ambiguity of myth, which hovers in a twilight zone between truth and falsehood, between time and eternity.

Some would say that these events are historicized myth, but this term is, I think, inept. It implies that the history of salvation, as set forth in the New Testament, belongs in the same category as stories about Greek and Hindu gods. This confuses the deliberate affirmations of Christian faith with the hazy dreams of a far less demanding type of religion. The central message of the gospel, which concerns the supreme intervention of God in the course of human history, is far removed from myth, but the good news had to be set forth in a way that would reach the whole man, including the very depths of human consciousness. Symbolic, and even mythical, forms of expression could, therefore, serve as vehicles for communicating the gospel. There is no need to deny that Christian believers in the first century, or even in the twentieth, have often thought and spoken about the contents of their faith in a somewhat mythical style. Something of the tension between *logos* and *mythos* which we have already noted in the Old Testament remains in the New, even after the Logos has Himself appeared on earth.

To identify the precise passages in which mythical thinking survives is a matter of detailed exegesis which would go beyond the limits of this essay. The New Testament scholar might consider, for example, whether there is not a mythical component in the Q-narrative of the temptation of Jesus in the desert. Perhaps this scene comes as close to anything in the Gospels to verifying the notion of myth proposed earlier in this article, but its collocation in the life of a historical individual, together with the heavy doctrinal and typological emphasis, prevents us from speaking, even here, of myth pure and simple.

Because of the power of myth to speak to man in the depths of his existence, it is quite intelligible that the apostles may have used mythical language in order to bring home to their hearers, and even to themselves, the full significance of the Christian kerygma. No one doubts that, in their preaching to the Jews, they exploited to the full all the Old Testament themes which seemed to fit their purpose. They applied to Jesus, with sovereign liberty, whatever the Old Testament had to say about the Messianic King, the Son of Man, the Son of God, or the Suffering Servant. In addressing pagans or converts from paganism, they might be expected to adopt similar techniques, explaining the gospel in terms of the religious thought characteristic of the Gentiles (cf. Acts 17.23).

It is presently controverted among New Testament scholars to what extent Paul and John were influenced by Gnosticism and the mystery religions. Without attempting to solve this disputed question, we may say that such influences should not be ruled out on a priori grounds. If the Gnostic myth of the redeemed Redeemer seemed to illustrate well the meaning of Christ's death and resurrection in its cosmic and heavenly dimensions, there is no reason to think that Paul would not have exploited it in the service of the exalted Christology which we find in Colossians and Ephesians. So too, in his efforts to bring the Hellenistic communities to appreciate the wonderful effects of Baptism and the Eucharist, Paul could have consciously borrowed from the language of the mystery religions.

Christ, in the perspectives of faith, appears as an answer to the hopes and prayers of all mankind, pagans as well as Jews. If Messianic prophecy expressed the hopes and longings of Israel, myth was the vehicle in which the Gentiles set forth their deepest anxieties and presentiments. "In daring to take over the language of myth," Schlier asserts, "the New Testament shows that Jesus Christ is the end, not only of the Law, but of myth besides."[45] Here we may recall the remark of Harnack: "In Christ the primal figure (*Urbild*) of all the myths has become history."[46]

This process of restating the Christian message in language influenced by pagan myth and mystery—the first beginnings of which may be indistinctly discerned in the New Testament itself—was to be carried much further, perhaps even too far, in the following centuries. Christian art and poetry did not hesitate to depict Christ in the form of Hermes, Orpheus, and Odysseus, and to apply to Him, the true Sun of Justice, what the pagan myths had undeservedly attributed to the sun-god Helios. The reasons for such procedures are apparent from the words which Clement of Alexandria addressed to the cultured pagans of his day: "Come, I will show you the Word and the mysteries of the Word, and I will give you understanding of them by means of images familiar to you."[47]

PERMANENT VALUE OF THE BIBLICAL SYMBOLISM

The boldness with which the early Christians transposed the gospel into new patterns of thought is highly instructive. At the beginning of this essay we raised the question, to which we may return in closing, whether the traditional Christian symbolism is not obsolete. The example of the early Christians themselves suggests that the symbolism may be changed; faith can never be bound to a single set of images. The overwhelming realities of revelation are such that they can never be contained within a single set of terms. Those who wished to evangelize and catechize in the Greek-speaking world found the terminology of Judeo-Christianity provincial and unintelligible. They abandoned titles such as "Son of Man," which was almost meaningless to Gentile Christians, and treated the title "Christ" almost as if it were a proper name. Their boldness should be an encouragement to the contemporary Christian who feels that his idiom has become strange to the secular mentality of our day.

Does this mean that the biblical symbolism is outmoded? The question cannot be answered by a simple yes or no. A balanced attitude must steer clear of both archaism and modernism. Archaism would treat beginnings as if they were final; it would take the fundamentalistic position that the Church can use no terms, images, or concepts not positively authorized by the Bible; it would practically convert preaching into Bible-reading.

The modernist extreme would say that the Church is not bound to her own origins, that she can devise new ways of thinking and speaking without having to justify them by an appeal to the past.

In a balanced view, the historical experience of the people of God, as enshrined in the Old and New Testaments, is recognized as perpetually normative. Foundations are given once for all; they cannot be replaced. Christianity, as a historical revelation, must always look back to its origins, and develop in continuity with them. Scripture, even in its imagery, pertains to the patrimony which God has permanently entrusted to the Church for its study, contemplation, consolation, and guidance, "that the man of God may be made perfect, equipped for every good work" (2 Tim 3.17).

It will, of course, be objected that the symbols of the Bible are based on a very naive and archaic world picture, but are they, for that reason, less valid? The ancient cosmology, which pictures the divine abode as above and the underworld below, while it is scientifically obsolete, retains much of its power as symbol. The picture of a God high above us corresponds well with the Christian doctrine of His transcendence. So likewise, the simple relationships of pastoral and patriarchal life, which supply so many of the biblical images, have close counterparts in ordinary human experience. Eliade can therefore say:

> We may even wonder whether the accessibility of Christianity may not be attributable in great measure to its symbolism, whether the universal Images that it takes up in its turn have not considerably facilitated the diffusion of its message. For, to the non-Christian, one question occurs first of all: how can a local history—that of the Jewish people and of the first Judaeo-Christian communities—how can this claim to have become the pattern for all divine manifestation in concrete, historical time? I believe we have pointed to the answer: this sacred history, although in the eyes of an alien observer it looks like a local

history, is also an exemplary history, because it takes up and perfects, these transtemporal Images.[48]

It seems clear, on the other hand, that the biblical images do not furnish sufficient materials for evangelizing the increasingly secular and urban world in which we live. It is therefore urgent, as Pope John XXIII declared, to restate the Christian message in "the literary forms of modern thought." But the challenge is not new. At no time in her history has the Church been content to reproduce mechanically the symbols of the Bible. It continually forges new ciphers to convey more adequately that which, in its full reality, bursts the bonds of any human language.

Abundant examples of the incessant creativity of the Christian imagination could be found in the visual arts or in poets such as Dante and Milton. To adduce but one example, we may note how the medieval artists, relying on the bestiaries of the time, depicted Christ as a pelican, feeding its young with its own blood. The image helped to bring home to medieval man what was already implied in the biblical images, which attribute our redemption to the blood of Christ, freely shed for our sake, and which represent Him as inviting us to drink of the blood of the Son of Man.

In a thriving Christianity the creation of secondary images of this sort goes on apace. At times they may even seem to overshadow the biblical imagery, somewhat as in New Testament times the symbol of the heavenly Lord assumed priority over the older symbol of the Son of Man. But the new images, devised for the needs of a particular culture, are never completely new. They look back to the great ideas and symbols in Scripture. Like new doctrines, they are ultimately controlled by the primary sources from which they stem.

There is no need to minimize the problem of bridging the cultural gap between biblical times and our emerging technopolitan civilization, but it would be a mistake, I suggest, to concede too quickly that the biblical images should be cast aside. If some of them are less immediately available for popular preaching, they can continue to nourish the thought of the preachers themselves. Remaining in historical and spiritual continuity with the people of God in biblical times, the Church will not wish to shelve the memory of the experiences by which God originally manifested Himself to the prophets and apostles. The biblical symbolism which enshrines these experiences will always remain a primary object of study and meditation. And it is doubtful that the faithful will ever cease to look upon God as their Father and Lord, or upon Jesus as the Good Shepherd and the Lamb of God. These inspired symbols form part of the patrimony by which the minds, imaginations, and emotions of the Christian people are to be formed and educated.

2

The Theology of Revelation

To a great extent the history of Catholic theology mirrors in reverse the history of heresy. In a panoramic view we can distinguish three great eras in the development of heresy, each more radical than its predecessors. Before the Reformation the chief point at issue was most commonly whether this or that particular doctrine was revealed, and creeds of ever-increasing complexity were framed to set forth orthodox tenets against heretical pretensions. In the sixteenth century, attention shifted to the norms of revelation. Whatever the first Reformers may have intended, the dispute between Catholics and Protestants soon became focused about the methods of finding out what was contained in revelation. It became urgent to ascertain the canon of Scripture, the value of "unwritten" tradition, and the authority of popes and councils. Finally, in the course of the past century, Rationalists and Modernists called into question the very existence of supernatural revelation, thus occasioning the pronouncements of Vatican Council I and the anti-Modernist documents on faith and revelation.

A CONTEMPORARY CONCERN

Corresponding to these three stages of heresy, we may distinguish three major periods in the development of theology. Prior to the

Reformation, primary attention was given to special dogmatics, which became systematically enshrined in the great medieval *Summae*. In the post-Reformation period, fundamental theology began to emerge as a distinct discipline. The treatises *De ecclesia* and *De locis theologicis* took shape. Most recently, the theological study of revelation itself has gotten under way. The present century has seen the first systematic efforts along this line.

Almost inevitably the initial studies in this field were strongly apologetical in tone. They sought to establish, against the caviling of adversaries, that God can reveal Himself, and has, in fact, done so in Christ. But the controversial tracts and seminary manuals produced in this polemical atmosphere gave all too little attention to the crucial dogmatic questions. Hardly anyone stopped to ask what revelation, concretely, is, what are its structural features, how it comes to man, and precisely how it is connected with grace and salvation. Is it, for instance, a system of speculative truths beyond the scope of philosophy, which nevertheless need to be known if man is to direct his life toward its last end? Or is revelation rather a living encounter in which man becomes linked in friendship with God, who opens up His heart to the creatures of His predilection? These and similar questions must be answered by a rigorous examination of the data of Scripture and tradition.

To construct a sound and credible notion of revelation is an urgent task in our day, both for the Church's dialogue with the surrounding world, and for her own internal development. It is increasingly apparent that the major religious cleavages among Christians are, in no small measure, due to divergent views concerning revelation. Even more obviously, the profound abyss between believers and infidels is constituted by the acceptance or denial of revelation itself. Those who deny revelation are always in danger of slipping into some form of atheism, for a God who does not speak can, with great difficulty, be recognized as personal. From a pastoral point of view, the Catholic faithful must be made more keenly aware of the salvific power of the word of God. A unilateral stress on the Sacraments as means of grace has, all too often, obscured this point. For the progress of

Catholic theology, likewise, a more intensive study of revelation is in order. Without it we can hardly hope to give a plausible answer to various pressing questions, such as the development of dogma, the uses of Scripture, and the nature of tradition. Recent debates about the so-called sources of revelation have often been rendered sterile by a lack of agreement about what revelation really is.

Protestants in our century have contributed importantly to this branch of theology. E. Troeltsch and H. R. Niebuhr wrestled earnestly with the problems inherent in the historicity of revelation. Barth and the dialectical school forged a dynamic theology of the word, conceived as a vertical intervention of the transcendent God, who never places Himself at man's disposal. Bultmann and the existential theologians have boldly faced the task of distinguishing between revelation itself and the time-conditioned world views of those to whom it comes. Contemporary Anglican divines are engaged in a deep exploration of the role of imagery and symbolism in God's speech to man. Catholic theologians have recently begun to take part in all these discussions; they are eager to assimilate the best insights of other Christian thinkers. Thus far, however, we have lacked a comprehensive survey of the problem of revelation as it now stands in Catholic theology.

René Latourelle, Professor of Fundamental Theology at the Gregorian University, has now given us a lengthy monograph on this subject, the fruit of a decade of unremitting labor.[1] He divides the main body of his treatment into five parts, corresponding to the standard phases of theological inquiry: the scriptural data (61 pp.), the Fathers (76 pp.), the theological tradition (94 pp.), the magisterium (63 pp.), and the author's personal speculation, including his reflections on Vatican II (176 pp.). The most conspicious qualities of the book are its comprehensive scope, and the familiarity it evinces with the pertinent literature in English, French, German, Italian, Spanish, and Latin. Accurate and up-to-date references are given to innumerable books and articles. This abundance of information is matched by synthetic power. Without oversimplifying complex issues, Latourelle succeeds in bringing the multiple data of tradition, and the paradoxical features of revelation itself into a measure of systematic unity. Notwithstanding a certain tendency to be verbose and repetitious, he has an attractive style of writing and a serene piety which make his book appealing, readable, and spiritually satisfying. In summary, it may be said that this book will go far to set the dogmatic treatise on revelation on a sound footing and to open the way for further detailed studies. It will presumably remain the standard Catholic work on the subject for some years to come. The publication of this study in the French original, before Vatican II completed its deliberations on the schema, *De revelatione*, was especially propitious.

THE BIBLICAL DATA

Latourelle's section on the Old Testament is an excellent recapitulation of the fruits of twentieth-century biblical theology. Beginning with the rather primitive manifestations of the patriarchal period (in which theophanies and oracles predominate, with divinatory techniques and dreams still playing a considerable role), a gradual progress is noted toward the high period of Israelite revelation. In the Sinai Covenant, the Law is grasped as God's revealed will; in the prophetic literature, God's promises and imperatives confront His people with dynamic urgency; and in the historical writings, the blessings and misfortunes of Israel are set forth as divine visitations. Finally, in the wisdom literature and the Psalms, we have the inspired response of human meditation and worship to God's gracious initiatives.

This portion of Latourelle's survey is an admirable introduction to the multiple strands of the Old Testament idea of revelation, bringing out the recurring themes of God's magnanimous liberty and man's duty to respond to it in trust and obedience. The progressive nature of revelation, slowly advancing toward its completion in the final age, is clearly shown. Perhaps it is not entirely evident how much authority Latourelle wishes to claim for the Old Testament ideas of revelation. He apparently has no wish to deny that primitive superstition, legend, and anthropomorphism have left certain traces on the sacred page. Such an admission in no way compromises the essential point: that the Old Testament in all its length and breadth is a divinely given adumbration of the definitive revelation which was to be accomplished in Christ. The New Testament revelation is intelligible only against the background of the Old.

Latourelle divides his discussion of the New Testament into five sections, concerned respectively with the Synoptics, Acts, Paul, Hebrews, and John. In the Synoptics, he notes, Christ's revelatory office is centered about His functions of preacher and doctor and His unique filial relationship to God. In Acts, the apostles are seen as heralds of Christ's revelation, thanks to their position as eyewitnesses, and the powerful help of the Spirit. The Pauline notion of revelation centers about the idea of *mystērion*: the disclosure of God's plan to restore all things in Christ. Hebrews contrasts the Old and New Covenants on the basis of the relations between the word of the prophets and the word of the divine Son. Finally, in his exposition of John, Latourelle gives an interpretation of the Logos-doctrine based largely on Boismard; he expatiates also on the Johannine theme of *martyrion*, showing how the Father and Son bear witness to each other.

This chapter, while containing many elements of value, is in some ways disappointing. The Synoptic Gospels are treated too much as if they were unsifted factual memories, although, as Latourelle elsewhere recognizes (pp. 350, 386, note 5), the entire Christian literature was deeply affected by the experience of the Church under the guidance of the Holy Spirit.[2] The Synoptic writers, moreover, have their own distinctive theologies of revelation, and cannot be reduced to a common pattern. Mark's Gospel, for instance, has been aptly characterized as "the book of secret epiphanies" (Dibelius, Bultmann), in which the "Messianic secret" plays a cardinal role. Matthew, whose aim is more catechetical, portrays Jesus as the new Moses, promulgating the perfect law of charity. Luke, the theologian of history, accents the role of the Holy Spirit, who descends upon the praying Jesus and prompts Him to herald the arrival of Messianic times.

In his discussion of New Testament Christology, Latourelle makes much of the passages which depict Jesus as revealer, but he overlooks the fact that the Evangelists seem to regard Him, also, as the recipient of revelation (Mk 1.11; Lk 10.17), and even allude to limitations in His revealed knowledge (Mk 13.32). Latourelle writes almost as if Christ's human words were a direct expression of His divine consciousness, and gives no attention to the psychological structure of Christ's human intellection. The matter is of some importance for the correct understanding of the traditional statement that the apostles, like the prophets, were recipients of immediate revelation.

A third lacuna in Latourelle's chapter on the New Testament is his failure to deal with the continuing process of revelation in the primitive Church. In his treatment of Acts and Paul he is much concerned with the "deposit" and its transmission, but says practically nothing about the new revelations being conceded to the apostles and prophets. In a study of the New Testament notion of revelation the "visions and revelations" received by Peter and Paul after Pentecost (e.g., Acts 9 and 10; cf. 2 Cor 12.1) ought not to be passed over in silence. In what cases, if at all, should these experiences be regarded as constitutive of the *depositum* itself? In view of the language of Trent (Denzinger-Schönmetzer, n. 1501) it seems doubtful whether these experiences should, in every case, be equated with the unauthoritative visions of the charismatics (1 Cor 14). During the first generation the dialectical tension between revelation as event and as institution was perhaps especially acute.

CATHOLIC THEOLOGICAL TRADITION

Part 2 of Latourelle's monograph gives a dense but highly stimulating summary of the patristic doctrine on revelation. Some twenty important writers from the Apostolic Fathers to St. Augustine are examined. Justin, it appears, made a bold step forward in applying the Stoic concept of *logos* to clarify the relationship of Christ to the pre-Christian pagan world. Irenaeus is outstanding for his historical grasp of revelation, which leads him to speak of the "economy," the "divine pedagogy," and the "recapitulation" of all things in Christ. Clement of

Alexandria held that the pagans were prepared for the Christian revelation by their philosophy, much as were the Jews by the Mosaic Law. Origen explored with fascinating subtlety the dialectic of Law and Gospel, history and Spirit. The Cappadocians and John Chrystostom dwelt on the divine incomprehensibility in a way that enriched the Catholic theology of mystery, and among the Western Fathers Augustine is remarkable for his mystical insight into the role of the Word as the interior teacher of revelation.

In this survey of the patristic territory Latourelle seems to do as much as is feasible in so brief a compass. In a larger treatment it would have been helpful to include some discussion of the early heresies; for even if they did not directly assail the traditional view of revelation, the Gnostics, Marcionites, Manicheans, Montanists, and Eunomians were not exempt from serious errors in this realm. Perhaps also, in view of the discussion of the theology of preaching later in the book, it would have been well to make some mention of Augustine's contribution to this field, in which he was so ably seconded by Gregory the Great.

Skipping over the entire period from Augustine to Bonaventure—in spite of the very evident riches offered by such figures as Erigena and Anselm—Latourelle next treats of the High Scholastic and neo-Scholastic theological tradition. St. Thomas, he finds, considerably advanced the psychology of revelation (notably in his treatise on prophecy), but failed to give corresponding emphasis to the historical progress of revelation, and to its culmination in Christ's revelation to His apostles. The post-Tridentine Scholastics (Suarez, de Lugo) shifted the focus of attention from active, immediate revelation to objective, mediate revelation and the guarantees needed to certify it as God's word. The leading theologians of the nineteenth century (Möhler, Franzelin, Newman, Scheeben) helped to revitalize the theology of revelation through a return to the Fathers, but their work was hampered by their involvement in anti-Rationalist and anti-Protestant polemics. The neo-Scholastics of the early twentieth century (Gardeil, Garrigou-Lagrange, and Dieckmann), for all their systematic acumen, are deservedly criticized by Latourelle for their excessively apologetical orientation, their abstract and propositional view of revelation, and their neglect of the biblical and historical data.

The contemporary period in Catholic theology, as Latourelle depicts it, is marked by an intense reaction against the rigidities of Scholasticism. A generation ago the manual theology was severely castigated by Chenu and de Lubac in France and by the advocates of kerygmatic theology in Germany and Austria. The current orientations in Catholic theology concerning revelation may be characterized as Christocentric, historical, interpersonal, and biblical. Although the neatness of Scholastic conceptual structures has been somewhat rumpled by the leading theologians of our day, we need not regard this as an unmixed evil. "This is a final proof of the fact that the reality of revelation will always be much richer than the constructions of the human mind, and that theology must vary her approaches in order not to be too unfaithful to this reality" (p. 244).

Part 4 takes up the pronouncements of the Catholic magisterium on revelation prior to Vatican II. Practically speaking, Latourelle limits himself to the Council of Trent, Vatican I, the anti-Modernist documents, and some recent encyclicals (especially *Humani generis*). This portion of the book conveniently assembles information which is, for the most part, accessible elsewhere. Latourelle shows very successfully that although the magisterium was not seeking to state positively the full notion of revelation, the condemnations of successive errors have, by implication, brought into relief the various aspects of God's word to man. As a result, one can gather from the Church documents a picture of revelation closely approximating that already culled from the biblical and patristic testimonies. In a fine concluding summary Latourelle constructs, on the basis of the magisterial documents, the following descriptive definition of revelation (p. 308):

the salvific activity, sovereignly wise and free, through which God, in order to lead man to his supernatural end, which consists in the vision of the divine essence, makes Himself known to man, together with the plan for salvation which He has conceived for humanity. This activity is the word of testimony of uncreated Truth, divine testimony demanding the homage of faith.

This admirable summary of the official documents of the Church leaves little to be desired except that the plan of the book has occasioned a certain neglect of the earlier Church pronouncements. "Anyone who studies the documents of the Church is immediately struck by the fact that errors concerning the notion of revelation are a recent phenomenon" (p. 247). This would seem to be an exaggeration. The writings of Paul and John bear witness to serious confusions even in New Testament times. Many of the early heresies, as mentioned above, had to do with the notion of revelation. Manicheism and Illuminism continued to plague the medieval Church, and were repeatedly condemned. The errors of Abbot Joachim, Wycliffe, and Hus, not to mention the Anabaptists and other Protestant sectarians, were based on misunderstandings in this area.

LATOURELLE'S PERSONAL REFLECTIONS

The last and longest part of the book presents the author's personal reflections. Without turning his back on Scholastic categories, Latourelle makes fruitful use of existentialist and personalist themes. To begin with, he ponders the traditional definition of revelation as *locutio Dei*, a notion which he greatly enriches by exploiting modern studies in the theory of language. Speech, he maintains, is a specifically interpersonal phenomenon; it involves, not simply the transmission of ideas or information, but also the self-expression of a speaker and an appeal to a personal addressee. Human speech employs language as its preferred medium, but makes use of other signs and gestures to bring about its full effect. God's speech to man, far from being a mere communication of supernatural information, is, above all, a gracious self-donation, an appeal for the obedience of faith, and an assumption of man into a transforming situation of divine friendship. The deeds by which God backs up His words give depth and realism to His testimony. These reflections, splendidly developed by Latourelle, are a powerful antidote to the jejune rationalism of some of the more popular manuals.

The relations between creation and revelation are next discussed. The production of the universe has a revelatory dimension insofar as it shows forth the power and goodness of the Creator, and calls for a response of adoration and worship. But in Latourelle's opinion this does not yet establish a dialogue situation, and hence falls short of being revelation in the strict sense. His statements on this point are reminiscent of Guardini, who remarks that the study of creation yields a knowledge of God comparable to that which one might gain of a proprietor from examining the home which he has built and furnished for himself. This differs vastly from the knowledge gained by personal encounter and conversation.[3]

Next, Latourelle addresses himself to the historical aspect of revelation. As many contemporary Protestants have insisted, God revealed Himself to Israel by His mighty salvific interventions on behalf of His elect people. But the "brute facts" of objectivizing history are not yet revelation. In Latourelle's opinion, which seems eminently sound, they are rather the raw material which receives its formal character as revelation from an inspired, prophetic interpretation. God must furnish the authentic commentary on His own action. "The structure of revelation is sacramental: facts, events, enlightened by word" (p. 349). This holds for the New Testament as well as the Old. Our Lord's career becomes an object of faith, and is believed by Christians, in the framework of the interpretation which He Himself placed upon it, and communicated to the Church. Christian revelation, therefore, is not crudely factual; it always has a doctrinal aspect. And conversely, Christian doctrine is not abstractly speculative; it is essentially linked to God's concrete, historical self-disclosure.

In the following chapter these points are underscored with special reference to Christ. In agreement with Karl Rahner, Latourelle adheres to the view of many of the Greek Fathers that the eternal Logos is "the only possible revealer" (p. 360).

In taking on human flesh, in speaking human language, and in living to the full the message which He preached, the subsistent Word has given the ultimate, unsurpassable revelation. The immeasurable gap between God and man—which Karl Barth will not allow us to forget—is in some sort spanned by the unfathomable condescension of God. According to the Catholic view of the Incarnation, Christ, the perfect witness, can guarantee the veracity of the human language in which He speaks of the divine.

In the remaining few chapters Latourelle discusses the role of the light of faith in man's assent to revelation, the miracles of Christ as symbolic deeds, the Church as the medium through which revelation becomes present in the world, the vision of God as the consummation of revelation, and the glory of God as the ultimate goal of the whole revealed economy. These closing chapters, while they do not introduce many ideas that have not been previously intimated, serve to round out the speculative portion of the book, and to bring it to a rhetorically effective conclusion.

The appendix to the English translation, dealing with the Vatican II Constitution on Divine Revelation, is in substance a clear, methodical, and reverent exposition of the first two chapters of *Dei Verbum*. The Council's view of revelation is well characterized by Latourelle as Trinitarian, personalistic, Christocentric, and ecclesial. On one minor point his interpretation of Chapter II will probably be contested. He apparently holds that, according to the Council, the content of tradition is materially wider than that of Scripture, at least insofar as the full canon of the biblical books is known by tradition alone (pp. 478 f.). But the language of the Council allows one to think that what tradition adds is clarity and certitude rather than substantially new knowledge. A number of modern Catholic theologians have maintained that the biblical books, to some degree, manifest themselves to the Church which, so to speak, hears God speaking in them, and that the definition of the canon, like other dogmas, results, not from tradition alone, but from a mutual coinherence of Scripture and tradition, comprising a single, indivisible, composite source. This point is of some ecumenical importance, since the standard Catholic tenet that the canon of Scripture is known only by tradition has long been rejected, and continues to be rejected, by the great majority of Protestant theologians.

SOME REMAINING QUESTIONS

This study of revelation, thorough and many-sided as it is, makes no pretense of being exhaustive. On the contrary, Latourelle protests that he regards it as a mere sketch and invites others to build on the foundations he has laid. As is evident from the preceding pages, I am convinced that he has made an enormous step forward, and my negative criticisms are quite incidental. But there are a number of major questions, raised especially by the last part of the book, which would seem to call for concentrated labor on the part of Catholic theologians. Several of these problem areas may now be mentioned.

This book is almost exclusively concerned with the historical Judeo-Christian revelation. Supernatural revelation is treated as coterminous with the series of salvific acts by which God manifested Himself to the prophets and apostles of the Old and New Testaments. But some discussion of whether and how God reveals Himself to the unevangelized gentiles would seem to be in order, for the sake of a more comprehensive concept of revelation, which might in turn throw light upon the essential properties of revelation itself. If St. Thomas, for instance, was correct in his doctrine of justification by a "first moral act" at the dawn of reason (*Sum. theol.* 1–2, q. 89, a. 6), it must be possible for men to receive supernatural revelation prior to any instruction about the facts of redemptive history and their doctrinal interpretation.[4] In such a perspective, the interior illumination of grace seems to take on a greater constitutive role in the process of revelation than Latourelle is inclined to allow it (p. 237, note 94; pp. 383–85). In order to explain how the faith of the unevangelized is structurally homogeneous with that of Christians, the patristic theme of the universal illuminative office of the Logos could perhaps be usefully invoked.

In setting forth the generic features of revelation, Latourelle rightly makes much of salvation history. The great acts of God are, so to speak, the material component of the revealed object. But it would be of interest to inquire just what is needed to make an event pertain to *Heilsgeschichte*. Latourelle holds that the history of revelation is not simply coincident with universal history; it depends upon God's free interventions. Yet these interventions, he remarks, need not be strictly miraculous; they would include God's special providence over the formation and fortunes of Israel, as attested by biblical history. But it may still be asked whether God has not manifested Himself by deeds to other peoples too, and whether He has not continued to act in a revelatory way since apostolic times. Tillich's view that Church history is a living channel of revelation, punctuated by decisive *kairoi*, seems closer to Catholic doctrine than the narrow biblicist view that salvation history ceased with the age of the apostles. Such an existential "filling up" of Christ's revelation in the course of later centuries would, of course, add nothing substantially new—inasmuch as the essential meaning of all history has been finally disclosed in the Christ-event—but it would continue to actualize God's message in new forms, adapted to new situations.[5]

Latourelle makes much of the role of doctrine as complementary to historical event in the process of revelation. As already mentioned, he holds that redemptive history does not exhibit its revelatory significance except in the light of a divinely communicated interpretation, which is at least seminally doctrine. In its finished form, as committed to the Church, the revelation takes on the form of a body of truths to be preserved, defended, and taught. While this may be admitted, it would be helpful to have a fuller discussion of how, in an inchoate manner, revelation can be communicated without doctrine, i.e., without precise conceptualization and carefully articulated enunciation. Inverting Latourelle's order of priorities (pp. 384 f.) I should be inclined to say that the ineffable experience of the Word holds a certain precedence over its doctrinal statement In the life of the individual believer and in that of the whole church, as Blondel observed, "it would be true to say that one goes from faith to dogma rather than from dogma to faith."[6] The Church itself, in formulating and judging doctrines, draws abundantly on its preconceptual knowledge gained through a mysterious vital contact with the divine Persons. Unless this were so, it would be most difficult to account for the dogmatic progress that has occurred.

The primacy of the preconceptual, to which we have just alluded, is of major importance for an "ecumenical" theology of revelation. In Catholic theology the faith of heterodox believers has too long been treated as an embarrassing anomaly. Canon Mouroux, in his stimulating study of the personal structure of faith, has done much to clear up the confusion. Through an act of faith, he points out, man surrenders himself to an overwhelming reality made present to him by God's grace. The spiritual plenitude of this total engagement issues in a "profound affirmation" that cannot be encompassed in words, concepts, or judgments. The judgments and formulas of faith, according to Mouroux, include a representative element that is always inadequate, and sometimes even incorrect, but since the affirmation has its basis in the ontological thrust of the whole person toward the Absolute, it is not canceled out by faulty expression. "The saving movement of the soul, initiated by grace, can pass through formulas, themselves pitifully inadequate, or even glaringly false."[7] While this observation bears more directly on the study of faith than on the theology of revelation, it helps to clarify the true role of doctrine in revelation.

Besides being historical and doctrinal, revelation is mysterious. Central to the theology of Paul, the notion of mystery has remained vital for Catholic theology, and was strongly re-emphasized by Vatican I. Latourelle's speculative section would have been enriched by a further treatment of this theme. Widely divergent understandings of mystery are current in Catholic theology—for example, those proposed by Lonergan and Rahner. From many presentations one gets the impression that mystery is a sort of insoluble problem, an impenetrable mass which remains after positive and speculative theology have exhausted their resources. This view overlooks the fact that the whole of revelation, insofar as it bears on the order of grace and beatitude, exceeds man's comprehension. Sacred history and sacred doctrine are themselves steeped in mystery. Far from being what is left over after theology has done its best, mystery is the very substance on which theology feeds and thrives. A statement free from mystery would hardly be, in the proper sense, theological.

The theology of revelation must seek to account for two things: both the special obscurity of the Christian mysteries, which are vastly more opaque than the "natural mysteries" probed in philosophy, and their luminosity, which renders them susceptible of an *intelligentia fructuosissima* (cf. *DS* 3016). Because God's revelation involves a personal approach to His creatures in finite forms, the God who speaks is more mysterious than the silent, absent God. The God of faith, precisely because He is more intimately known than the God of philosophy, is more inscrutable. The revealed light exhibits the profundity of what Newman called the "revealed darkness."[8] To the unbeliever, the Christian mysteries may appear as mere conundrums, but thanks to the inner dynamism of grace, which comes to man together with the revealing word, these mysteries are singularly luminous to the eyes of faith. They evoke a total response in which the thrill of fascination, as Rudolf Otto noted, is dialectically conjoined with a sense of holy awe. In terms of man's vital relationship to them, mysteries possess an intelligibility in their own order which does not depend upon clear conceptualization, but surpasses it. This elusive type of knowledge will appear crude and "prescientific" only to those who hold up scientific explanation as the ideal toward which all knowledge should aspire.

Considerations such as these have a direct bearing on the problem of the transmission of revelation. It is often argued that the logic of analogy, as taken over from the philosophical disciplines, is unsuited to revealed mysteries. A friendly Lutheran critic, for instance, has this advice for Catholics:

> The Church must be willing to be led by the Holy Spirit back to a "polar" or "dialectical" thinking and teaching about the mysteries of God. This dialectic alone is suitable for the "Mysterium" of the events of God's grace. Up to the present time, and

under the pressure of a justifiable defense against dangerous errors, the Church has abandoned such dialectic in favor of an all too rationalistic oversimplification of its dogmatic and theological statements.[9]

Latourelle, insisting on the value of the *analogia entis*, accuses Barth of an agnosticism that "does away with all real communication between God and man" (p. 446), but in his own treatment of the theology of preaching, Latourelle avoids any facile rationalism. He recognizes that to communicate the gospel is a supernatural action in which the power of the Spirit must energize the servant of the word (p. 411). In a recent essay Karl Rahner has raised the question whether all doctrinal utterance must not participate in the supernatural quality of kerygmatic utterance; whether even theology does not risk falsifying its nature if it merely talks about mystery as a kind of "object," and fails to "conjure up the gracious experience of the absolute mystery itself."[10] Perhaps the profound intention of dialectical theology was to forge a language better suited to this evocative task than the *analogia entis*, or at least the oversimplified version of analogy, often presented in elementary manuals, against which Barth so fiercely protested.

Closely connected with the foregoing is the question of symbolic language, which ought to find a place in any full treatise on revelation. As is evident, figurative speech and imagery hold a place of prime importance in Scripture, in the liturgy, and in many creeds. Rationalistically oriented theologians may look on this as a merely pragmatic or rhetorical device designed to impress on untutored minds and wayward hearts the "straight" truths of revelation. Spinoza held this view, but St. Thomas takes a more nuanced position (*Sum. theol.* 1, q. 1, a. 9). Recent language theory finds riches in the "latent meaning" of metaphorical expression that defy transposition into the "manifest content" of scientific cognition.[11] Hence we must ask whether the supernaturally given images in Scripture and tradition may not have an irreplaceable role in the communication of God's word to man. Austin Farrer, among others, vigorously contends that we cannot grasp the biblical message apart from the images in which it is clothed; that "we cannot by-pass the images to seize an imageless truth."[12] The veil of faith, he asserts, is impenetrable indeed, but far from blank. "It is painted with the image of God, and God himself painted it, and made it indelible with his blood, when he was nailed to it for us men and for our salvation."[13]

The principal proponents of the theology of symbol, including E. L. Mascall, M. Eliade, and G. Vann, have no intention of reducing the whole of revelation to poetic imagery, to the exclusion of historical fact and doctrinal truth, but they would insist that the biblical images cannot be discarded to make room for purely scientific discourse. This position, if valid, is of great significance, both for the theory of revelation, and for theological method. What must revelation be, we may ask, if it cannot be adequately communicated without imaginative symbols? Can theology itself ever really leave imagery behind? The debates at the Vatican Council II concerning the various images of the Church give grounds for the view that correct imagery is a perennial concern of dogma and theology.

In his chapter on miracles Latourelle touches lightly on the theme of symbolism. The prodigies worked by our Lord, he points out, were not merely substantiations of His authority, but also figures or symbols of the new order which He came to bring. Once miracles are looked upon as God's symbolic gestures, the problem of imagery appears in a new light. The mutual disclosure of persons is normally accomplished more through symbolism than through propositional speech, more through gestures and accents than through formal statements. If revelation, as Latourelle insists, is not simply a transmission of new knowledge, but a personal encounter between God and man, it is not surprising that imagery should be so abundant. The Catholic theologian may heartily concur with Alan Richardson when he writes: "Once we have discarded the dogma that scientific knowledge is the only kind of truth, we shall realise that the imagination, using the word in such a way as to include the act of the will, is the only means by which ultimate or existential truth can be apprehended and communicated."[14]

In singling out these various points which require more extensive investigation, I do not wish to imply any fundamental inadequacy in Latourelle's book as it stands. Like any author, he is entitled to place limits to his inquiry. He has given us a very useful and substantial introduction, and has not aimed at a final summation, which would evidently be premature in the present state of theology. The fact that his work stimulates more questions than it answers is a tribute to its thought-provoking power. And the author gives such evidence of scholarship and theological skill as to leave little doubt that he himself, in future years, will carry the theology of revelation far beyond the point where he leaves it in this book.

3

Reflections on "Sola Scriptura"

Until recently the majority of Catholics and Protestants would perhaps have agreed that the formula *sola Scriptura*, as aptly as any other, epitomizes the ultimate parting of the ways. This has been notably true as regards the relations between Lutherans and Catholics. At the Leipzig Disputation in 1519 Luther laid down the basic principles—namely that popes and councils are subject to error and that "no believing Christian can be coerced beyond Holy Writ." This was erected into a confessional norm in the Formula Concordiae of 1577, in which we read: "We believe, teach, and confess that the prophetic and apostolic writings of the Old and New Testament are the only rule and norm according to which all doctrines and teachers alike must be appraised and judged." "The Holy Scripture remains the only judge, rule and norm according to which as the only touchstone all doctrines should and must be understood as good or evil, right or wrong."[1] Such is the Protestant and Lutheran *sola Scriptura*. It is often called the "formal principle" of Reformation Christianity, as contrasted with justification by faith, which is designated the "material principle."

In a polemical work published in 1638, the Anglican, Chillingworth, who had been a Catholic for a time, effectively reduced the whole of Protestantism to this one doctrine:

> ... by the religion of protestants, I do not understand the doctrine of Luther, or Calvin, or Melanchthon; nor the confession of Augusta, or Geneva, nor the catechism of Heidelberg, nor the articles of the church of England, no, nor the harmony of

protestant confessions; but that wherein they all agree, and [to] which they all subscribe with a greater harmony, as a perfect rule of their faith and actions: that is, the Bible. The Bible, I say, the Bible only, is the religion of protestants![2]

Corresponding to these Protestant affirmations, we can find many affirmations from the Catholic side that the claims of the Church stand or fall with the doctrine that revelation comes to man by a twofold channel, namely, Scripture and tradition. The Council of Trent began its proceedings in 1545 by laying down as the foundation of all its subsequent decrees the sources of revealed truth that all should recognize. After declaring that Christ, our Lord, appointed his apostles to be the source of all saving truth and moral teaching, the Council went on to declare: "This truth and teaching are contained in written books and in unwritten traditions that the apostles received either from the mouth of Christ Himself or from the dictation of the Holy Spirit and passed on, as it were, from hand to hand."[3]

Trent did not actually define the relations between the contents of these two sources, but it was widely interpreted as teaching that there were at least some points of Christian doctrine that were not contained in the Bible. Many Catholic theologians of the Counter Reformation period asserted as much. Melchior Cano, for instance, wrote: "The doctrine of faith was handed down by the apostles not all in writing but partly by word [of mouth]"[4] Robert Bellarmine takes the same position:

> Scripture, even though it was not produced primarily to be a rule of faith, is a rule of faith, not total, but partial. For the complete rule of faith is the word of God, or the revelation of God made to the church, which is divided into two partial rules, Scripture and Tradition.[5]

This view is repeated again and again in Catholic textbooks down to our own day. A widely used contemporary textbook, *De Ecclesia Christi*, by Joachim Salaverri, published in Madrid in 1952, has a thesis that reads: "The primary font of revelation is divine apostolic tradition, which outstrips Holy Scripture in antiquity, completeness, and sufficiency."[6] In evidence of the insufficiency of Scripture the author states that there are a number of revealed truths, such as the sevenfold number of the Sacraments, which are not found in Scripture[7].

In polemical writings from the sixteenth to the twentieth century, Catholics have been trying to convince Protestants that there are revealed truths not recorded in the Bible; Protestants have been trying to convince Catholics that there is no reliable access to the word of God except through Holy Scripture. The arguments on both sides can be found in practically any theological manual, and need not be reviewed here.

What is more interesting by far is the shift of position that has been occurring in both Protestant and Catholic positions in the present century, especially since World War II. This unexpected change of climate is dramatized in two recent important assemblies. At Vatican Council II, in November 1962, a schema was presented by the theological commission, dealing principally with the sources of divine revelation. It espoused the view, not simply that revelation was in both Scripture and tradition (which Trent had already said), but that these were two separate sources—which Trent did not say—and further, that there are some revealed truths which could be found only in the latter. A declaration to this effect would have, so to speak, canonized the common textbook teaching of the past 300 years. Yet, astonishingly, the majority of the Council Fathers objected that the draft schema was unsatisfactory, since it was too polemical and went beyond what was settled Catholic doctrine. The proposed decree was withdrawn from discussion, and Pope John XXIII ordered it to be reworked. The new draft, circulated to the bishops during the summer of 1963, avoided saying that tradition is a source independent of Scripture, or that there are any revealed truths not contained in Scripture. This view, as we shall see in the next chapter, prevailed in the Constitution on Divine Revelation adopted in the fall of 1965.

Outside the Catholic Church a development of comparable magnitude took place within the predominantly Protestant Commission on Faith and Order of the World Council of Churches. At the Fourth World Conference on Faith and Order held at Montreal in July 1963 a report was adopted on the subject, "Scripture, Tradition, and Traditions." It emphasizes the inseparability of Scripture and tradition, and gives primacy to the latter. It states, in part:

> Our starting-point is that we are all living in a tradition which goes back to our Lord and has its roots in the Old Testament, and are all indebted to that tradition inasmuch as we have received the revealed truth, the Gospel, through its being transmitted from one generation to another. Thus we can say that we exist as Christians by the Tradition of the Gospel (the paradosis of the *kerygma*) testified in Scripture, transmitted in and by the Church through the power of the Holy Spirit. Tradition taken in this sense is actualized in the preaching of the Word, in the administration of the Sacraments and worship, in Christian teaching and theology, and in mission and witness to Christ by the lives of the members of the Church.[8]

In an earlier draft of this report, the second sentence of the preceding quotation had been worded: "Thus we can say that we exist as Christians *sola traditione*, by tradition alone."[9] Several prominent theologians at the Conference stated that, although they personally could subscribe to the formula *sola traditione* in this context, they thought it was too inflammatory in the minds of Protestants accustomed to the Reformation battle-cry, *sola Scriptura*. The dangerous phrase was therefore expunged, but the memory of its presence in the draft declaration will probably have continued influence.

The strong emphasis given to tradition in the Montreal Conference displeased some of the more Biblically minded commentators. Carl Henry, for instance, called the conference "a major debacle whose defacing scars may long embarrass the ecumenical movement."[10] The renewed stress on tradition in the Faith and Order Conference, however, represents the rather general drift of thought in ecumenically minded Protestantism today. It would be an exaggeration to say that Catholics and Protestants have switched positions, as though Catholics were, today, the spokesmen of *sola Scriptura*, and Protestants were championing *sola traditione*. But there are many signs that it is no longer accurate to say that the basic difference consists in the fact that Protestantism advocates Scripture as the one source of revelation, whereas Catholicism looks to Scripture plus tradition. With the recent theological developments within both branches of Christendom, the Protestant-Catholic dialogue has entered a new phase.

What is responsible for these dramatic shifts? Is it, simply, that people are getting tired of other old positions, and want to roll over, like a patient on a hospital bed? I do not think it is a matter of mere theological restlessness. Is it, then, an ecumenical spirit of good will that makes Protestants and Catholics want to drop their past polemical orientations and go as far as possible in saying the same thing? Ecumenism, I think, is a contributing factor, and rightly so. Four centuries of bickering brought us no closer to agreement; perhaps it is time, then, to make a real effort to see the other's point of view, and to go as far as we can in accepting his insights. Historically, the ecumenical movement has had a lot to do with toning down the oppositions—and in this connection it is only right to take account of the new dialogue between the Protestants and Eastern Orthodox in the World Council of Churches.

If Protestants and Catholics have begun to review critically their own previous positions, it is no doubt because they have detected some flaw in what they were saying, and some truth in what other Christian groups have been advocating. I should like, then, to discuss first, some of the intrinsic reasons which have persuaded many Protestants that the biblicist formula, *sola Scriptura*, is inadequate; and second, some of the motives why Catholics today are hesitant to affirm that there are any revealed truths found, not in the Bible, but only in tradition.

PROTESTANTS ON THE NEED OF TRADITION

The main reasons influencing Protestants to change their position may, I think, be gathered under two headings, the first having to do with the origins of the Bible, the second with its interpretation.

Until modern methods of historical research were applied to the Bible, theologians often gave a quite unrealistic, and even incredible, account of its origins. They insisted strongly, and quite rightly, on the doctrine of biblical inspiration, but explained it in such a way as often to give the impression that inspiration took the place of human activity in acquiring and expressing knowledge. It was naively assumed that the sacred authors must have received their message, and even the very words in which they were to state it, by dictation direct from heaven. In recent decades, critical scholarship has made it clear that the historical writers of the Old and New Testaments made use of sources, both written and oral, and sometimes, in fact, did little more than compile materials already in tradition. Thus nearly everything that we now read in the Synoptic Gospels, for example, was already professed in the Christian community before the sacred authors went about composing their Gospels. Once this became apparent, the primary focus of attention shifted from the evangelist-editors to the process by which the traditions were formed.

This shift of interest was largely the fruit of Form Criticism, a new approach to the Gospels introduced by Martin Dibelius, Rudolf Bultmann, and others shortly after World War I. Whatever the defects in the presuppositions and methods of the early form critics, a question far too complicated to be discussed here, they at least made scholars conscious of the enormous importance of the oral Gospel which lies behind the written Gospels. The French Protestant exegete, Oscar Cullmann, recognized that this had immense significance for interconfessional debate concerning the roles of Scripture and tradition. As early as 1925 Cullmann wrote: "Although Catholicism never completely forgot that tradition is prior to Scripture, the theologians descended from the Reformation no longer reckoned with the fact that between the time of Jesus' life and that of the composition of the Gospels there was an interval of at least thirty years during which there was not yet any written life of Jesus."[11]

The early form critics, as is well known, tended to be quite radical in denying the historical reliability of the Gospel tradition, much of which they attributed to the creative imagination of the early Hellenistic community. Today many historians of the early tradition, especially in Germany and Scandinavia, regard the Gospel traditions as the result of a remarkably faithful process of transmission going back to the earliest Palestinian community. The extent to which the recollections of the apostles were over-painted by the concerns of the primitive Church is still under discussion, but in any case the Gospels are viewed as crystallizations of the approved traditions of the primitive Church. The same may be said, with the necessary adaptations, concerning large parts of the Old Testament. Hence, the opposition between Scripture and tradition can no longer be sharply drawn. One cannot attribute religious authority to the Bible without, at the same time, having a high regard for the tradition which precedes and envelops it. It is evident that the Church, in the first few generations, lived primarily by the preaching of the apostles and other ministers of the oral Gospel. Only in the latter half of the second century do we begin to get anything like a canon of the New Testament.

The second factor which has made Protestants reluctant to separate tradition from the Bible is the problem of correct interpretation. The standard Catholic doctrine on this point has always been that Scripture ought to be interpreted according to the sense "which holy mother Church has held and holds, for it pertains to her to judge concerning the true sense and interpretation of the sacred scriptures."[12] The Church emphatically rejects any interpretation that is contrary to the general consent of the Fathers. The classical Protestant formula, on the other hand, was "Scriptura sui ipsius interpres." In his work on the *Bondage of the Will*, Luther, replying to Erasmus, seemed to favor this position. The Catholic hermeneutic, then, puts the accent on tradition—the authentic tradition being that which the Church has held and does hold. The Protestant formula, in this sharp expression of it, by-passes tradition, and affirms that the Bible not only contains the entire revelation, but that it is a self-interpreting document. It is not only the Constitution but the Supreme Court in the republic of faith.

In recent Protestant studies one finds a tendency to soften

this extreme position. To single out one author, I might refer to Jaroslav Pelikan. In his *The Riddle of Roman Catholicism* he notes that the question of interpretation is intimately connected with that of the genesis of the New Testament.

> Tradition, which was a term of opprobrium for the reformers, is now becoming an acceptable concept among Protestant theologians and biblical interpreters. If, as Protestant interpreters like Dibelius and even Bultmann concede, the Christian community, through its tradition, shaped the forms of the New Testament, then it might well follow that the Christian community, again through its tradition, ought to have some voice in the interpretation of the New Testament.
>
> It is for this authoritative voice of tradition that Roman Catholic theology and Orthodox theology have been contending against Protestantism for four hundred years. Suddenly now, Protestant theology has begun to listen to tradition as it has not since the Reformation.[13]

In his introduction to Luther's exegetical writings for the American edition of Luther's works, Pelikan maintains that Luther himself moved, and intended to move, within the context of tradition. "Luther," he writes, "could not have been the exegete he was without the help of the Church's tradition. The tradition gives him a footing on which he could and did move and shift, but which he never lost."[14] Tradition at its best, according to Luther, was the voice of the Church, obediently listening to the Word as the Spirit gave it understanding and utterance. Luther would never have thought of questioning the articles of the Creed; to do so was, in his view, blasphemous. If he opposed merely human traditions, he did so in order to defend what he viewed as the authentic and true tradition. In other writings, Pelikan has argued that Melanchthon and Chemnitz were still more explicit in their acceptance of a sacred and binding tradition.

Quite apart from the historical question as to the extent to which the classical Protestant theologians accepted tradition, it must be asked whether it is possible for any Christian today to do

without it. Numerous and weighty Protestant voices in our day
answer this question in the negative. Paul Tillich, for instance,
expresses this unequivocally:

> It is obvious . . . that the radical biblicistic attitude is a self-
> deception. No one is able to leap over two thousand years of
> history and become contemporaneous with the writers of the New
> Testament, except in the spiritual sense of accepting Jesus as the
> Christ. Every person who encounters a biblical text is guided in
> his religious understanding of it by the understanding of
> all previous generations. Even the Reformers were dependent
> upon the Roman tradition against which they protested. They
> directed special elements of the ecclesiastical tradition against
> others in order to fight the distortion which had affected
> the whole tradition, but they did not and could not jump out
> of the tradition into the situation of Matthew and Paul. The
> Reformers were aware of this situation, and their orthodox
> systematizers were still aware of it. Evangelical biblicism, past
> and present, is unaware of it and produces a "biblical" theology
> which actually is dependent on definite dogmatic developments of
> the post-Reformation period. Through historical scholarship the
> difference between the dogmatic teaching of most American
> evangelistic churches and the original meaning of the biblical
> texts can easily be shown. Church history cannot be evaded;
> therefore it is a religious as well as a scholarly necessity that the
> relationship of systematic theology to the ecclesiastical tradition
> be stated frankly and pointedly.[15]

In voicing these ideas Tillich reflects a large segment of
contemporary Protestant thinking. Much the same point of view
may be found in the statements on tradition issued by the
Montreal Conference, as quoted above. There is a growing consensus that every Christian, whether he wills or not, is immersed
in some sort of tradition. The only alternative to authentic tradition is bad tradition.

Several extrinsic factors in our time have been making
Protestants increasingly aware of the ecclesiastical and traditional factor in faith. For one thing, the extreme individualism
which was born in the Renaissance, and reached its apex in the
nineteenth century has begun to decline in favor. The image of

the solitary believer nourishing his faith on a private study of the Bible has lost some of its appeal. Christian life appears once more as a life within the community of the new people of God. The return to tradition among Protestant Christians is intimately connected with the revival of a sense of the Church.

As another contributory factor one might mention the manifest inadequacies of Fundamentalist exegesis as practiced in the first quarter of the twentieth century. The extreme biblicists in the American churches of Calvinist lineage imagined that it was possible for the individual believer, without any special training, to achieve an adequate understanding of God's message to mankind by a simple reading of the Bible. But the doctrines proclaimed in the name of pure biblical teaching were so mutually contradictory and so incompatible with the findings of the natural sciences that the Fundamentalist stand was totally discredited, at least among intellectual believers. The extravagances of Pentecostalism, Seventh Day Adventism, and the Jehovah's Witnesses are a living demonstration of the perils of such naiveté in exegesis. Private judgment in the exposition of the Scriptures leads ineluctably to sectarianism. Anyone who thinks he finds a new religious position in the Bible feels authorized to set up a new denomination. Just as Luther and Calvin opposed the Enthusiasts and Sectarians of their day, so conservative Protestantism in the twentieth century is emphasizing the authority of confessional traditions against the rabid individualism of the fanatics.

CATHOLICS ON NEED OF BIBLE

While modern Protestantism has been placing stronger emphasis on tradition, Catholicism in our day has been experiencing a biblical renewal. A generation ago nothing seemed more evident than that the Catholic Church stood for unwritten tradition as a separate channel of doctrine, conveying truths not ascertainable from Holy Scripture. Today, however, Catholics are inclined to seek a biblical basis for every doctrine, and to be extremely critical of every idea and institution which seems foreign to the Bible. The older polemical arguments for the sufficiency of unwritten tradition now seem logically inadequate, and what is still more decisive: we Catholics have been experiencing, individually and collectively, the salvific power of the biblical word.

The idea that tradition is a separate channel of information, running parallel to Scripture, seemed tempting for apologetical reasons. As everyone knows, the Church teaches many dogmas which are not evidently contained in Scripture—for instance, that there are seven Sacraments (neither more nor less), that the Blessed Mother was immaculately conceived and assumed corporeally into heaven, etc. If asked where these dogmas come from, many unreflecting Catholics would no doubt reply, "from sacred tradition," meaning by this that they were known to the apostles and passed down from generation to generation by word of mouth, or at least by some channel other than the canonical Scriptures.

The more one examines this position, the less plausible it appears. In the first place, it involves a *deus ex machina*. The existence of these alleged traditions cannot be verified by historical evidence, but is postulated for the sake of the argument. Secondly, the thesis is actually contrary to all probability. It is almost incredible that if the early Fathers had known all these facts they would have written so vaguely about the Sacraments, about Mary, etc. In fact it took a thousand years of keen theological analysis to hammer out the technical notion of sacrament, as understood in modern Catholic theology. If St. Paul or Ignatius of Antioch has been asked whether matrimony was a Sacrament they could hardly have understood the meaning of the question. The same is true, even more conspicuously, of a doctrine such as the Immaculate Conception, which involves the highly sophisticated notions of original sin and preservative redemption. Finally, even if we did grant the existence of such traditions in apostolic times, contrary to all appearances, it is most difficult to see how they could be utilized by the modern Church as doctrinal sources. A tradition cannot be a valid source unless its existence and contents can be established with some assurance

Many Catholic theologians, therefore, hold that dogmas, such as the ones mentioned, are no better attested by oral traditions dating back to the apostles than they are by the Bible itself. Hence, it seems otiose to postulate apostolic tradition as a second stream of revealed doctrine, running parallel to the Bible.

This is not to say that the modern dogmas are simply inventions of the Church in later centuries. It is a firm tenet of Catholic theology that all revelation was given, at least in embryonic form, before the end of the apostolic age, but this completion of revelation does not reduce the Church to a state of inertness. On the contrary, the Church throughout the centuries has the task of meditating constantly in order to plumb the depths of the revelation already given. The closing of the deposit is a beginning as well as an end; it ushers in a new era of religious history in which the development of dogma occurs. Because we accept the principle of development, we are not compelled to seek, in the original fonts, fully formulated propositions matching every tenet of the contemporary Church. The relationship is rather that of a seed to a flower, or that of an acorn to an oak. It is pointless to object that the apostolic Church is vastly different in appearance from the Church today. This is no argument that it has changed its inner nature. There is nothing substantially new in the modern Church, any more than there is anything substantially new in an adult man that was not germinally present in the foetus.

This paradox of stability within change is most commonly explained by the biological analogy of the development of an organism. The metaphor is a useful one, and can claim a certain foundation in John and Paul, but like all analogies it limps. Dogmatic development is not something that occurs automatically according to a biological law of growth. The vital principle responsible for the increase is not an immanent form inhering in the Church, but rather the Spirit of God, who acts with sovereign liberty in his dialogue with the Church. The Church, in her search for understanding, must constantly listen to the Spirit. Only if she does so will she be able—like the scribe instructed in the kingdom—to bring forth out of her treasures "things new and old" (Mt 13.52).

According to the view just propounded, the modern dogmas of the Church can be explained as the result of a development from a seed no larger than the Bible itself. There is no need, then, to appeal to oral tradition as a second deposit, but this does not mean that tradition is not at work. On the contrary tradition, in the modern theological understanding, is often identified with the entire process by which the data of revelation—including the Bible itself—are transmitted with the help of the Spirit in the Church of God. Tradition is to be understood primarily, in an active sense, as the sacred process of handing on; secondarily, in an objective sense, as the complex of insights gained through this process. There is continuity in tradition because the deposit of faith remains the same, because the same Christ remains Lord of the Church, and because the same Holy Spirit directs the Church in every age. But there is growth in the tradition because the Spirit is constantly leading the Church, as Paul expressed it, "to the deep knowledge of the Son of God, to perfect manhood, to the mature measure of the fullness of Christ" (Eph 4.13).

THE PLACE OF THE BIBLE

In the light of these reflections on tradition let us now consider the place of the Bible in the scheme of revelation. The Bible is not absolutely necessary—under all conditions—for faith to be born. Rather, the biblical books are, themselves, products of a preexistent faith; many of them, as I have said, are little more than a sedimentation of the holy traditions in which the convictions of the early community were expressed. Nor does the Bible appear to be sufficient as a source of faith. It is always handed to the individual by the Church, and the Church, in drawing up the canon, made some use of tradition. She inquired as to the external testimonies concerning the books to be canonized, and examined their contents in the light of her own faith, but the Church has never looked upon herself as superior to the Scriptures. That is a misunderstanding of Catholic doctrine. In reality, the Church gratefully receives these books as a special gift from God. Once she has recognized the books, and placed them in her canon, she reveres and venerates them; she reads them, so to speak, on her knees. In these books she finds an original and divinely guaranteed record of prophetic and apostolic tradition. As a tangible part of the original deposit, the Bible holds a place of unique honor as a source of her preaching and theology. In liturgical proclamation, and in silent meditation, the Scriptures have been, and still remain, a living source of faith for countless generations of Christians.

Is there any sense in which the Catholic, like the Protestant, can say that his faith and that of the Church are based on the Scriptures alone? In facing this crucial question we must make many distinctions. Obviously a particular individual may come to Christian faith without having read the Bible himself, or heard it read to him verbatim, provided the biblical message has reached him in some words. But the preaching of the Church is only a proximate rule of faith; it is itself drawn from authentic Christian sources. If we press the question to its last implications, must we not say that the declarations of creeds and councils, popes and bishops, Fathers and theologians, must have their ultimate foundation in the Bible, or else be judged to have no sufficient warrant in God's revealing word? Because the Bible is the only original source we have, in which the prophetic and apostolic faith is embodied, the Church always looks to it in formulating her faith. She looks to tradition too, but not in the sense that it contains other truths in no way found in the Bible. Hence, it would seem correct to say that the Church's faith is thoroughly and primarily biblical. Its original matrix is the Bible alone. For this reason the Catholic need not deny the view of Lutherans that the Bible is the *norma normans*, the *norma non normanda*, of the Church and dogmatic theology.[16]

In confirmation of what I have said, it may be noted that, in her dogmatic definitions, the Church has always made much of the biblical foundation; but she often finds in a sacred text more than would appear to the eye of a scholarly exegete investigating the original meaning as understood by the sacred writer. The Church's interpretation of Scripture is not bound by the laws of merely philological exegesis. Having the mind and spirit of

Christ, she can find in the Bible things that would not be discernible to the outsider. The precise method by which the Church interprets the Scriptures is very difficult to describe, and constitutes one of the most pressing problems of current Catholic theology. The Church may be said to have a charismatic sensitivity for what God intends to communicate by the book, and cannot be held to justify all her affirmations by reference to particular texts. This power of discernment is, no doubt, due to a special intimacy with the divine author of Scripture, who unceasingly guides the Church, and gives her a kind of instinct for the real meaning of the Bible. Scripture becomes, for her, the Word of God because she hears the divine Word speaking through it.

In seeking to formulate this mysterious event, Catholics are still groping for an adequate terminology. There are elements in the Protestant tradition that may help them in this task. For instance, there is the Calvinistic doctrine of the inward witness of the Holy Spirit, and the Barthian doctrine that the Bible becomes the Word of God when and as it pleases the Word himself to speak through it. While Catholics reject the actualism and occasionalism that seems latent in the Barthian position, they cannot but applaud his recognition of the charismatic factor in a genuinely theological interpretation of the Bible.

However difficult these points may be to explain, they should not astonish or scandalize any believing Christian. The Church's use of the Bible is certainly no more free than the use which the New Testament authors made of the Old Testament. Throughout the Gospels, Acts, and Epistles the point is repeatedly made that the Jews could not understand the deeper meaning of the Law and the Prophets; indeed, not even the apostles were able to do so until the Risen Lord, by sending His Spirit, opened up to them the hidden sense. The same Spirit that descended upon the apostolic Church is ceaselessly at work in the Church of God, helping her to fathom the divine message.

These considerations concerning the meaning of the Bible bring us squarely back to the problem of tradition. The secret operation of the Holy Spirit disclosing the divinely intended meaning of the Bible is the well-spring of tradition. The monuments of tradition—including the writings of the Fathers and theologians, and the decrees of Councils and bishops—constitute a chain of witnesses to the teaching of the Holy Spirit. By confronting the witness of the Church in previous ages, the contemporary Church becomes better disposed to receive the intimations of the Spirit today.

Bringing together the fruits of these reflections on Scripture and tradition, we can conclude that they are not really two separate sources, but two facets of a single source. The Bible is not revelation unless it is read in the light of Church tradition; the tradition is not revelation unless grounded in the Bible. The one channel by which revelation is available today is Scripture enveloped in the atmosphere of living tradition. Theologians in our time sometimes speak of a mutual coinherence of Scripture and tradition—a "circumincession" that causes each to be present in the other. This view has been rapidly gaining ground over the post-Tridentine view that Scripture and tradition were two independent sources, standing side by side, which could be examined one at a time.

The position to which we have come is, I believe, fully Catholic, but not exclusively so. I seem to note, among many distinguished Protestant theologians—including Lutherans such as Pelikan and Skydsgaard—a tendency to say much the same thing. The essential point of difference between Protestants and Catholics, as I understand it, does not lie in their respective views on Scripture and tradition. If that was ever the great issue dividing us, it need not remain so. Today, the main point of contention will rather be: where and how is authentic tradition to be found?

In answer to this question the Catholic will reply: the Church as a visible, organized society is the divinely appointed organ that can speak in the name of God himself, exacting the obedience of faith. The hierarchy can, at opportune moments, give expression to the mind of the Church. This it has done in the ancient Creeds and Councils, and continues to do in the living magisterium today. When the Church finds it necessary, she may totally engage her authority, thus demanding a sincere and unqualified assent on the part of all her faithful. The distinctive note of the faith of Catholics is their acceptance of the Church's claim to speak with finality about matters of faith. The Catholic theologian or exegete has no desire to be anything but a Catholic. He wishes to read the Bible and understand it within the Church, as a faithful member of the Church, and in perfect subordination to those whom the Holy Spirit has appointed as shepherds in the Church of God.

The Protestant position, as I understand it, is opposed to this. It holds that bishops, popes, and councils, being dependent on the Scriptures as the source of their faith, have only provisional or relative authority. All their decisions are subject to revision and correction when measured against the original underived norm, the Holy Scriptures. However much the Protestant may esteem the creeds and councils, or even the doctrinal standards of his own denomination, he feels that they are, in principle, liable to error, and in need of being tested by the Bible. While the mediation of the Church can never be eliminated, it can and must be criticized and purified.

These differing views on church authority give a somewhat different slant to the formula *sola Scriptura* when it is enunciated by a Catholic or a Protestant. The Catholic can accept it in the sense that the Bible is the nuclear source from which all true doctrine develops, but he cannot accept what the Protestant will wish to add—the further statement that every Church decision is subject to error and must be reviewed in the light of the Bible itself. Without attempting to solve this further problem of Church authority, we may take satisfaction in the degree of agreement which is possible. In our views of Scripture and tradition, Catholics and Protestants—or at least many Catholics and many Protestants—are closer together today than we have been at any time since the Reformation. The progress achieved along these lines gives rise to the hope that our other disagreements may not be as insuperable as we are wont to suppose.

4

The Constitution on Divine Revelation in Ecumenical Perspective

The ecumenical significance of Vatican II's Constitution on Revelation, *Dei Verbum*, will best appear if we begin with a glance at the historical background. Prior to Vatican II, the general Councils and the Roman magisterium never dealt with revelation at any length except for the purpose of condemning errors. The most important statements came from the Councils of Trent in the sixteenth century and Vatican II in the nineteenth. In opposition to the Protestant Reformers, Trent taught the divine authority of Catholic tradition, and drew up a definitive list of books to be included in the Bible. Vatican I made a strong statement on the supernatural and gratuitous character of revelation in opposition to the Rationalists and Semi-Rationalists of the time, who spoke of revealed truth as though it might be discovered by unaided human effort.

When preparations were begun for Vatican II the Theological Commission drew up a schema "On the Sources of Revelation" written in much the same style as Trent and Vatican I. This document, had it been adopted, would have narrowed down the positions tolerated within the Church, and correspondingly exacerbated the long-standing controversies between Protestants and Catholics. On the disputed point of the relations between

Scripture and tradition, the schema took the view that there are some revealed truths ascertainable by tradition alone, apart from Scripture—a position denied by many Catholics and by practically all Protestants. In its approach to other questions, such as the inspiration and inerrancy of Scripture, and the historicity of the Gospels, the proposed document was negative and defensively apologetical. By canonizing the tenets of a particular theological school within the Church, this schema would have seriously restricted Catholic theologians and exegetes, and made it difficult for them to collaborate with other Christian scholars. This first draft, therefore, represented a hindrance, not a help, to unity.

At the first session in 1962, the schema on the Sources of Revelation was debated from November 14 to 21. The speeches of that week were perhaps the most dramatic and crucial test of the mood of the Council. Although the schema had its defenders, a multitude of bishops rose in succession to protest that the proposed Constitution was totally lacking in that ecumenical spirit which, according to the desire of John XXIII, should inform the entire Council. The most eloquent summary of the case of the Liberals, as they came to be called, was made by Bishop De Smedt of Bruges, who took the floor on behalf of the Secretariat for Promoting Christian Unity. In the judgment of the Secretariat, he declared, the proposed schema had "grave faults from an ecumenical point of view: it would not encourage a dialogue with non-Catholics; it would represent not progress but a retreat." "If the schema prepared by the Theological Commission is not modified," he continued, "we shall be responsible for causing Vatican Council II to destroy a great, an immense hope . . . for . . . the unity of those for whom Christ Our Lord offered this prayer: *ut unum sint*."[1]

After almost a week of spirited argument, a vote was taken as to whether the existing schema should continue to be debated or withdrawn for total redrafting. The majority of the Fathers, though not the required two-thirds, voted for adjournment of the debate. The next day Pope John himself took the initiative, and ordered the schema withdrawn. At the same time he set up a new commission to draft a substitute document that, he clearly indicated, should be pastoral in tone, ecumenical in spirit, and free from binding declarations on matters still under discussion among Catholics. This new commission he placed under the joint presidency of Cardinal Ottaviani of the Theological Commission and Cardinal Bea of the Secretariat for Unity. The step of bringing Bea and his Secretariat into the drafting of the schema on Revelation indicates the great ecumenical importance which Pope John attached to this Constitution.

A totally new text, prepared during the following winter, was circulated among the Council Fathers in the spring of 1963. Although this schema was not publicly debated at the second session, a number of suggestions were submitted in writing, on the basis of which the text was again reworked before the third session in the fall of 1964. The amended version distributed at the close of the third session was once more retouched during the interval before the fourth, the most important changes being three proposed by Pope Paul himself. Finally, at the fourth session, the Constitution was adopted by a vote of 2,344 to 6 and officially promulgated by the Pope on November 18, 1965.[2] It is officially designated by the first two words of the Latin text, *Dei Verbum* (The Word of God).

The Dogmatic Constitution, as finally adopted, consists of six chapters which I shall briefly discuss in order, from the point of view of their ecumenical significance. The chapters are entitled: (1) Revelation Itself; (2) The Transmission of Divine Revelation; (3) The Divine Inspiration and the Interpretation of Holy Scripture; (4) The Old Testament; (5) The New Testament; and (6) Holy Scripture in the Life of the Church.

THE NATURE OF REVELATION

As regards the first chapter, the very fact of Catholic concern with the doctrine of the word of God has unquestionable ecumenical import. Traditionally, Protestantism has been identified as the religion of the word; Catholicism has been rather the religion of institution and sacrament. Father Latourelle has put the matter well:

> Now among Protestants primarily, since Scripture is the only center of attention, we can see that the Word of God is the foundation of their spiritual life just as it is at the foundation of theological research. In Protestant teaching man is alone before the Word of God; this is the medium and environment for his interior life, which is nourished and renewed by daily contact with Scripture. The theology of the Word of God, consequently, stands out in boldest relief, and receives a privileged treatment. As a matter of fact, all the great names of contemporary Protestant theology (K. Barth, R. Bultmann, E. Brunner, P. Tillich, R. Niebuhr, H. W. Robinson, etc.) have devoted chapters, and even entire works, to the theme of revelation. Thus, giving the Word of God all the importance it deserves among the Christian realities means contributing, in some manner, to an understanding among Christians.[3]

It is evident, however, that some ways of conceiving revelation are more apt to promote ecumenical dialogue than others. Human concepts about revelation have greatly changed in the course of the centuries. In classical Protestant theology, which reached its zenith in the seventeenth century, the tendency was to look upon revelation as a collection of doctrines set forth in Scripture. It was therefore understood as coming from God in the form of written or spoken words, and as embodying truths that could be expressed adequately in propositional form. But the trend in twentieth century Protestantism is to regard revelation primarily as a personal encounter with God himself, and to hold that this encounter is effected, not simply by words, but also by events—most importantly by the great deeds of God to which biblical history bears witness.

A parallel evolution has been going on within Catholic theology. Until recently we have been inclined to think of revelation in rather static, doctrinal terms, as one may see from consulting the statements of Trent and Vatican I or almost any of the older textbooks. But the new Constitution, in its opening paragraphs, moves far away from any narrowly conceptual or propositional view. It takes as its fundamental text the words of 1 Jn 1.2–3, "We announce to you the eternal life which was with the Father and has appeared to us. . . . " Revelation is presented, not simply as a communication of knowledge, but as the dynamic process by which the divine persons invite men to enter into a relation of fellowship. In describing the manner in which this event takes place, the Council calls attention to the role of both words and deeds. "This plan of revelation is realized by deeds and words having an inner unity: the deeds wrought by God in the history of salvation manifest and confirm the teaching and realities signified by the words, while the words proclaim the deeds and clarify the mystery contained in them" (art. 2). This view of revelation, which harmonizes well with much modern Protestant biblical theology, should facilitate interconfessional dialogue.

The biblical and historical emphasis, so evident in the passages already quoted, would seem to correspond to a genuine ecumenical need. The Danish theologian, Kristen E. Skydsgaard, in his address to Paul VI on behalf of the observer delegates at the third session of the Council (November 1, 1964), pleaded for the cultivation of a "biblical theology, concentrated on the study of the history of salvation, in the Old as well as in the New Testament."[4] The Constitution *Dei Verbum*, especially in its discussion of the nature of revelation, would seem to fulfil this stipulation.

One asset of a biblical and personalistic approach to revelation is that it serves to accentuate the great central truths of revelation on which Christians commonly agree, rather than the later and more refined developments of doctrine. In this connection it is well to recall what the Decree on Ecumenism has to say about the unequal importance of different truths of revelation. "There exists an order or 'hierarchy' of truths, since they vary in their relationship to the foundation of the Christian faith" (art. 11 § 3). If we keep in mind the primary role of biblical history in effecting a salvific encounter between God and man, we can better appreciate the riches to be shared by all Christians despite the existing doctrinal divisions, which are by no means unimportant.

TRADITION

The second chapter, on the Transmission of Divine Revelation, takes up the mutual relations between Bible, tradition, and the teaching Authority of the Church. Since this is probably the most crucial issue dividing Protestants and Catholics, it was not to be expected that the Council, in its statement of the Catholic doctrine, would produce a formula which Protestants would be prepared to sign. But it was to be hoped that the Council would raise no new obstacles, and would possibly indicate some ways in which the existing tensions could be eased.

The Council of Trent had already made it clear that, in the Catholic view, the Bible, apart from tradition, is not a sufficient guide to revelation. But Trent did not settle precisely what tradition is. Many Fathers at Trent undoubtedly conceived of it as a second channel, parallel to Scripture, but independent of it, affording access to certain truths not derivable from Scripture. This view became quite widespread in Catholic theology in the next two centuries and would have become official Catholic doctrine if the first schema of Vatican II had been accepted. But it was this point, more than any other, which moved the Council Fathers to repudiate the first schema. It embodied a view of tradition unacceptable, not only to Protestants, but also to many of the leading Catholic theologians of our time, who maintain that post-apostolic tradition is, by its very nature, a kind of reflection or commentary upon Scripture.

The final text of the Constitution emphasizes the inseparability of Scripture and tradition, and avoids affirming that there are any revealed truths transmitted by tradition alone. The whole question of what truths are, or are not, contained in Scripture is probably unanswerable, since Scripture says different things to different people, depending on the dispositions and previous knowledge which a given interpreter brings to it. According to the Catholic view, the Bible does not yield its full meaning unless it is read in the context of the life and experience of the Christian community—or, in other words, in the Church.

The Council is therefore content to say that tradition is

necessary for the proper transmission and explanation of the word of God, so that "it is not from sacred Scripture alone that the Church draws her certainty about everything which has been revealed" (art. 9).[5] In this sense, the Council firmly rejects the Reformation slogan, *"sola Scriptura."* This rejection might seem to raise a new barrier between Catholics and Protestants, but in fact it does not, because the Catholic Church has been committed for many centuries to this position, and few Protestants today would wish to defend "Scripture alone" in the sense in which the Council here rejects it.

Many Protestants now recognize that some kind of authoritative tradition is necessary for an adequate understanding of the Gospel. As an indication of the current trend one may consult the reports on "Tradition and Traditions," submitted to the Fourth World Conference on Faith and Order at Montreal in the summer of 1963. The American section of the Commission on Tradition at Montreal declared, in a report signed by Albert C. Outler as chairman:

> The actual history of Christianity since the Reformation has made the formal anti-traditionalism of the Reformers obsolete. To defy the accumulated traditions of the medieval Church in the name of the freedom of God and of the renewing Spirit, the Reformers could speak as though traditions were always consequent upon Scripture, both logically and chronologically, and as though it were possible to preclude the development of traditions by firm adherence to the Scriptures as both the source and the norm of Christian teaching. Such defiance makes less and less sense as the several Protestant communions themselves spawn traditions of teaching and usage that are no more (and no less!) scriptural in their origin and validation than were the *consuetudines ecclesiasticae* against whose claim to apostolicity the Reformers protested so vehemently. Abundant examples from the history of Orthodox, Protestant, and Roman Catholic theology, liturgy, piety and policy support the thesis that for better or for worse, or for a combination of the two, traditions are inevitable.
>
> Yet, in the open face of this history of Protestant traditions many theologians continue to insist on the anti-traditional formulae of early Protestantism, thus maintaining the tradition of *sola Scrip-*

tura despite the historical actuality of *Scriptura nunquam sola*! Scripture is nowhere by itself alone.[6]

The present state of the question, in the light of Montreal and Vatican II, is no longer whether or not tradition is legitimate and necessary. We agree that it is both, but the current problem is: what is tradition? The older conception that it is a parallel source of verbal doctrine handed down from apostolic times is being rapidly abandoned by all who have not yet abandoned it. Today, it is more commonly conceived as a kind of atmosphere produced by the Holy Spirit in the Church, permitting it to understand the full biblical witness.

In an important speech at the third session of the Council, the Melchite Archbishop, Edelby, called attention to the value of the Oriental conception of tradition, as found both among Catholics and Orthodox, for showing a way out of the impasse in Western theology. Tradition, according to this Eastern view, he said, is to be identified with the Church itself insofar as the Holy Spirit empowers it to understand Holy Scripture in the light of the Risen Christ. Without tradition, he observed, Scripture would be "the letter which kills."[7] This "pneumatological" view of tradition, in many respects, agrees with what Cardinal Cervini maintained at the Council of Trent, as well as with some of the ideas of Johann Adam Möhler and the Catholic Tübingen School of the nineteenth century. It quite evidently corresponds to the teaching of Vatican II, which sees in the vital and dynamic character of tradition the key to the progressive development of doctrine in the Church. "This tradition," says the Council (art. 8 §2), "which comes from the apostles, develops in the Church with the help of the Holy Spirit. . . . For as the centuries succeed one another the Church constantly moves forward toward the fullness of divine truth until the words of God reach their complete fulfilment in her."

The function of tradition in the Church is stated more precisely in the following paragraph (art. 8 §3): "The words of the Holy Fathers witness to the living presence of this tradition, whose wealth is poured into the practice and life of the believing and praying Church. Through the same tradition the Church's full canon of the sacred books becomes known, and the sacred writings themselves are more profoundly understood and unceasingly made active in her. And thus God, who spoke of old, uninterruptedly converses with the Bride of His Beloved Son, and the Holy Spirit . . . leads unto truth all those who believe, and makes the word of Christ dwell abundantly in them (cf. Col 3.16)."

While espousing a dynamic and progressive view of tradition, the Council is careful to insist on continuity with the past. In particular, *Dei Verbum* takes pains to show that the magisterium of the Church is not, as some have falsely imagined, the author of tradition. The Church's teaching authority, says the Constitution, "is not above the word of God, but serves it, teaching only what has been handed on, listening to it devoutly, guarding it scrupulously, and explaining it faithfully. . . . It draws from this one deposit of faith everything which it presents for belief as divinely revealed" (art. 10 §2). Thus the function of the magisterium is not to decide what the faithful are to believe, but rather to formulate accurately beliefs which already exist in the Church thanks to the apostolic witness, originally embodied in Scripture, and ever freshly understood through the living presence of the Spirit of the Truth which Christ promised and bestowed upon his Church.

I have discussed Chapter II at some length because it is ecumenically the most important chapter in *Dei Verbum*. Without attempting the impossible task of bridging the gap between Protestants and Catholics on the norms and channels of revelation, it succeeds in offering a very irenic and moderate statement of the Catholic position. By calling attention to the inseparability of Scripture and tradition, and by explaining the limits within which the magisterium operates, it goes far to remove those misunderstandings which have unnecessarily troubled the relations between Protestants and Catholics in the past. Protestants will, no doubt, feel that even the teaching of *Dei Verbum* puts too few controls on the magisterium of the Church, but Catholics will reply that the magisterium is divinely directed in interpreting, just as the biblical authors were in composing—and on this point the ecumenical discussion must continue to focus.

The remaining four chapters of the Constitution (chs. 3–6) deal with the Bible under various aspects. Since all Christians accept, in substance, the same Bible, these chapters are of obvious ecumenical significance. The Bible has been called a bond of union, but sometimes it has looked more like an apple of discord or a bone of contention among rival Christian groups.

Chapter 3, on the Inspiration and Interpretation of Sacred Scripture, takes the place of a chapter in the original schema "On the Inspiration, Inerrancy, and Literary Composition of Scripture." The word "inerrancy" was dropped from the title because the Fathers wanted to accent the positive values of the Bible rather than the merely negative point of immunity from error.

In past centuries the inspiration and inerrancy of the Bible were basic planks of common accord between Protestants and Catholics, but today most Protestants deny the inerrancy of the Bible, and many reject its divine inspiration. The chief defenders of these doctrines are the Fundamentalists, who understand inspiration and inerrancy in a rigid and mechanical way. The original Vatican II schema would have come very close to Fundamentalist teaching, but the doctrine of the final text opens up new possibilities of fruitful encounter with non-Fundamentalistic Protestants.

The first paragraph of this chapter makes it clear that inspiration does not mean that the ideas or words of the Bible were dictated from heaven, but that the writers were given a special divine help in using their own powers and abilities. The Bible is not a meteorite which descended from another world, but something which grew out of a particular religious and cultural context through divinely assisted human effort. The Council's teaching on this matter should dispel the widespread impression that the Church is committed to the obsolete mechanical view of the inspiration which many erroneously identify with inspiration itself.

Turning then to inerrancy, *Dei Verbum* makes an important advance over most current theological textbooks. Up to the present many Catholics have felt obliged to maintain that the biblical writers made no mistakes on any matter—even astronomy, biology, or secular history. The present Constitution, by pointing out that the scope of inerrancy is governed by the purposes of inspiration, makes it unnecessary to defend this exaggerated view. To quote: "The books of Scripture must be acknowledged as teaching firmly, faithfully, and without error that truth which God wanted put into the sacred writings for the sake of our salvation" (art. 11 §2), i.e., truths important for man's religious relationship to God.[8] And inerrancy is attributed to the Bible as a whole, rather than to each biblical writer as an individual. Any particular sentence, chapter, or biblical book must be read in its total context. As the Constitution puts it, "Serious attention must be given to the content and unity of the whole of Scripture if the meaning of the sacred texts is to be correctly brought to light" (art. 12§3). No one chapter, book, or author is to be read as if it, alone, were the Bible. This larger and more flexible concept of inerrancy will permit Catholic exegetes to feel free to interpret individual texts with complete honesty. Too often in the past non-Catholic biblical scholars have been put off by the dogmatic and apologetical attitudes of some Catholics who sought to find in each biblical writer a full and balanced view of Christian truth.

The question of inerrancy leads naturally to that of the interpretation of the Bible, considered toward the end of chapter 3. This has been a hotly disputed issue among Catholics themselves in recent years. A diminishing, but still powerful group of theologians have resisted all efforts to open up the Bible to scientific critical study. In an important encyclical of 1943 (*Divino Afflante Spiritu*), Pius XII pointed out the necessity of reckoning with the characteristic modes of thought and expression in use in the ancient Near East as an essential step in getting at the true meaning of the inspired text. But the conservative opposition continued to attack Catholic biblical scholars, so that it became imperative to have a strong statement from the very highest authority, defending the freedom of exegetes to work conscientiously and responsibly with all the tools of modern research.

Article 12 of the present Constitution gives Catholic exegetes this needed charter, and points out the importance of their work for the development of Catholic doctrine. Their preparatory research, says the Council, helps to mature the judgment of the Church regarding the contents of revelation. This observation is of great importance because many theologians have one-sidedly stressed the necessity for Scripture scholars to be obedient and submissive to the teaching of the magisterium. It is now clear that the relation between scientific exegesis and the teaching authority must be one of mutual respect and mutual listening.

All these problems, while they are in the first instance internal to the Catholic Church, have important repercussions in the ecumenical field. To a great extent the ecumenical movement, as it has developed in Europe and the United States, is an outgrowth of conversations between exegetes of different confessional traditions. It is no accident that Cardinal Bea, the leading ecumenical figure at Vatican II, is by training and profession a biblical scholar. The Constitution on Revelation, by its first defense of scientific biblical scholarship, assures the continuation of this dialogue among exegetes of different Christian traditions.

Chapter 4, a brief but inspiring statement on the Old Testament, need not delay us, since it does not seem to raise any serious problems regarding the ecumenical relations among Christians. Protestants and Catholics are generally agreed that the Old Testament is an essential part of the Christian Bible and that it receives its full religious significance in the light of the New Testament fulfilment. The Constitution on Revelation wisely cautions against going indiscriminately to the Old Testament for guidance, since God revealed himself only gradually with the passage of centuries. While some of the doctrines and precepts contained in the Old Testament are incomplete and provisional, it has perennial value.

Chapter 5 on the New Testament is remarkable because of its differences from the chapter on the same subject in the 1962 schema. The early draft insisted that the four Gospels were actually written by Matthew, Mark, Luke, and the Apostle John, and that they were strictly historical, even in their reporting of particular incidents. The final text abandons this apologetical approach, and emphasizes rather the religious and salutary value of the Gospels. The facts, it tells us, are recorded as seen in the full light of the Church's Easter faith, and are presented in such a manner as to bring home their religious importance to Christian communities of the second generation. In its teaching on the Gospels, the Constitution closely follows the 1964 Instruction of the Biblical Commission on the same subject, which therefore provides the best available commentary on this section. To guard against the exaggeration of certain form critics who have been overinfluenced by modern existentialism, the Constitution points out that the "kerygmatic" concern of the Gospels by no means cancels out their historical truth, even though the historicity here in question is not precisely that of disinterested factual reporting.[9]

In opening up the Gospels to dissection in the light of modern form criticism, the Constitution merely sanctions what has been the practice of the best Biblical scholars for several decades. But this official approval is important for the protection of exegetes who have, too often, been unjustly accused of dangerous innovations. Abbot Butler of Downside Abbey, a New Testament scholar who is also a member of the Secretariat for Christian Unity, pointed out the ecumenical significance of this forward step. "We do not want the childish comfort of averting our gaze from the truth, but a truly critical scholarship which will enable us to enter into dialogue with non-Catholic scholars."[10]

The sixth and final chapter, dealing with the place of the Bible in the life of the Church, is rich in ecumenical import. It begins with a bold comparison between the way in which the faithful are spiritually nourished by the word of God and by the Sacrament of the Altar. This idea had already been suggested in the Constitution on the Liturgy, which declared that Christ "is present in his word, since it is he himself who speaks when the Holy Scriptures are read in the Church" (art. 7). According to the Constitution on Revelation this salvific presence of Christ occurs even outside the liturgy, whenever believers devoutly apply themselves to the reading and study of the Bible. "For in the sacred books, the Father who is in heaven meets his children with great love and speaks with them" (art. 21). Oscar Cullmann, in citing this phrase, remarks on its meaningfulness to Protestants. "Against Protestant views," he writes, "Catholics have all too often objected that the Bible is a 'dead letter' while tradition alone is a living element."[11] But this respect for the salutary power of Holy Scriptures is by no means new in Catholic theology. The theme has been broached in several of the biblical encyclicals of the past century, which are accustomed to quote in this connection *Heb* 4.12: "For the word of God is living and effectual and more piercing than any two-edged sword."

Chapter 6 then goes on to speak of the role of Scripture in the life of the faithful, and especially in the study and prayer of priests and religious. To make the Bible readily accessible to all, modern translations are strongly recommended. The Council also states its approval of common Bibles, produced in collaboration by Christians of various confessions, for the use of the faithful without distinction of denomination. By endorsing this idea the Council powerfully contributes to making the Bible become, as it should be, a bond of union among all Christians. Toward the end of the chapter the Constitution, extending its horizons still more widely, recommends editions of the Bible with suitable explanations for the use of non-Christians (art. 25 § 3).

EVALUATION

The Constitution *Dei Verbum* is a relatively brief document, consisting of some ten pages of text and three or four pages of footnotes. It obviously makes no pretense of being a complete treatise on revelation. Some might find it defective because of what it omits. For example, it gives no definition of revealed, as distinct from naturally acquired, knowledge. It does not seek to prove the possibility or reality of revelation, or to show why Christianity should be accepted as a revealed religion. Beyond presenting the Christian revelation in an attractive way, it makes no effort to render the notion of revelation meaningful or credible to the modern secular mind. In short, this document is unconcerned with the apologetical problem.

For the full doctrine of Vatican II on the subject of divine revelation one would have to study many other documents besides *Dei Verbum*. This Constitution concentrates primarily on the Bible as a record and medium of revelation. It, therefore, says little about how God reveals Himself to non-Christians who have no contact with the biblical religions. The bare hint given in Article 3 of *Dei Verbum* on this point is clarified by several passages in other documents. For example, the Constitution on the Church in the Modern World (*Gaudium et spes*) declares explicitly that "all believers of whatever religion have always heard His [God's] revealing voice in the discourse of creatures" (art. 36, §5). The Declaration on the Non-Christian Religions says that these religions "often reflect a ray of that divine Truth which enlightens all men" (art. 2, §5). And the Constitution on the Church implies that even men who "without blame on their part, have not arrived at explicit knowledge of God" may receive sufficient grace and revelation to attain eternal salvation (art. 16, §3).

While asserting that revelation achieves its fullness in Christ, the Constitution on Revelation says little about whether, or how, God continues to reveal himself in subsequent generations. The passage we have quoted about how God speaks uninterruptedly to his children through the Bible (art. 21) gives one suggestion in this regard. The Constitution on the Church supplements this eloquently by calling attention to God's continued self-revelation through the saints: "In the lives of those who share in our humanity and yet were transformed into especially successful images of Christ (cf. 2 Cor 3.18), God vividly manifests to men His presence and His face. He speaks to us in them, and gives us a sign of His kingdom, to which we are powerfully drawn. . . " (art. 50, §3).

Gaudium et spes is the boldest of the Council documents in bringing out the secular and cosmic dimensions of revelation. It frequently refers to Christ as the light in whom it is possible to interpret history in its full breadth, and the soul of man in its inmost depths (art. 10). The Church has the task of distinguishing and interpreting the many voices of our age and judging them in the light of the divine Word (art. 44, §4). In order to do so, the Church must accurately discern the signs of the times, through which God communicates Himself in a new way in every epoch of history (cf. art. 4, §1). The events of world history, viewed in the light of Christ, help to mature our understanding of what was initially revealed in Christ. Revelation, therefore, comes to fulfillment in the course of history, and through contact with the various forms of human culture, which bring out one or another aspect of the divine message. "For God, revealing himself to his people to the extent of a full manifestation of Himself and his incarnate Son, has spoken according to the culture proper to different ages" (art. 58, §1). By its positive attitude toward the variety of human cultures, and especially toward the technical and scientific resources of our age, *Gaudium et spes* counterbalances the primarily biblical orientation of *Dei Verbum*. It provides important clues for the unending process of distinguishing between the permanently valid content of Christian revelation and the time-conditioned formulations in which it necessarily comes to us. These hints will prove most helpful in dealing with the so-called problem of demythologization, an agonizing one for Protestants and Catholics alike. The wide opening to the world in *Gaudium et spes* lays the basis for a broader, if more amorphous, type of ecumenism than that envisioned in *Dei Verbum*, which is chiefly concerned with the dialogue with biblically minded Protestants.

It would be unfair to condemn *Dei Verbum* in terms of what it does not try to do. At least its silence on these matters is not damaging to the present ecumenical dialogue. On the contrary, this very reticence implicitly invites theologians to work at these problems with full freedom, unhampered by premature directives. Because it closes no doors, the Constitution assures that the problems which face all Christians alike will continue to be discussed in an ecumenical way.

Does the Constitution in any way inhibit ecumenical relations between divided Christians? Quite evidently, not all Christians will agree with everything said in *Dei Verbum*. The Fundamentalists will think its doctrine on inspiration and inerrancy too lax, and its endorsement of form criticism too bold. On the other hand, the more venturesome form critics will find the statements on the historicity of the Gospels too timid. Protestants in general will find that too much scope is given to tradition, and too much discretion to the magisterium as its official interpreter. But on all these points the Constitution does not go beyond settled Catholic doctrine, which it sets forth in a moderate, but uncompromising manner. The discretion and ecumenical spirit so evident in this document should help the Church's critics to see the reasonableness of the Catholic position, even if they do not feel that they can personally accept it.

The limited scope of *Dei Verbum* is perhaps its greatest source of strength. In deliberately concentrating on the biblical aspects of revelation, this document achieves a unity and compactness which contrasts favorably with the rambling and repetitious character of several other Conciliar statements. The biblical language and emphasis of the Constitution will make conservative Protestants as well as Catholics feel at home. By its reverent treatment of the Bible as a channel of revelation, *Dei Verbum* will undoubtedly serve to strengthen the ties among all biblically oriented Christians, and to facilitate a fruitful exchange of ideas and insights among exegetes of every denomination. Taken as a whole, the Constitution splendidly illustrates the truth of the statement in the Decree on Ecumenism (art. 21, §4): "The sacred word is a precious instrument in the mighty hand of God for attaining to that unity which the Saviour holds out to all men."

PART TWO

THE CHURCH AND THE
TRANSMISSION OF REVELATION

5

The Church and the Faith of Catholics

Pope John XXIII, in his inaugural encyclical of June 29, 1959, expressed the hope that Vatican Council II might become for non-Catholic Christians a "gentle invitation to seek out that unity which Jesus Christ prayed for so ardently from his heavenly Father." The divisions among Christians which are so great a scandal to the modern world are, tragically, divisions in faith. This has raised in many minds the suspicion that faith is itself the divisive factor that must be abandoned if mankind is to achieve its goal of unity. And yet we Christians dare to affirm just the opposite. Though we are divided in faith, we are not divided by faith. Whatever divisions exist among believers can, indeed, be only in spite of faith, for faith itself is a force that makes for union.

In the classical treatises on the act and virtue of faith, which have come down from the great neo-Scholastic theologians of the Counter Reformation, and are reflected in the seminary manuals of our day, this social and unitive aspect of faith is commonly neglected. One gets the impression that faith is the act of an isolated individual, prompted by the secret workings of grace in the recesses of his consciousness. That there should be a plurality of believers, all professing the same creed, would seem to be a purely accidental fact, in no way connected with the very nature of faith. Each believer is treated as a lonely traveler to God, like so many trains on parallel tracks. If the role of the Church is mentioned at all, it is viewed as quite extrinsic to faith itself. The Church is taken to mean the magisterium, and its function is limited to that of proposing the revealed datum and the various arguments of credibility. But this action of the magisterium, we are reminded, is neither sufficient nor strictly necessary, since the interior workings of grace are the only true cause of faith. Thus, the act of faith may be described, in the last analysis, as a wholly spiritual transaction between the individual soul and its God.

Without seeking to minimize or deny the role of interior grace, I should like to concentrate on the "ecclesiastical," or "ecclesial" dimension of faith. As an act and virtue, I shall maintain, it inheres primarily in the whole Church as a body, and only secondarily in individual persons. Men cannot come to Christian faith except by relating themselves positively to the Church which, by her life and doctrine, preserves and transmits the revelation she has received. The Church, moreover, must be looked upon as a true cause of faith wherever it exists. Any analysis of faith which overlooks this mediation of the Church is basically at variance with the theological data, and with the data of Christian experience.

In the present essay I shall speak only of the faith of Catholics, leaving for our next chapter the faith of non-Catholic Christians.

THE CHURCH AS BELIEVER

The whole question can be approached, first of all, from the point of view of the believing subject. Who is it, really, that believes? A man can say, "I believe." He can also say, "the Church believes." But is this latter expression strictly accurate? Is it anything more than a figure of speech, like the statement, "the government is in mourning" or "the State is angry?" If the Church does really believe, is her faith something other than the sum-total or result of the faith of her members? All these questions, I shall maintain, should be answered in the affirmative.

The idea of a solitary believer, perhaps, contains no inherent absurdity, but in point of fact no such person has ever existed. Man's whole progress toward faith is positively influenced at every turn by social factors. The very thought of becoming a Christian arises through contact with other believers. At least in the case of Catholics, it is obvious that a man's approach to faith runs *pari passu* with his approach to the believing community. So long as he remains outside the Church it is possible for him to see powerful motives for believing, and to gravitate in a tentative way toward the Catholic faith. But this faith remains vacillating and inchoate until he enters into believing association with others, identifying himself with what he recognizes as the Church of God.

If space permitted, we could abundantly illustrate this communal aspect of faith from the biblical teaching. In the Old Testament, faith is viewed as the normal accompaniment of membership in the Israelite people. For a gentile to become a worshiper of Yahweh, he must in some way become a naturalized Israelite. In the Gospels the Church becomes heir to the old Israel. The confession of Peter, as described by St. Matthew, splendidly exhibits the connection between the faith of the apostles and their role in the Church. St. Thomas, in his commentary, calls attention to this. "Super hanc petram, scilicet confessionis tuae, aedificabo Ecclesiam meam."[1] Peter became the foundation stone of the Church by reason of his belief and confession. Later, according to St. Luke, Christ prayed for the security of Peter's faith in order that he might be able to confirm his brethren (Lk 22.32). Throughout the Acts and Epistles, the Church is portrayed as the community of believers. To become a believer, and to be incorporated into the Church by baptism are regarded as virtually synonymous.[2]

In our own day, the baptismal liturgy still expresses, in dramatic form, the communal character of faith. When the catechumen approaches the door of the Church, asking for admission, he is stopped with the interrogation, "What do you ask of the Church of God?" "Faith," he replies, for faith achieves itself through baptismal incorporation in the community.

If the social character of the act of faith is manifest in the Baptism of adults, still more is this true in the case of infant Baptism. St. Thomas, in his treatment of the question, raises the objection that since Baptism is the Sacrament of faith, only those who can actually believe ought to be baptized. In his reply, he compares the baptized infant to an unborn baby. Just as the foetus in the womb receives physical nourishment from the mother, without any personal activity, so the newly born infant, incapable of any personal act of faith, can benefit from the faith of the whole Church. "Fides autem unius, immo totius Ecclesiae, parvulo prodest per operationem Spiritus Sancti, qui unit Ecclesiam et bona unius alteri communicat."[3]

Just as faith initially engrafts the individual into the people of God, so the entire life of faith finds its natural environment within the Church. The example and influence of the believing community are often required to make perseverance morally possible. The fellowship of the faithful, as Karl Adam has said, means more than the loyal submission of all to the same authorities. "It means that there is a solidarity and partnership of faith, a reciprocal interaction and fruitful influence, which by intimate and pervasive action make their external union an inward communion in the faith, a communion which out of the depths of the common experience of the faith is ever expressing itself anew in a single 'credo' of the mystical Christ."[4]

The Creeds are, in fact, a privileged source for the communal faith of the Church. Some of them are written in the third person singular, beginning with phrases such as "Sacrosancta Romana Ecclesia . . . firmiter credit, profitetur et praedicat" (*Pro Jacobitis*, *DS* 1330). Others, perhaps more typical, are introduced by the first person plural, "credimus," "credimus et confitemur," or the like (e.g., *DS* 21, 40, 41, 42, 44, 46, 48, 51, 71, etc). The Baptismal Creeds, for obvious reasons, use rather the singular, "credo." The same is true of the Creed we recite at Mass, presumably because it is derived from an ancient Baptismal liturgy. The common liturgical recitation, however, imparts a sense of community. When we stand at Mass for the Credo we are conscious that we are giving utterance to no private doctrine, but to the faith of the whole Church, which is coming to expression on our lips. Our words and thoughts bind us into unity with other believers in a solidarity which extends to the whole congregation, and beyond it to all faithful Christians across the face of the earth, both today, and in ages gone by, and in centuries yet to come. As St. Thomas splendidly expresses it, "Confessio fidei traditur in symbolo quasi ex persona totius Ecclesiae, quae per fidem unitur."[5]

To appreciate the social character of the ancient Creeds we should bear in mind that they were not forged out of solicitude for academic correctness, to become objects of scholarly study and classroom instruction. Before all else, these Creeds are solemn, cultic acts in which the Church liturgically lives out her relationship to the triune God whom she invokes and adores. They were not fashioned in order to impose new articles of faith, but to assert what the Church had always known and believed. They are phrased, often in highly figurative language, to be recited, and even sung, on festive liturgical occasions, but because common worship presupposes a union of minds, the symbols were also professions of orthodox belief. When there was question of heresy, they might even be adopted to serve as a test of pure doctrine. They were sometimes regarded as a kind of pass-word, or identification for mutual recognition among the faithful, and were not infrequently imposed on dissidents as a condition for ecclesiastical communion.[6]

What the Creeds express, therefore, is the faith of the whole Church. The ancient writers, according to Fr. de Lubac, designated this as *fides ecclesiastica*,[7] but because this term was put to new uses as a result of the Jansenist controversy, other terms gradually came into use. Some contemporary writers, for example, use the term *fides collectiva ecclesiae*.[8]

Is this faith of the Church, as such, anything real, as distinct from the faith of individual Catholics? In a certain sense, we must admit that it is, for it does not have the same attributes as individual faith. The collective faith is indefectible. To the whole Church, and not to any individual, Christ gave his promise, "I will be with you all days, even to the consummation of the world" (Mt 28.20). Any member, even though he be a bishop or pope, can conceivably apostatize, but the society itself will endure. The universal Church, moreover, is inerrant, although any doctor or theologian, as a private person, can deviate from sound doctrine. The corporate faith of the Church is a participation in the intuitive knowledge proper to Christ as Son of God (cf. Jn 1.18). In Him, as head, the whole truth is actually known, and through His Holy Spirit it is constantly being supplied and sustained in the members of the Church militant.

It is no mere metaphor, then, to say that the Church, herself, believes. All too often, while recognizing that the Christian revelation is a public one, we think of faith as a merely private response. We look upon the official Church as our teacher, and think of the faithful as individuals, but to the public character of revelation there corresponds a public faith—the infallible and indefectible faith of the universal Church. This faith of the Church is, in some sense, prior to that of any of her members. While it comes to life only in particular individuals, they are believers by virtue of their association with the Church itself.

The collective faith which permanently inheres in the Church as a whole must, of course, come to fruition in individual souls. It is not simply inserted into them from outside as a foreign substance. The Spirit of Christ, interiorly vivifying the whole Mystical Body, stirs up within them a Catholic instinct. This *sensus fidei* is granted to all, but not in a uniform manner. Each receives insight in a manner and degree proportioned to his office, and to the free munificence of the Spirit. These charismatic graces, however various they may be, never rend the Body apart. On the contrary, all the gifts of the Spirit are aimed to build up the whole Body in unity "until we all attain to the unity of the faith and of the deep knowledge of the Son of God."[9]

There are two types of deviation from full participation in the Church's faith. The first is an excessive collectivism, which would treat the faith of the community as a substitute for personal engagement. In many Catholic countries (and doubtless in some Protestant areas too) it has been noted that individuals often cease to practice their faith once they move outside the strongly religious atmosphere in which they have been reared. Does this not tend to show that their faith was too much a matter of social conformity, and never became for them a fully responsible commitment?

The opposite deviation would be to construct a faith of one's own rather than submit to the revelation which was delivered, once and for all, to the saints. This homespun type of faith, the very hallmark of sectarianism, often reflects a high degree of moral fiber, but it is an erratic and ambiguous thing; it overlooks great portions of God's revelation to mankind and all too often identifies transient human opinions with the saving message of God. The sordid harvest of doctrinal dissension, often accompanied by serious moral and psychological deviations, confirms the Catholic in his distrust of such religious individualism.[10]

THE CHURCH AS WITNESS

Having seen the extent to which faith, itself, is a social act, we may now consider briefly the transmission of faith. In the practical order, to believe and to bear witness are almost interchangeable terms. To confess one's faith is to deepen and strengthen it. To keep it bottled up in oneself is to warp and obfuscate one's own vision. Thus the Scripture can say: "With the heart a man believes unto justice, and with the mouth profession of faith is made unto salvation" (Rom 10.10). The spoken word, or its equivalent, is the spark by which the faith of others is ignited. "Faith depends upon hearing" (Rom 10.17).

In confessing her faith the Church becomes, after Christ, the great witness. She is God's abiding herald, unfailingly strengthened by his indwelling Spirit. The whole Church, like the Apostle, can apply to herself the Psalmist's phrase, "I believe, and so I spoke" (Ps 115.10; 2 Cor 4.13).

Any act of confession is two-pronged. It takes place in the presence of God and of man. In its Godward dimension it is an act of religious worship. In its human dimension it is an appeal to others to share in one's faith and in the blessedness which faith bestows.

Every witness claims to be, in his way, an authority. He professes to know what he is talking about, and asks others to rely on his word. To be a witness in the full sense means to speak in the presence of transcendence, to seal one's words, at least implicitly, with an oath. To bear false witness is a form of sacrilege.[11]

All this is eminently true in the case of the Church. She speaks as the society to whom God has manifested His innermost thoughts; she is conscious of being His elect people. More than this, she has been divinely commissioned to bear witness to the world—to publish to all mankind the wonderful counsels of God. Like the prophets of old, she has a message which she cannot contain within her breast (cf., Jer 20.9). Like her divine Master, she must say, my message is not mine, but His who sent me (Jn 8.28; 14.24, etc.). Obviously, no merely human agency could, without blasphemy, claim that its message was the very word of God, but the Church must do so because she has heard God's voice, and knows that she speaks by His power. She is a mere mouthpiece by which God communicates with mankind. Where matters of faith are concerned, *Vox Ecclesiae est vox Dei*.

In a wide sense, the apostolate is the task of the whole Church, but in order that the Church may speak with a united voice, she needs a regulative organ. God has provided for this need by establishing the hierarchy. No individual can claim to speak for the Church except insofar as he submits his personal word to her hierarchical supervision. The magisterium is not the sole font of initiative in the Church, but it plays an indispensable role in deciding what new directions are sound, and which should be rejected. If there were no such official teaching body, the misconceptions of individual believers would become inextricably confused with the doctrine of the Church as such.

How does this teaching function of the Church affect the very structure of the individual Catholic's act of faith? Is faith a submission of the mind to God, to the Church, or to both?

According to Catholic theology the authority of the revealing God, and it alone, is the true motive of faith, specifying it as a theological virtue. Faith is a total assent to the testimony of another, and could not, with propriety, be accorded to the word of anyone but God. No man or group of men, not even the Church as a created reality, deserves such an unqualified submission. On the other hand, the testimony of God comes to the believer through the Church. Her authoritative proclamation is a created reflection, or echo, of the divine testimony. Both are received in one and the same act. In the normal situation, then, faith is both divine and catholic. It has these two dimensions, since it embraces God's word as attested by the living Church. "He cannot have God for his Father who does not have the Church for his mother" (Cyprian).[12] We submit to God precisely by acknowledging the witness whom he has commissioned and certified.[13]

In the first section of this essay we spoke of the Church as believer; we saw that she is the great believer, and that no one can come to faith, at least in a secure way, without uniting himself to her. But now it is also apparent that the Church, precisely because of her faith, is the great witness. As witness she is the instrumental cause and norm of the faith of her members.

SIGN OF CREDIBILITY

No witness tries to prove his own testimony. If he did so, he would abdicate his dignity, and descend to the level of a school teacher. The Church as an authoritative witness makes no attempt to demonstrate the mysteries that God has put into her keeping. She confidently proclaims them, assuring men that her word is reliable.

Any witness, however, must be able to show the credibility of his message; otherwise men could not prudently believe. In exhibiting the credibility of her message the Church points to supernatural signs—signs by which God himself marks her out and accredits her to mankind. These signs are all, in some sense, miraculous.

Among the signs of credibility there is one which exceeds all others in its universal accessibility. That is the sign which the Church, herself, is. By her wonderful vitality, and her abundant fruits of holiness she is a visible reflection of the Lord whom she preaches, and a visible token of the kingdom which she announces. Her steadfastness, her patience, her devotion to all that is humanly good, and, in short, her imitation of the manifold virtues of her Master render her singularly attractive. These qualities have a greater drawing power, it would seem, than the numerous physical miracles which God is pleased to work in the Church.

Vatican Council I called attention to the function of the Church as a sign raised up among the nations, an irrefragable testimony to her own divine origin.[14]

Vatican Council II was convened in order to renew and refurbish the sign which the Church is, and must be, for it is possible that the sign should, at times, become dim and tarnished. Through a kind of obsolescence, some of the Church's institutions and practices may lose their relevance. With the passage of time they may cease to serve any real purpose, or carry any clear meaning. The sins and laxity of Catholics, moreover, can become a scandal, positively repelling persons sincerely in quest of union with Christ. According to Pope Adrian VI, the faults of Catholics were primarily responsible for the defection of so many Christians at the time of the Protestant Reformation. Since that time the indifference and worldliness of Catholics has greatly contributed to the perpetuation of Christian disunity. In order to attract all those in whom the grace of Christ is at work, the Church must become more in practice what she already is in principle; she must be more evidently a sign of the peace and charity of Christ.

It would be easy to cull from the Council documents a lengthy catena of passages accenting the need for interior renewal in order that the Church may become a more effective sign of Christ in the world. According to *Lumen gentium*, for example, the Church "exhorts her sons to purify and renew themselves so that the sign of Christ may shine more brightly over the face of the Church" (art. 15). *Gaudium et spes* reminds the faithful that "to the extent that they neglect their own training in the faith, or teach erroneous doctrine, or are deficient in their religious, moral, or social life, they must be said to conceal, rather than reveal, the authentic face of God and religion" (art. 19). As a remedy, Christians are exhorted to practice justice and charity toward all men. "What does the most to reveal God's presence, however, is the brotherly charity of the faithful who are united in spirit as they work together for the faith of the gospel and who prove themselves a sign of unity" (*ibid.*, art. 21). Later in the same Constitution (art. 43) we read:

> Although by the power of the Holy Spirit the Church has remained the faithful spouse of her Lord and has never ceased to be a sign of salvation on earth, still she is very well aware that among her members, both clerical and lay, some have been unfaithful to the Spirit of God during the course of many centuries. In the present age, too, it does not escape the Church how great a distance lies between the message she offers and the human failings of those to whom the gospel message is entrusted.

The Decree on Ecumenism calls attention to the close connection between unfaithfulness within the Church, and the Christian disunity that so often results from, or is perpetuated by, it. For this, Catholics must bear much of the blame. "For although the Catholic Church has been endowed with all divinely revealed truth and with all means of grace, her members fail to live by them with all the fervor they should. As a result, the radiance of the Church's face shines less brightly in the eyes of our separated brethren and of the world at large, and the growth of God's kingdom is retarded" (art. 4).

To make the Christian message credible is the task of the whole Church and of each member, insofar as he allows himself to be transformed by her. To the Philippians St. Paul wrote that the faithful "shine like stars in the world" in the midst of a "depraved and perverse generation" (Phil. 2.15). This is what the Church of every age and locality must do if she is to achieve her mission. She must become a radiant symbol of all that human nature can attain to with the assistance of divine grace.

MYSTERY OF FAITH

The Church, insofar as she is a visible community, can be a manifest sign of Christ, but she is not wholly visible. Her true beauty is from within, and does not appear to flesh and blood. Her life, now hidden with Christ in God, will not become manifest until the last day. This must be so, because the Church is a mystery, a part of the great mystery which she herself announces.

That there are bishops, priests and laity who call themselves Catholics, is an evident fact, but that they comprise a divinely fashioned community, the new Israel, the elect people of God, the temple of the Holy Spirit, the first fruits of the final kingdom, all this we do not see. No matter how brilliant the sign of Catholic holiness becomes, there will always be a gap between what we see and what we believe. We can never say *video Ecclesiam catholicam*, but only, *credo Ecclesiam catholicam*. To accept the Church as a supernatural society is a daring leap that goes far beyond all that reason can hope to demonstrate. It is an act of faith.[15]

PRIESTLY MEDIATION

I have concentrated, in these pages, on the Church's prophetic ministry, which is directly ordered toward the response of faith, but this is not the full picture. In any full treatment it should be noted that the transmission of revelation involves also the priestly ministry—that is to say, those activities of the Church which directly aim at sanctification. For the acceptance of faith is a supernatural work, an effect of grace. Through her prayers and sacramental rites the Church is incessantly at work, mediating God's grace to men. Thanks to her life of worship, her preaching itself is fecundated from above, so that the Church can say, like her divine Lord, "my words are spirit and life" (Jn 6.63). In the liturgy the Church prays frequently for the conversion of infidels (e.g., in the Good Friday intercessions), and for an increase of faith in her members (e.g., in the Prayer of the Assembly for the thirteenth Sunday after Pentecost). To those who come to her she administers the Sacraments of faith. Baptism is the Sacrament of faith par excellence; it imparts the basic attitude. But all the other Sacraments are, in their way, channels of faith. They serve to nourish and strengthen the supernatural convictions of those who devoutly receive them.[16]

CONCLUSION

The Church's relation to the faith of her members is complex, even paradoxical. As mediator, she participates in the extremes which she unites. She does not present herself as a third party, interposing herself between the faithful and their Lord, but as a bridge or meeting ground, sharing in the functions of the Redeemer and the redeemed. Thus it is possible for her to be both subject and object of faith, believer and believed. She can call for faith in her word, and yet tell men to believe in God alone. She can point to herself as a manifest sign and yet declare that she is a mystery hidden in God. She implores the Lord for the grace of faith, and sacramentally imparts the grace which she petitions. Compressing all these data into a single formula, we may sum up. The Church, through her prayers and sacramental action, receives and bestows the grace whereby she infallibly heralds, and herself indefectibly believes, on her own assurance,· confirmed by the sign of her own vitality, that she herself is the very people of God, redeemed and sanctified by the most precious Blood of His only begotten Son.

6

The Church and the Faith of Protestants

In the preceding chapter we have seen that Christian faith, at least in its Catholic manifestations, has an essentially ecclesial structure. Our main conclusions may be summarized in three propositions. First, faith is ordinarily a submission of the mind, not simply to the revealing God, but also to the Church as his authorized representative. Second, faith is sustained by the visible life of the Church, which constitutes for the Catholic an unfailing motive of credibility. Third, the individual's faith is a participation in the collective faith which exists in its fullness in the whole Church as the Bride of Christ. Hence faith, of its very nature, draws men into communion with the Church. At the end allusion was made to the priestly mediation of the Church as a source of the grace which arouses and strengthens faith. Thus the links between faith and the Church are numerous and important.

In the present chapter I should like to deal with another aspect of this question. Is this ecclesial structure a necessary property of Christian faith as such, or is it a peculiarity of the faith of Catholics? I shall deal particularly with the faith of Protestants, since they constitute the majority of non-Catholics, and are best known in the United States. It might seem that Protestant faith is a sheerly personal relationship between the individual and Christ, and that consequently the ecclesial dimension is here lacking. I shall contend that, while the churchly aspect is less obvious in the faith of Protestants than in that of Catholics, it is by no means absent; in fact, it tends to become increasingly prominent as the faith of Protestants grows in vigor and self-awareness. While the limits of this chapter will preclude a full exploration of the question, I think it will be possible to outline the structure of the problem, and to show how this dimension of church-relatedness provides a convenient standard by which to compare and contrast the faith of Catholics and Protestants.

PROTESTANTS AND CHURCH AUTHORITY

Let us begin, then, with the most conspicuous difference between the faith of Protestants and Catholics, namely, the relation of each to the authoritative witness of the Church. The Catholic, when he believes, submits to the Church as God's representative in the world, the bearer of his revealed word. To him it seems almost self-evident that if God's revelation is to be perpetuated in its purity and integrity there must be an infallible rule of faith. It is not enough for men to preach their own personal convictions; their word must be a faithful and guaranteed echo of God's word.

St. Thomas, speaking of formal heretics, says that they cannot have divine faith at all because they do not accept the divinely given and infallible rule of faith, namely, the teaching of the Church.[1] Some theologians, extending this principle to all non-Catholics, have thought it impossible for anyone to make an act of Christian faith unless he submits to the magisterium of the Church. To come across such views it is not necessary to go back to the seventeenth century, for instance, to John of St. Thomas[2] and the Carmelites of Salamanca.[3] We can find the same position strenuously defended in Orestes Brownson's article entitled, "Faith Not Possible Without the Church," which takes the position that no one can make an act of supernatural faith unless he acknowledges the infallible authority of the Catholic hierarchy.[4] Even such a distinguished theologian as Cardinal Newman, in his *Discourses to Mixed Congregations*,[5] eloquently maintains that Protestants, in rejecting the living magisterium of the Church, are, in consistency, forced to bargain for private judgment. And since private judgment is the very antithesis of faith it follows that, in Newman's opinion, Protestants, generally speaking, cannot have faith, at least in the Christian meaning of the term.

The Catholic theological consensus of the twentieth century, ratified by numerous statements in Vatican Council II, may be said to have settled the question by maintaining that Protestants can, and often do, have supernatural Christian faith. This presents the theologian with the challenge of explaining how men can believe in the Christian revelation with a supremely firm assent if they do not accept the authorized magisterium of the Church. Does not Christ Himself say in the Gospel, "He who hears you hears Me and he who rejects you rejects Me" (Lk 10.16)? Does not St. Paul teach that faith cannot arise except through the preaching of one who is duly sent (Rom 10.14–15)? And reason itself would seem to indicate that if there is no infallible organ of revelation faith will not have the guarantees necessary to command our unwavering assent.

As a first step toward a reply to this difficulty we may note that Protestants do not normally deny the existence of all authoritative human testimony concerning Christ. Liberal Protestantism in the nineteenth century did make an effort to separate faith in Christ from faith in His appointed witnesses. Harnack and others, applying critical scholarly methods to the New Testament, sought to reconstruct the teaching of Jesus by the techniques of scientific history, but the quest for the historical Jesus failed to produce any agreed upon or well-defined picture of Jesus. If it yielded any "assured results," it proved that one must either accept the New Testament portrait of Jesus substantially, as it stands, or else renounce any hope of attaining Him as a clearly delineated and religiously significant figure.

Thanks to the initiative of theologians such as Karl Barth, the twentieth century has witnessed a notable revival of biblical faith in the Protestant world. Protestants today generally feel committed, not simply to the historical Jesus, but to the Christ of faith portrayed in the Gospels. This Biblical faith involves a certain commitment to the Church—that is, to the apostolic Church whose doctrine and devotion are enshrined in the New Testament.

For many Protestants, Christian faith has a still broader basis in ecclesiastical authority. Anglicans, Lutherans, and Calvinists, appealing to the early confessional writings of their respective denominations, not uncommonly hold that the decisions of the early Ecumenical Councils and the ancient Christian Creeds are authentic interpretations of Scripture, constituting for all subsequent generations an irrevocable rule of faith.[6] No Christian today, they would maintain, may call into question the great trinitarian and christological decrees of Nicaea and Chalcedon. These orthodox Protestants do not, of course, regard the late medieval or modern Councils as equally authoritative, but this denial does not cancel out the essentially ecclesial quality of their faith. They do feel definitively committed to certain Church decisions.

The great difference between Catholics and Protestants is, of course, that the former do, and the latter do not, recognize an infallible, living magisterium. Practically speaking, there is no authority in the world today which can command the assent of Protestants in the name of divine faith. The decisions of all existing ecclesiastical bodies are regarded as having a merely relative and provisional value. They can, perhaps, oblige the individual in the name of prudence or obedience, but not—it is felt—in virtue of faith itself. To question the decrees of a bishop or council, they would say, is not necessarily to doubt the word of God.

As previously noted, some Catholics have exaggerated the importance of this difference, maintaining that the lack of an infallible voice in the Protestant world must make all faith impossible. A fallible teacher, according to this view, is in no position to call for the unqualified assent of faith, but this objection, pressed to its logical conclusion, would prove too much. It would prove that practically no Catholics could have faith, for it is extremely rare that Catholics hear the infallible pronouncements of the magisterium at first hand. The normal way in which a Catholic learns what to believe is through the very fallible mediation of parents, parish priests, and catechism teachers. Hence, we may argue *a pari* that the fallible nature of Protestant churches and preachers does not prevent them from being channels by which believers arrive at divine and Christian faith in the biblical doctrines endorsed by the apostolic Church. The fact that the word of God is sometimes mingled with errant human opinions is not fatal to faith itself. Thanks to the interior testimony of the Holy Spirit it is possible for Christians to assent with all their heart to the data of revelation proposed in this imperfect form.

Granted that the absence of an infallible, living magisterium does not prevent the inception of faith, still it does have important effects. To be sure, there is no essential difference between the faith of Protestants and Catholics. For each, the formal object is the same—the authority of the revealing God. For the Catholic, however, faith involves submission to the living magisterium of the Church, acknowledged as God's voice in the contemporary world. This does not mean, merely, that he will accept certain doctrines which Protestants generally regard as unrevealed, such as the Assumption of the Blessed Virgin. More fundamentally, it means that a new modality is added to faith itself. When the Catholic and the Protestant profess materially the same propositions, they do so in qualitatively different ways. The Catholic accepts the central dogmas of the Trinity, the Incarnation, and the Redemption, and indeed the whole complex of revealed truths, as vouched for by the teaching Church. Implicit faith in the whole profession of the Church is, for him, logically prior to the acceptance of any particular doctrines.

The Catholic's unconditional commitment to the authority of the living Church profoundly affects the phenomenological quality of his faith. He does not simply believe in what he has himself examined and found true. He accepts a given doctrine because it is taught by God's official organ of revelation. Whenever the magisterium solemnly enunciates a new doctrinal formula as being an implicit element in the revealed deposit, the convinced Catholic accepts it with a spontaneity which the Protestant finds incomprehensible. For the Protestant the objective rule of faith is something already given, primarily in the Bible; for the Catholic, the complete rule of faith includes the free and partly unpredictable—though by no means arbitrary—decisions of the living magisterium. This puts the believer in what is, naturally speaking, a rather uncomfortable position, but it purges his faith of any self-opinionated attitude and requires him to remain completely docile.[7]

Why does not the Catholic's intellectual obedience to the Church involve a new formal object, making his faith specifically different from that of the Protestant? Quite clearly, because the Church itself is believed on the authority of God. To the eyes of faith, the sovereign light of God's truth shines through the teaching Church. Just as the Church testifies to God, so God testifies to the Church. Each manifests the other. Because Christ commissioned and equipped the Church, the Catholic's submission to the Church is not something strictly additional over and above his submission to Christ. Indeed any Christian, in his general will to conform his mind to Christ's teaching, already adheres, in a vague and implicit way, to the Church. Thus even the faith of Protestants can be called implicitly Catholic.

The relation between implicit and explicit Catholicity must, however, be rightly understood. It is not a mere matter of logical implication, such as obtains between the two propositions, "Peter is a man" and "Peter is capable of laughter." One cannot deduce from the fact that Christ was the Son of God the further truth that the Roman Catholic Church teaches with divine authority. To discern that the Catholic Church represents Christ in the modern world is a new discovery, for which additional light is needed. It is a progress similar to that made by a believing Jew when he discovers that the Old Testament bears witness to Christ. Just as the Old Testament, to any Christian reader, is full of testimony to Christ, so the Christian dispensation, for the Catholic, finds its historical fulfilment in the Church to which he belongs. The Protestant will not be able to see this without an insight into the inner life of the contemporary Church. For him to accept Catholicism would be simultaneously a fulfilment of the faith he previously had, and a conversion to something radically new.

THE CHURCH AS MYSTERY AND SIGN

As we noted in the preceding chapter, the Church is both a mystery hidden in God and an evident sign of credibility. It is at once an object of faith and a miraculous proof on which our faith rests. Of these two aspects, Protestants tend to stress the former. Without denying the visibility of the Church, they prefer to dwell on its hiddenness. They would not normally say that the historical Church, as an organized society, constitutes a miraculous evidence for the truth of her own teaching. To the minds of some Catholics this suggests the question whether Protestants can have a sufficient rational basis to render their faith, by human standards, a fully prudent act.

In answering this question we should not overlook what Protestants themselves say about their motives for believing. Lutherans and Calvinists commonly place little emphasis on the external motives of credibility; they accentuate rather the freedom and obscurity of the act of faith, as an assent made possible by the grace of God. Their principal motive of credibility, on their own showing, would seem to be the inner witness of the Holy Spirit. No Catholic, of course, would deny the role of the Holy Spirit in the act of faith.[8] In individual cases, God can so incline men's minds from within that no external grounds of persuasion are strictly necessary, but it seems unlikely that Protestants generally believe by virtue of these interior motives alone. As a matter of fact, Protestants themselves often speak of supporting external evidences, which render their faith entirely reasonable and prudent.

Catholic polemicists, anxious to expose the inner weaknesses in the Protestant position, often quote the dictum of St. Augustine: "Ego vero Evangelio non crederem, nisi me catholicae Ecclesiae commoveret auctoritas."[9] But this statement can hardly be taken as meaning that Augustine thought that faith was impossible outside the Church. Such an interpretation would be contrary to his own express statement that non-Catholics can have faith.[10]

In systematic apologetics it has long been customary to establish the messiahship and divinity of Jesus on historical grounds, without reliance on the authoritative testimony of the living Church.[11] The arguments have something less than apodictic force, but are not worthless. The Protestant can use historical evidences of this type, but is by no means limited to them. Like the Catholic, he too can appeal to the wonderful expansion and stability of the Christian religion, its marvelous fruits of sanctity, its coherence with the highest human wisdom. Such arguments are part of the stock in trade of Protestant, as well as Catholic, apologetics manuals.

In considering the motives of credibility available to Protestants, we may appropriately ask whether the faith of Catholics and the vigor of Catholicism are not an important item. Some Catholic theologians have made this claim. Msgr. Journet, for instance, approvingly paraphrases Cardinal Billot as follows: "If the Church, which is ever the pillar and the ground of truth, should ever, by impossibility, be wiped out, and her perpetual profession of faith suddenly silenced, we should soon witness the disappearance of all that remains of divine truth in the separated Churches."[12] Notwithstanding the apparent complacency and the polemic tone of this statement, it deserves serious consideration. The Lutheran Pastor Max Lackmann in a recent work quotes and endorses the views of a nineteenth century Lutheran, who expresses himself in almost identical terms. According to this author, A. F. C. Vilmar, "The total collapse of the papacy, were this possible (a fact which we neither envision nor desire), would bring down upon us the dissolution of all the denominations into smaller and smaller groups, the atomization of the Church, the reign of raw unbelief, and finally the total destruction of Christianity."[13]

Even if these statements are exaggerated—as may readily be admitted—it does seem that the strength and durability of the Catholic Church has a salutary effect on the faith of Protestants. This very fact, besides consoling us Catholics, should remind us that we have too often neglected our responsibilities toward Christians of other confessions, taking a cold and contentious attitude toward them, perhaps even secretly hoping for their religious decline. We should seek to strengthen them in all that is good, and at the same time be ready to acknowledge our own debt to them. We Catholics are frequently encouraged and sustained in our faith by seeing the religious convictions and fervent lives of our separated brethren.

THE COLLECTIVE FAITH OF THE CHURCH

Thus far we have studied the relation of the Protestant's faith to the Church as an authoritative witness, and as a motive of credibility. We still have to consider a third aspect, namely, to what extent does the Protestant's faith integrate him into the divinely founded community of believers? Does it make him a sharer in the collective faith of the true Church?

Many observers have detected a qualitative difference between Protestantism and Catholicism in this regard.[14] The Protestant, they would say, believes as an individual making a personal act of responsible commitment; he utters on his lips what he himself perceives through the enlightenment of the Spirit; his faith is primarily a vertical communion with God and with Christ the Lord. The Catholic, on the other hand, puts the accent more on historical solidarity with other men in the believing community. He allows the faith of the whole group to come to expression in his mind and on his lips. He therefore accepts with implicit faith whatever the Church believes, and feels no need to investigate personally the grounds of each particular doctrine. To make a neat opposition, it might seem proper to say that Protestant faith exists first in individual persons and only subsequently in the community as a gathering of like-minded believers; whereas Catholic faith is primarily an attribute of the divinely founded community and only derivatively the act of individuals who aggregate themselves to it.

This contrast contains a nucleus of truth, but it should not be pressed too far, lest we should fall into the error of identifying Protestantism itself with some of its Liberal and Sectarian manifestations. Whatever some Protestants may have thought, especially in the nineteenth century, it remains a fact, generally acknowledged today, that Protestants do not come to believe as autonomous individuals; they do so within a believing community—a family, a parish, a regional church—which introduces them to the faith and educates them in it. Nor do the Protestant Churches commonly look on themselves as free societies constructed by the organizational genius of their respective founders. Today, as in the sixteenth century, most Protestants take the note of apostolicity very seriously. They have no desire to frame new doctrines and ecclesiastical structures, but simply to adhere to the one foundation which has been laid, Christ and the apostolic Church (1 Cor 3.11, Eph 2.20).

It should be evident, then, that the faith of Protestants is not just a private encounter between the individual and the Lord. It has a communitarian and ecclesial dimension. However incomplete and faulty the teaching of certain Protestant groups may be—a question far too complex for discussion here—it must be recognized that their determination to persevere in the faith of the apostles forges a powerful bond between themselves and the earliest Christians. It gives them a real participation in the faith of the apostolic Church.

In view of this fact, it would be insufficient to say that the faith of Protestants is formally Christian, but only virtually Catholic. The apostolic Church with which Protestants wish to remain in continuity is already, in essence, the Catholic Church. Hence, the Protestant possesses, through his faith, a powerful bond with Catholicism—not, indeed, directly with the Church of today, but with that of apostolic times. In this sense his faith may be called formally Catholic. Many Lutherans and Calvinists, not to mention Anglicans, have insisted on this. They frequently express the desire to be called, not Protestants, but evangelical Christians, or even evangelical Catholics.[15] This is a development which we may welcome and approve. While holding that the fullness of Catholicity cannot exist without union with the Petrine See, we may concede that other Christian churches can have a certain share in Catholicity. The fact that they have come to cherish their Catholic heritage is a hopeful sign.

The faith of Protestants and Catholics, then, has greater structural similarity than is usually recognized. It is false to imagine that Protestants are committed only to the Gospel, Catholics only to the Church. Protestants adhere to the Gospel, and therefore to the Church in which the Gospels have their place of origin and their permanent home. Catholics adhere to the Church, and therefore to the Gospel which is both the source-book of her faith and the central theme of her preaching. The evangelical Churches in our day are anxious to reaffirm their Catholic heritage. The Catholic Church is seeking with equal zeal to renew itself according to the Gospel. These twin tendencies are bringing about a vast increase of mutual understanding. As evangelical Churches become more Catholic, and the Catholic Church more attentive to the Gospel, the separation narrows. We cannot say whether the gulf between us will ever, through God's grace, be bridged, but in the meantime we can rejoice in that partial solidarity which we already possess. As believing Christians we all share, at least imperfectly, in the one faith of the one, holy, catholic and apostolic Church.

CONCLUSION

In this chapter it has not been possible to do more than sketch the outlines of our subject. Even the sketch is incomplete. I have said nothing, for instance, of the relation of Protestants to the Church's life of worship. Actually they benefit from, and participate in, the worship of the Catholic Church. Whenever they validly confer any Sacrament we say that the Catholic Church is active in and through them. Because the Sacraments and the whole life of Christian worship have an unbreakable relationship to faith, this observation has an important bearing on the ecclesial quality of the faith of Protestants. In a fuller treatment we should have to discuss this matter at length.

From the preceding pages I hope at least one point has become clear. The existence of faith among our separated brethren is not something which we Catholics should find painful or embarrassing, something which we should gloss over or minimize. On the contrary, it is a fact which we can explain on our own theological principles, and when so explained, it increases our understanding, love and esteem of Catholicism itself. For the faith of Protestants, like every supernatural gift they receive, is a bond between them and the Church, giving testimony that the vital influence of the Church extends far beyond her juridical borders. Wherever the Gospel is sincerely preached and the Sacraments are faithfully administered, something of the Church is present. Wherever Christian faith is found, something of the Church has taken root in human minds. And the Catholic will say that this is the true Church, found in its substantial plenitude in the Catholic communion. This Church, as a supernatural force, is mysteriously at work in all believing hearts, and eagerly looks forward to the day when the Lord of the Church will return to establish, in its manifest beauty, His final, glorious Kingdom.

7

The Protestant Preacher and the Prophetic Mission

One of the most important theological advances of Vatican Council II was the explicit recognition given to the ecclesial character of Christian communities outside the Roman Catholic Church. The Decree on Ecumenism (n. 3) affirms that "many of the most significant elements which together go to build up and give life to the Church herself can exist outside the visible boundaries of the Catholic Church." In view of the Christian elements which constitutively pertain to them, these communities can "carry out many of the sacred actions of the Christian religion." These actions, moreover, "can truly engender a life of grace and can be rightly described as providing access to the community of salvation." For this reason, these "separated Churches and Communities . . . have by no means been deprived of significance and importance in the mystery of salvation." Article 1 of the same Decree throws further light on the ecclesial character of these communities by asserting that the separated brethren invoke the Triune God and confess Jesus as Lord and Saviour "not merely as individuals but also as members of corporate groups in which they have heard the gospel . . ."

Among the authentic Christian elements which subsist in the separated communities of the East and West one must reckon, most importantly, the twofold ministry of word and Sacrament. Protestant churches insist rather less than the Catholic and Eastern Orthodox on sacramental practice, but they claim to be, in an eminent sense, churches of the word. We must therefore ask ourselves whether, and to what extent, the word of God can be proclaimed with salvific power within Protestant Christianity. An investigation of this question will enrich our understanding, both of Protestantism, and of the theology of preaching.

In Catholic theological thinking, the Church heralds the gospel in the name of Christ its founder, by His command, and as a living organ vitally conjoined to His Spirit. But Catholic theologians are reluctant to admit that Protestant Churches have been divinely commissioned to proclaim the gospel, or that they are, as institutions, instruments of the Holy Spirit. Hence it seems problematical whether Protestant Churches can speak with the grace and unction of the Spirit, in a manner apt to elicit from their hearers the supernatural response of faith. The full force of this difficulty will become evident if we first propose a brief theological analysis of the nature of preaching and of the preacher's need for a divine mission.

THE NECESSITY OF A MISSION FOR THE PREACHER

The entire proclamation of the Christian revelation is, in a wide sense of the word, preaching. More precisely, preaching may be defined as the public proposal of the word of God in the name of the Church. The primary form of preaching is oral communication, in which there is a living, personal confrontation between the witness and his audience. Written preaching is a derivative form. Here we shall therefore attend chiefly to oral preaching.

There are many different types of preaching, such as the evangelization of infidels, the catechetical instruction of children and uneducated believers, pastoral exhortations, and the mystagogical sermons which often accompany the Church's public worship. As regards its immediate goal, preaching may seek to promote any of the various functions of the Church—faith, worship, or Christian conduct. For present purposes we shall confine our attention to preaching in so far as it is intended to generate or to perfect Christian faith.

The Christian tradition has recognized that the office of preacher is essentially prophetic. St. Albert the Great observes that preaching is "a kind of prophesying or exposition of prophecies."[1] St. Thomas calls it "quasi prophetare."[2] Modern theologians rather commonly take the same position. Thus Abbe Moeller writes: "Preathing in the strict sense pertains to the prophetic mission of the Church. . . . The preacher is a witness and interpreter of God, just as were the prophets of old."[3] Abbé Rauch likewise declares: "The preacher is a prophet in the original sense of the term—one who declares what God has taught him."[4]

The prophet, however, is one who speaks in obedience to a call, or mission, received from God. He acts, not on his own initiative, but as moved by God, whose envoy he is. His mission includes not simply his original designation, but the divine afflatus which is upon him when he speaks. Thus the prophet is an instrument—a living, conscious, rational instrument—of God, who speaks in and through him. Because of this dynamic presence of God, the prophet's words have a divine fecundity surpassing that of merely human eloquence. They are not empty speech but events of the supernatural order. They are, according to many theologians, always efficacious—either unto justification or unto judgment, depending on the response of the hearer.[5]

The concept of preaching which appears in the New Testament is thoroughly prophetic. This is apparent from the terminology alone. As Przywara remarks, "The formal root-term, for ancient prophetism as for the new evangelism, is the *kērygma*."[6] The Greek term *kēryx*, as is well known, designates an official herald or crier. "*Kērygma* means, therefore, official messenger announcing the official message."[7]

The prophetic notion of preaching is eminently verified in Jesus' proclamation of the kingdom of God, as described in the Gospels. His public mission begins with the descent of the Spirit upon Him in His Baptism. He preaches in virtue of this mission, inasmuch as "the Spirit of the Lord is upon me" (Lk 4.18). He says nothing on His own authority, "but He who sent me, the Father, has commanded me what I should say and what I should declare. ... The things, therefore, that I speak, I speak as the Father has bidden me" (Jn 12.49–50; cf. 8.28). His words possess a mysterious unction. "All bore Him witness, and marveled at the words of grace which came from His mouth" (Lk 4.22). But those same words have power to condemn whoever does not believe: "The word that I have spoken will condemn him on the last day" (Jn 12.48; cf. 15.22).

St. Paul displays a profound consciousness that, in preaching, he is discharging a commission laid on him by God (cf. Tit 1.3) and that he does so with special assistance from heaven. He informs the Corinthians that he speaks as an "ambassador of Christ," that "God exhorts through us," that "Christ speaks in me" (2 Cor 5.20; 13.3). He congratulates the Thessalonians for having welcomed his gospel "not as the word of men but, as it truly is, the word of God" (1 Th 2.13).

A special mission from God is not simply a property of Paul's own preaching but a permanent attribute of Christian preaching itself. Paul clearly teaches this in his letter to the Romans, where he asks the rhetorical question, "How are men to preach unless they be sent (*apostalōsin*)?" (Rom 10.15). The great tradition of Christian theology has interpreted this as requiring a special mission in any Christian preacher. In their exegesis of this text St. Thomas[8] and Luther are equally emphatic in declaring that whoever should pretend to preach without being sent by God would be in a class with the false prophets of whom God said to Jeremiah: "I did not send them, yet they ran" (Jer 23.21). Luther, who wrote his commentary as a Catholic in 1515–16, goes so far as to declare: "This is the mighty arrow that strikes down the heretics."[9]

Modern commentators, both Catholic and Protestant, generally interpret the Romans text in much the same way. The comment on the text in Kittel's *Wörterbuch* may be taken as representative:

> God does not send books to men; He sends messengers. By choosing individuals for this service, He institutes the office of

proclamation. Not every Christian is called to preach. ... A preacher is not a reporter who recounts his own experiences. He is the agent of someone higher whose will he loudly and clearly makes known to the public. Without calling and sending preaching is a self-contradiction and even a deception. It holds out something which has no reality. If there is no sending, the preaching of Christ is propaganda, not mission.[10]

The term "preaching" may, of course, be used in a descriptive sense to include what Friedrich here calls a "fraud," but in the theological sense preaching essentially involves a divine mission. Hence we may subscribe to the definition of Fr. Rock: "Preaching is an act of the ministry whereby one *duly sent* publicly announces the truths of the faith in order that men might be moved to believe and to do what is necessary to be saved."[11]

THE MISSION AND THE EFFICACY OF PREACHING

Having established the absolute necessity of a mission for authentic Christian preaching, one may ask what kind of necessity is here involved. Is it merely a precept or also a necessity of means? We shall attempt to show that the latter is the case.

The New Testament makes it clear that Christ, in commanding the apostles to spread the gospel, engaged Himself to provide them with a special assistance for this task. This assistance was conferred in plenitude when the Spirit descended in the form of fiery tongues. After Pentecost the Holy Spirit, working in and through the apostles, gave their words a superior force and efficacy. Clothed with power from on high (Lk 24. 49), they preached with boldness (*parrēsia*: Acts 4.13, etc.), with power (*dynamis*: 1 The 1.5, etc.), and with persuasive force (*plērophoria*: *ibid*.). Their words pierced the hearts of their[17] hearers (Acts 2.37) and were more piercing than a two-edged sword (Heb 4.12).

One cannot, of course, infer that what was given to the apostles is necessarily the property of every Christian preacher. As founders of the Church, the apostles had special graces, but analogous graces are needed by Christian preachers in every generation if the Church is to discharge her mission throughout the ages. The preacher is something more than a mere occasion of faith for his hearers. According to the doctrine of St. Thomas, he is an external disposing cause of faith.[12] The proper effect of his activity—namely, the positive disposition toward faith in the soul of the hearer—is, according to many theologians, a reality of the supernatural order. A supernatural disposition could not, it would seem, be the per se effect of a purely natural activity. Hence it is clear that the preacher, in order to accomplish his appointed task, must be divinely assisted in his proposal of the word of God.[13]

St. Thomas expressly teaches that a special charism—the *gratia sermonis*—is ordinarily given to those who are charged with teaching and persuading publicly in the Church.[14] Thanks to this gift, the preacher's tongue can become, as it were, an instrument of the Holy Spirit.[15] The proper effect of the *gratia sermonis* is to lend spiritual power to a man's words ("quod quis efficaciter loquitur," in the phrase of St. Thomas). Such a gift is required in order that those who possess revealed knowledge may be able to communicate it according to the needs of their hearers.[16] In brief, it enables a man to communicate his faith to others.[17]

There has been considerable discussion recently among theologians as to the precise kind of supernatural causality at work in preaching: whether it is *ex opere operantis* or *ex opere operato*, whether it results in actual or sanctifying grace, etc. These questions need not concern us here. The essential point, which would be accepted by the majority of theologians, is that the Christian sermon is a supernatural action—a true *Heilsgeschehen*—and must be so in order to fulfil the essential purposes for which Christ instituted the preaching office.

Once one adverts to the function of the *gratia sermonis*, the prophetical quality of Christian preaching is obvious. Yet this charism does not of itself turn every preacher into a prophet in the proper sense of the word. For one thing, it does not necessarily render him infallible. Only in her most solemn preaching is the Church entirely exempt from error.[18] The pastor or curate preaching an ordinary Sunday sermon is not entitled to exact the "obedience of faith" for every word he utters. His word is not, simply speaking, the word of God. Nevertheless, his office or delegation guarantees him certain charisms which, if he cooperates, can render his word supernaturally efficacious. As Mura has said: "The divine mission of which the preacher of the gospel can avail himself is the first guarantee of his apostolic fecundity."[19]

It is evident, then, that preaching, as a solemn communication of the faith of the Church, requires a proportionate charism in the herald. Since this charism is a divine gift essentially ordered toward the proclamation of the word, we may conclude that the divine mission is for the preacher a true necessity of means.

CATHOLIC DOCTRINE ON HOW THE MISSION IS RECEIVED

We have seen that a divine mission is necessary, with a necessity of means, in anyone who claims to preach the Christian gospel. In order to approach the question whether Protestants can have any such mission, we must inquire more particularly how this divine mission is conferred.

According to Catholic doctrine Christ vested in His apostles, as those who "were with Peter," the total responsibility for the propagation of the gospel, including the right and duty to oversee the whole process of the evangelization of non-Christians and of the instruction of the faithful. In discharging this mission the apostles could, and did, take others into their company. The episcopal college, as the successor of the apostolic college, had inherited the plenitude of its transmissible functions. In being invested with his office, the bishop receives a share in the apostles' own mission. "Just as Christ was sent by God, and the apostles by Christ, so the bishops and all who have succeeded the apostles have been sent by the apostles."[20]

The fulness of the preaching power is and necessarily remains proper to the episcopate.[21] Just as the ministry of the word was the principal office of the apostles (cf. Acts 6.2; 1 Cor 1.17), so, according to St. Albert and St. Thomas, the bishops' primary task, which they should be reluctant to delegate to others, is the work of preaching to their flocks.[22] Nevertheless, it is not practicable for the bishop to reserve the whole work of preaching exclusively to himself. He may, therefore, suitably co-opt fellow workers to assist him in a subordinate capacity. By ordaining and empowering deacons and priests the bishop can, as it were, extend his activity to places where he cannot be personally present. Although some measure of teaching authority can be conferred upon laymen and clerics in minor orders, they do not have that special fitness to receive the delegation to preach which deacons and priests possess through their ordination. According to present canon law, laymen may not be appointed to give sermons in church.[23]

Frequently in the history of the Church the question has arisen whether the right to preach could not come through some channel other than "canonical mission." Subject to certain distinctions which we shall subsequently explain, the Church has regularly replied in the negative. As Scheeben profoundly observes, the doctrine that there can be some doctrinal mission independent of the hierarchical magisterium is the beginning, or at least the end, of all heresies.[24]

Some heretics have maintained that every Christian has the right to preach the word of God; some have asserted that this is the inalienable privilege of every priest; others have claimed to have received directly from the Holy Spirit a divine call which exempted them from the need of any ecclesiastical recognition. Against all these classes of heretic, the Church has steadfastly affirmed that anyone, in order to preach, needs a legitimate mission, "and this cannot be given except by the bishop."[25] Such was the doctrine of the Council of Verona, reasserted by the Fourth Lateran Council,[26] against the Waldensians; such, likewise, was the teaching of Constance against the Wycliffites and Hussites;[27] such, finally, was the doctrine of Trent against the Protestants.[28] The same view is reflected by the present Code of Canon Law.[29] Summarizing the canonical provisions on this point, Fr. McVann declares:

No interior urge to preach the Gospel, no sense of a divine call, no sacred order or religious profession, can make up for the lack of proper authorization. Only one, the Pope, is above all need of canonical mission, for he receives his power to preach directly from his assumption of the papacy.[30]

To preach without canonical mission is not merely to be deprived of the added graces which such a deputation would guarantee. As McVann points out, it is a serious offense to intrude into the pulpit without due authorization. The sinfulness of the act is apparent once it is understood that preaching, as an official ecclesiastical function, pertains only to those who have public authority in the Church.[31]

To preach is not an act of spiritual government, and thus does not involve jurisdiction strictly so called, but St. Thomas, using the term "jurisdiction" in a wide sense, was able to write: "To preach and to hear confessions are acts involving both power of jurisdiction and power of order."[32] To preach without faculties is, therefore, as Fr. Stanley remarks, "analogous to the hearing of confessions without faculties."[33] The action is both illicit and, in a certain sense, invalid, since the public and ecclesial quality of the action is not duly verified.

THE PROBLEM OF PROTESTANT PREACHING

From what we have already said concerning the necessity of a divine mission and the manner in which it is derived, the problematical situation of the Protestant preacher is evident. The Protestant Churches, having lost both the regular apostolic succession and communion with the primatial see, can confer no mission on their preachers. The Protestant minister possesses neither valid orders nor the delegation required for preaching. It would seem evident, then, that he can have no divine mission to preach. And since preaching without a mission is an absurdity, it apparently follows that there can be no such thing as Protestant preaching. Is it not obvious, then, that the Protestant who mounts into the pulpit is a mere pseudo preacher—a modern successor of the pseudo prophets assailed in Scripture? His sincerity or human eloquence, great though they may be, cannot equip him for the supernatural work of preaching. If he lacks the *gratia sermonis*, he cannot be a disposing cause of grace in his hearers. At best he will be a merely accidental occasion for any spiritual good which they may derive from his words.

Some Catholic writers have taken approximately this view of Protestant preaching. Pierre Charles, S.J., has sought to show that the entire Protestant system collapses because of the impossibility of establishing an authoritative mission for the Protestant preacher.[34] According to the Reformation, Fr. Charles maintains, the only justification for the Church is the preaching of the word. Ordination is conceived to be nothing other than the rite of constituting preachers; all ceremonies are regarded as mere adjuncts to preaching. But Protestant theology cannot, without involving itself in contradictions, explain how the minister gets any valid title to preach the word of God. He cannot receive it from the Protestant Church as an organization, for the visible structure of the Church is of human institution. Hence he can receive only what the community as a group of believers can delegate. "But that men should delegate to men the *ministerium verbi* can be nothing but an open contradiction."[35]

With polemical dexterity Père Charles turns against the Protestants in general the questions asked by Karl Barth:

> What are you doing, you man, with the word of *God* upon *your* lips? Upon what grounds do you assume the role of mediator between heaven and earth? Who has authorized you to take your place there and to generate religious feeling? And to crown all, to do so with results, with success? Did one ever hear of such overweening presumption, such Titanism. . . [36]

A look at the actual situation, according to Père Charles. verifies what the theological principles would lead one to expect. Anglicanism, he finds, has escaped the "anéantissement du sermon," but only because it has retained a considerable portion of the old Catholic tradition. Elsewhere within the Protestant world the sermon has collapsed. "I believe that we may, without being uncharitable to anyone or engaging in cheap apologetics, recognize that the Protestant sermon is the *reductio ad absurdum* of the idea that gave it birth."[37]

This empirical confirmation is precisely the point that many observers, both Catholic and Protestant, would contest. Not all reporters are agreed that Protestant preaching is so obviously inferior to that of Catholics. Abbé Moeller, in fact, suggests the contrary: "In the field of preaching our Protestant brethren have considerably surpassed us, because they have elaborated a 'theology of the word.'"[38] And he gives particular credit to Barth for this achievement.

Propst Asmussen has squarely put to Catholics the problem of how they judge Protestant preaching.[39] According to the Catholic theory, he remarks, the ministry of Protestants, not coming from the apostles, does not come from Christ; their preachers would be mere delegates of the community and hence would not really possess any preaching office. But many Protestants, according to Asmussen, hold with the Augsburg Confession (and against the early Luther) that the ministry is of divine institution, and not a mere creation of the community. While frankly admitting that it is difficult to show the full legitimacy of Protestant ministries, Asmussen asks whether Catholics, in their concern for legitimacy, do not overrate the importance of organizational and juridical factors. Cannot extraordinary modes of ordination under certain circumstances be equivalent to normal modes at other times? Cannot God, when He so wills, dispense with the ordinary institutional machinery? The fact that Protestant ministers, whether regularly or irregularly, have some kind of divine mission is, in Asmussen's view, proved by the results. Referring to Rom 10.14–15 he writes:

> Now you might say: your mission is not in order; you are not legitimately sent. I should have understanding for that objection. But I doubt whether you can seriously say: preaching, faith, and invocation do not occur among you Protestants. For even if we show very imperfect evidence of our mission, still it must be

hard for you to question the proofs of power which have been
furnished by Protestant preaching.... The phenomenon of our
Kirchentage simply does not fit into the framework in which you
generally consider our ministry. The spiritual efficacy which
has been achieved is not explicable without a *de facto* antecedent
mission.[40]

It would be quite beyond the scope of this essay to pass judg-
ment on what goes on at a contemporary German *Kirchentag*:
whether the results could be accounted for on natural grounds
or call for a supernatural cause. But we must squarely face
Asmussen's questions on the level of theological principle.
There seem to be three possible positions: (1) that Protestants
have no mission and hence cannot preach fruitfully; (2) that
Protestants have a mission and can preach fruitfully; (3) that
Protestants have no mission and nevertheless preach fruitfully.
All of these positions offer their difficulties, but perhaps, by
introducing certain distinctions we can outline a solution that
does justice to all the data of the problem.

ECHOES OF AUTHORIZED PREACHING

Prescinding, for the moment, from the titles of the Protestant
preacher, we may note that the Protestant believer is not
entirely beyond the reach of authorized Catholic preaching.

Most obviously is this true with regard to Holy Scripture.
The prophets and apostles whose words are preserved in the
Bible were authentic preachers of the faith, sent by God. As
recent Scripture scholarship has made clearer than ever, the
New Testament is, in large part, a crystallization of the official
preaching of the primitive Church. Not only is this true of books
like 1 Peter (which may have been a Baptismal homily), but even
the Gospels are, to a great extent, records of Christian sermons.
The Lutheran Althaus hardly goes too far when he declares of
all the biblical accounts of Jesus: "They are a portion of Christian preaching, which calls for faith."[41] Scripture, inspired
by God, represents the very prototype of Christian preaching,

and is charged with a mysterious power to evoke and sustain the life of faith. Some would even hold with Father (now Cardinal) Bea that "the very words of Holy Scripture, read and explained with the necessary dispositions, possess an inherent light and force which surpass the light and force of human words, and give them singular and unique authority and power."[42]

Thus the Protestant reader, when he ponders the Bible, makes contact with Catholic preaching. And it is not merely in private and silent reading that the Bible manifests its salutary power. When it is read aloud and discussed in a study group, or in a meeting of communal worship, its efficacy is not lost. We should say, even, that Protestant sermons, when they contain quotations and echoes of the Bible, convey something of its grace and unction. And since Protestant preaching at its best is thoroughly biblical, this observation is not lacking in importance.

Besides the Bible, other Catholic preaching may have a notable influence on Protestants. The Fathers and Doctors of the Church inspired many of the best thoughts and phrases in the writings of the Reformers, and are still read in the original by some Protestant ministers. The contemporary Catholic magisterium—including the declarations of bishops, councils, and Popes—comes to the attention of Protestants through the radio and press, and does much to sustain and deepen their faith. Thus there are many ways, direct and indirect, in which authorized Catholic preaching, with its *gratia sermonis*, has an impact on the faith of Protestants.[43]

These echoes of authorized preaching are important for seeing how the faith of Protestants is related to the prophetic office of the Catholic Church, but the question which presently confronts us has to do with the functions of the Protestant minister. He presumably does something more than mechanically repeat what others have said. He makes an effort to express his own earnest convictions concerning the word of God. He seeks, moreover, to adapt the eternal message of the gospel to the needs, capacities, and particular situation of the audience before him. In the remainder of this essay we shall consider whether it is possible that in this task he will be divinely assisted for the benefit of his congregation.

NONHIERARCHICAL PREACHING

We have pointed out that preaching in the proper sense of the word (as most Catholic theologians understand it) is a public heralding of the Gospel, such as can be done only by one who has positive authorization from the Church. Those who receive the commission for public preaching, and they alone, receive the special charisms corresponding to this function.

It does not follow that those who lack the office or delegation of preacher receive no *gratia sermonis* at al!. St. Thomas teaches, on the contrary, that women, although they cannot be preachers in the Church, can receive a *gratia sermonis* to perform such apostolic tasks as may be within their competence. They may, for example, engage in "doctrina privata," addressing "one person or a small group, speaking informally."[44]

Catholic theology recognizes a vast field of Christian witness, instruction, and exhortation which requires no special mandate from the hierarchy. While this type of activity is not unrelated to the preaching of the hierarchy, and ordinarily tends to bring men into more effective contact with the latter, it has a dignity and importance of its own. This is attested by Scripture, and by the common consent of theologians.

In the New Testament the term *kēryssō*, as we have already observed, normally designates the official proclamation of the gospel by a herald specially appointed for the task. But there are many other terms, such as *prophēteuō, euaggelizomai, didaskō, katēcheō, martyreuō,* and *homologeō,* which are not restricted to the apostles nor, it would seem, to those positively deputed by them. Especially is this evident regarding the last of these terms. The Gospel makes it clear that all Christians are obliged, under certain circumstances, to make an open profession of faith: "Everyone who acknowledges (*homelogēsei*) me before men, I also will acknowledge him before my Father in heaven"

(Mt 10.32). By his Baptismal confession of faith the Christian enters upon the path of salvation: "With the heart a man believes unto justice, and with the mouth profession of faith is made unto salvation (*homologeitai eis sōtērian*)" (Rom 10.10).[45]

The doctrine that the laity, as such, possess a certain apostolic mission was frequently expressed by the Fathers. St. Augustine, in fact, repeatedly says that all Christians have the duty, so far as in them lies, to preach. The following quotation is typical:

> Which of the faithful can keep silent about Christ? Listen to me, brethren. Do you think that we should stand here alone and announce Christ, and that you should not preach Him? Whence do those come to us, wishing to be Christians, whom we have never seen, whom we do not know, to whom we have never preached? Did they perhaps believe though no one announced the truth to them? The Apostle says: "How shall they believe unless they hear? How shall they hear unless someone preaches to them?"
>
> Therefore, the whole Church preaches Christ.[46]

St. Thomas gives considerable scope to the laity in the field of Christian witness and instruction. To confess one's faith, he holds, is mandatory whenever the honor of God or the needs of one's neighbor require it.[47] The task of instructing potential converts may be incumbent on any believer. Godparents, moreover, have the duty to school their charges in Christian conduct.[48] Elsewhere he points out that fraternal correction, in so far as it is an act of charity, pertains, not simply to prelates, but to all who have the virtue of charity.[49] He adds that, when necessary for the defense of the faith, a Christian subject should publicly admonish his religious superiors.[50] Hence St. Thomas teaches that simple laymen have a positive responsibility to profess, defend, and extend their faith by private conversation and sometimes by public declarations.

Vatican Council II, in its Constitution on the Church (n. 35), expressly teaches that lay persons, as "living heralds of the faith," must evangelize the world, both by speech, and by the living testimony of their conduct.

LAY WITNESS OF PROTESTANTS

Granting, then, that there is a certain kind of testimony and instruction proper to the laity which is an exercise of specifically Christian virtue, it may be asked whether Protestants can share in this type of activity. To reply, it will suffice to examine the theological foundation for the power and duty of such Christian witness.

"It cannot be denied," writes Fr. Congar,[51] "that apostleship is an obligation laid on every Christian by his baptism and by charity." This opinion agrees with the statement of the French bishops in their meeting of 1946: "The laity do not have to wait to be empowered in order to discharge their individual apostolic mission: it is enough that they are the faithful, with the demands made upon them by their Baptism and Confirmation."[52] In other words, the mission of the laity to conduct the kind of apostolate we have been considering is antecedent to, and independent of, any positive deputation from the hierarchy. It is neither created by the hierarchy nor could they, if they should so desire, totally suppress it. The obligation to profess one's faith arises by operation of divine and natural law, granted that a man is a baptized or confirmed believer.

In this theological foundation one may distinguish between an individual and interior aspect on the one hand, and a social and sacramental aspect on the other. These two aspects are mutually complementary, and in the normal case both will be verified. But for the sake of clarity we shall consider them separately.

(1) The subjective foundation is apparent from the doctrine of St. Thomas summarized on the preceding page. It consists in faith animated by charity. A realistic appreciation of the spiritual needs of one's neighbor will arouse an impulse to instruct him to the best of one's ability in the truths which seem to be necessary or important for his salvation.

Even more fundamentally, men profess their faith because faith demands expression: "I believed, and so I spoke" (2 Cor 4.13). By the very law of its being, a living faith is radiant.

The Scholastic maxim, *bonum est diffusivum sui et communicativum*, applies here. Once it takes root in souls, the gospel tends to grow, to bear fruit, and to propagate itself. The joy and force which the believer experiences in his commitment to Christ flow into his words and actions. The testimony of the Christian, prompted by faith and charity, is at all times a supernatural act, wherein the Spirit co-operates. In times of persecution, when the profession of faith becomes most difficult, its supernatural strength will shine forth most brilliantly. The *gratia sermonis* will at such times be given most abundantly. "The Holy Spirit will teach you in that very hour what you ought to say" (Lk 12.12). The witness of a Christian, when threatened by suffering, becomes a glorious deed, charged with contagious power.

How far does all this apply to Protestants? Clearly, they too can have the infused virtues of faith and charity. Their faith, to be sure, is defective, and seriously so, in so far as they fail to acknowledge the true Church and profess certain positive errors. But such a faith, faulty though it be in content, can be living and intense. It can, therefore, express itself in words and conduct. The Protestant will have the power, and at times the duty, to profess his supernatural convictions. How could his faith remain a purely interior thing, bottled up in himself?

We are not speaking here of a merely subjective obligation, such as arises from an erroneous conscience. The Protestant's obligation to suffer rather than deny his Lord, to convert his unbelieving neighbor to a belief in God or in Christ, or to instruct the ignorant in those revealed truths which he really knows, may be an objective duty, in conformity with God's will. When he performs this duty with the help of grace, his action can be impressive. The constancy of many Protestants in the face of the Nazi persecution, especially in the concentration camps, aroused admiration and praise from Catholics.[53]

As Catholic theologians have often observed, there is no a priori reason why a Protestant in good faith cannot be, in the theological sense, a martyr.[54] Vatican II, in its Decree on Ecumenism (n. 4), praises those separated brethren "who are bearing witness to Christ, sometimes even to the shedding of their blood." If they can be martyrs, it seems evident that Protestants can also be confessors, since the greater includes the less.

(2) The socio-sacramental foundation of the power of Christian witness consists in Baptism and Confirmation. Most fundamentally, Baptism, the Sacrament of faith, is the Sacrament of the external confession of faith. Already at the baptismal font, before receiving the bath of regeneration, the neophyte must make a solemn profession of his firm adherence to Christ.

Through the working of this Sacrament, faith and the other supernatural virtues are infused or deepened. The recipient is, moreover, marked with an indelible character whereby he is consecrated to the service of Christ. Henceforth he has the duty to profess his faith in his words and actions, and a sort of title to the graces he will need to fulfil this obligation. Speaking of the relation between Baptism and the apostolate, Monsignor Philips writes: "Even the least of the elect undergoes a total transformation through Baptism. . . . It is no longer the witness who bears the message, but rather the message which bears him, stimulates him, and guarantees him a surprising efficacy."[55]

That Protestants may be, and often are, validly baptized, is universally admitted by Catholic theologians and is strongly reaffirmed in the Vatican II Decree on Ecumenism (n. 22). And there can be no doubt but that their reception of the Sacrament places them under a special regime of graces, enhancing their power to adhere to Christ and confess his name. Father Lombardi, among others, has noted this fact: "As God's children, they will certainly be aided by their Father with abundant graces, so that they may preserve their state of adopted sons, and therefore be able to profess the true faith, at least in the indispensable articles. . . ."[56]

The fact that they are baptized, moreover, gives a certain liturgical dimension to the confession or martyrdom of Protestants. Whether they know it or not, they are sacred persons, persons who have received a share in the triple office of Christ as Prophet, Priest, and King. Even with reference to formal heretics, St. Augustine was able to write: "The sign of

Baptism, when it remains unaltered, suffices even among heretics to confer a consecration, though not a participation in eternal life."[57] The Protestant, therefore, has a share in Christ's priestly power, thanks to which he can, for example, administer and receive the Sacrament of Matrimony. So, likewise, he is more intimately incorporated into Christ the Prophet than is the unbaptized believer. His confession of faith is more intimately linked to Christ's prophetic office.

The Christian initiation, begun with Baptism, should normally be completed through Confirmation and the Eucharist. These three Sacraments together constitute the total Christian initiation. Confirmation is par excellence the Sacrament of Christian testimony. By deepening the Christian's faith it tends to transform him—according to the measure of his cooperation with the sacramental grace—into a perfect witness. As St. Thomas explains, "the confirmed receives the power, *quasi ex officio*, of publicly professing the Christian faith by his words."[58]

The Protestant does not receive the Sacrament of Confirmation *in re* and hence does not receive the quasi office to bear public witness, but there is no reason to doubt that those Protestants who long to be faithful witnesses to Christ have an implicit desire for the Sacrament and thus receive some of the graces ordinarily conferred in Confirmation. In this way the Sacrament can benefit even those who do not have access to it and are perhaps unaware of its reality as a Sacrament.

We conclude, therefore, that the Protestant, thanks to the theological virtues of faith and charity and his sacramental Baptism, is able to render a truly Christian witness, analogous to that which can be rendered by the Catholic layman without special empowerment from the hierarchy. But there are differences between the Christian witness of a Protestant and that of a Catholic, and these must be noted.

The Protestant does not possess the full Catholic faith. In some ways his profession actually contradicts the faith of the Church. For this reason his witness will be mutilated. He does not give testimony to the *whole* Christ—to Christ living on in His

Mystical Body, which according to Catholic doctrine subsists today in the Roman Catholic Church. His confession, then, will tend to engender in his hearers a faith no more perfect than his own; that is to say, a dogmatically incomplete faith, insufficient for full membership in the Mystical Body, as specified in *Lumen gentium*, n. 14.

The Protestant's testimony, moreover, will not dispose his hearers to receive the full apostolic witness of the hierarchy. When he speaks as a Lutheran, or Calvinist, or simply as a Protestant, he testifies to some extent against the truth. Hence his act of confession is, objectively speaking, ambivalent. While it tends to instil a genuine Christian faith, it at the same time disposes men against the plenitude of that faith and the Church which God had made necessary for salvation (cf. *Lumen gentium*, n. 14).

In some respects the testimony of Protestants impedes the spread of Christianity even at the most rudimentary level. It augments the picture of Christian disunity. The Vatican II Decree on Ecumenism (n. 1) pointed out that such discord "inflicts damage on the most holy cause of proclaiming the good news to every creature." The Churches meeting at Evanston likewise frankly acknowledged this: "Our divided witness is a necessarily defective witness, and indeed a scandal in the face of the non-Christian world."[59] Many souls are deterred from believing in Christ because of the spectacle of mutually contrary Christian confessions.

While maintaining, therefore, that the Protestant, as a baptized believer, can and sometimes must be a witness to Christ, we must add that the value of his testimony is ambiguous and that it can do harm as well as good.

PROTESTANT MINISTRIES: THE PROBLEM

We have examined the general vocation of Protestants, simply as baptized believers, to express and propagate the faith which is theirs. We have seen that this mission exists, although in a deficient manner, and that a Protestant can therefore have a divine call, under certain circumstances, to "preach" in a very wide sense of the word.

Doubtless the power of the average Protestant to radiate his faith goes far to explain the continued existence and vitality of Protestant Christianity, but it does not seem to us to be the principal factor. In the Churches of the Reformation, as within Catholicism, the great bulk of Christian testimony and education is performed by a special class of men whose lives are primarily dedicated to the work of the ministry. These men are set apart from the "laity," considered as the great body of Christians living in the world. The choice of the ministry, in the sense of a special vocation, involves assuming a new status in which the mode of one's existence is dictated by the needs of the apostolate. It is evident that many Protestants adopt the ministry as a calling. The Catholic theologian must therefore ask himself whether the Protestant, while remaining Protestant, can be called by the Lord to leave his nets and become a fisher of men (cf. Mt 4.19–20). Can he be "separated for the gospel" (Rom 1.1; cf. Gal 1.15)? Can he be entitled to exclaim with St. Paul, "Woe to me if I do not preach the gospel" (1 Cor 9.16)?

The question is of some urgency in the present phase of the ecumenical dialogue. The German Lutheran, Hans Asmussen, has insistently put the question to Catholics: "What is our ministry according to your conceptions?"[60]

The question of Protestant ministries is extremely obscure and complicated. Part of the difficulty comes from the lack of any agreement among Protestants themselves as to the nature of their ecclesiastical offices. Some would hold with Tillich that "there are in Protestantism only laymen; the minister is a layman with a special function within the congregation."[61] The great majority, however, at least among conservative Protestants, would agree that there is a class of ministers who are set apart by a special vocation. As to their powers, there is again no unanimity. But it would be agreed that the public ministry of word and sacrament is normally the task of this special class. Traditionally. Protestantism has put predominant emphasis on the ministry of the word. The early Luther, in fact, virtually reduced ordination to the process of selecting preachers.[62] Many modern Lutherans, however, deplore this as too narrow.[63]

What constitutes the special vocation which the minister must have? In Protestant, as in Catholic, theology, two aspects are recognized: the interior (or "vertical") and the exterior (or "horizontal"). Religious individualism tends toward the view that the vocation is essentially complete with the interior call, and that ordination is nothing but "a corporate recognition of the grace-gift, investing with the authority of the Church the exercise of that gift within the community."[64] But orthodox Protestants, making more of the social dimensions of Christianity, tend to regard the ecclesiastical side of the vocation as no less important than the "vertical." These ecclesiastically-minded Protestants, however, are far from agreed as to how ministers are legitimately constituted in the Church. Some would hold that every local congregation can issue a "call" and that the laying on of hands is unessential. Many of the older Presbyterians, on the other hand, held that ordination by the ordained was indispensable. Some Lutherans still hold in principle that only bishops can rightly ordain (although they generally admit of exceptions in abnormal cases).

Even among those who insist on ordination, there are wide divergences of opinion about what this ceremony accomplishes. Many would say that the rite itself effects nothing; but High Church factions tend to look upon it as actually conferring special charisms and powers.

Lutheran Church polity is particularly indecisive and eclectic. Many Lutherans proclaim that their Churches are not committed to any definite type of organization, that they can adopt an episcopal, presbyteral, or congregational order, or any combination of these, as they see fit.[65]

In the face of such vague and various theories, it is most difficult for a Catholic to reply to Dr. Asmussen's question. How can one place a theological interpretation on a ceremony which remains so equivocal in the minds of those who use it? One is tempted to retort by asking: "What do you Protestants hold concerning your ministries?" But notwithstanding the obscurity of the matter, certain general statements can be made.

As we have mentioned, there are two aspects to be considered—the interior and the exterior. The interior vocation and its working may be called charismatic, prophetic (in a special sense), or pneumatic. The exterior aspect may be called juridical, institutional, and in some cases sacramental.

Ordinarily these two aspects go together. The interior vocation urges one toward assuming a particular state in the visible Church. And legitimate induction into that state, especially when effected through the Sacrament of Order, itself confers interior graces. But there is no perfect equivalence between interior and exterior. The interior call normally precedes the exterior in time. The Holy Spirit, moreover, preserves a certain liberty in the Church: He can distribute many of His gifts to those who lack physical access to the normal institutional apparatus.[66] Conversely, it is possible for the recipient of an external call and of a Sacrament to refuse the grace that is offered him, and hence to lack certain charisms normally pertaining to his office.

Because of the relative independence of the pneumatic and the institutional, it will be possible for us to consider each of these aspects separately.

PROTESTANT MINISTRIES: THE CHARISMATIC ASPECT

Christianity since the earliest days has been characterized by free and sporadic manifestations of the Spirit. In reading Acts or 1 Corinthians, we cannot fail to be struck by the abundance of charismatic irruptions in the primitive Christian community. St. Paul mentions a whole series of graces of knowledge and utterance, culminating in a gift called "prophecy" (1 Cor 12–14). Prophecy, in this sense, was a purely charismatic grace enabling one to speak intelligibly for the profit of the Church. In the communal services of worship the prophets were permitted to discourse as the Spirit prompted them, subject to certain rules of good order (1 Cor 14.26–33).

While these "prophets," unlike the apostles, were not official heralds of revelation, they had an important function in the life of the community. It was their task to speak for the "edification, encouragement, and consolation" of their fellow believers (1 Cor 14.3). Occasionally they predicted the future or revealed the secrets of hearts. When unbelievers happened to be present, the utterances of the prophets were likely to convince them that "God is truly among you" (1 Cor 14.25). Thus, while these prophets did not precisely give sermons, they spoke with spiritual power. A prominent exegete has recently pointed out that good Christian preaching should have some of the qualities of prophesying as St. Paul here describes it.[67]

The unpredictable gifts of the Spirit, so characteristic of the apostolic and subapostolic Church, have not ceased in modern times. *Mystici corporis* asserts that they will never be lacking in the Church. The structure of the Church, according to this encyclical, consists neither of hierarchical grades alone nor of charismatics alone; both are essential.[68] In any sound ecclesiology, therefore, room must be left for the gratuitous interventions of the Spirit.

Does the Spirit bestow such charisms outside the visible body of the Church? Certain affirmations in *Mystici corporis* might lead us to hesitate before answering. The Holy Spirit, we are told, is the soul of the Roman Catholic Church alone; hence, no separation should be made between the spiritual and the juridical, between *Liebeskirche* and *Rechtskirche* (§62). The Spirit of Christ, moreover, refuses to dwell with sanctifying grace in members that are wholly severed from the Body (§55). These affirmations, however, by no means exclude the activity of the Spirit, *intuitu ecclesiae*, among non-Catholics. It is Catholic doctrine, indeed, that the interior grace and movements of the Spirit extend beyond the limits of the visible Church. Otherwise, as Franzelin points out, conversions would be impossible.[69]

More than this, the Spirit frequently dwells with sanctifying grace in non-Catholics who are united to the Church by the bonds of unrecognized desire. Especially is this true of the baptized. Referring to Acts 10.44, Father Sartory remarks that if the gifts of the Spirit could be poured out on pagans before their baptism, there is far more reason to suppose that His charisms may be found among baptized Protestants.[70]

Catholic theology has traditionally admitted the existence of charismatic, including prophetic, graces outside the visible society of the Church. The New Testament calls the Cretan poet, Epimenides, a prophet (Tit 1.12). The Fathers of the Church quite freely declared that the gentiles had their prophets.[71]

The Old Testament makes it clear that the charism of prophecy was not confined to members of the Chosen People. Newman, in his discussion of the prophetic gifts which seem to be found among Evangelical Protestants, recalls that the prophet Balaam, though neither an Israelite nor a sharer of its faith, had a genuine prophetic mission.[72] And Father Congar, developing a similar thought, observes that the tribes of the Northern Kingdom, after they had lost the Levitical priesthood through their schism with Judah, continued to possess prophets in great abundance. This fact, he remarks "is the proof for us that God does not cease to visit and to guide through his prophets that part of his people which has fallen into schism."[73]

Recently Father Rahner has touched briefly on the subject of charismatic graces outside the Church. All charisms, he affirms, have their true home in the Catholic Church and are therefore found in greatest abundance within her. Yet it is also possible for genuine charismatics to arise outside her visible limits.

> The idea of special spiritual gifts, at least when each individual case is viewed separately, does not include that of being an exclusive privilege.... For the Christian knows, confesses and feels it in no way a threat to the uniqueness and necessity of his Church, that there can be and is God's grace and the grace of Christ outside the Church. He does not prescribe to what heights that grace can raise a human being without, and before, incorporating him or her into the sacrament of grace, the Church.[74]

The Roman magisterium has likewise given support to the view that prophetic charisms can exist among non-Catholic Christians. The "Instructio" of the Holy Office, *Ecclesia catholica* (1949), referring to the ecumenical movement, affirms that the intense desire for Christian unity which has manifested itself among non-Catholics is inspired by the grace of the Holy Spirit.[75] This would seem to indicate that the leaders of this movement have been, at least in some measure, guided by the Holy Spirit. Vatican II, in its Decree on Ecumenism (n. 1), likewise attributes the ecumenical movement to the grace of the Holy Spirit.

It might be thought that if non-Catholic religious leaders could have prophetic graces, this would be an adequate substitute for the hierarchical authority which they lack. Is not the prophet, by definition, an authentic messenger of God? Under the Old Testament, it is true, the prophets had, among other functions, that of establishing the faith, but since the fulness of revelation has been given in Christ, the authoritative teaching office has passed to the hierarchical Church, which possesses *ex officio* a certain prophetical status. The sporadic gift of prophecy exists rather, as we have mentioned, for "edification, encouragement, and consolation" within the Church. The charismatic prophets of the New Testament, therefore, are not authoritative teachers. Although they may occasionally discourse on doctrinal matters, they do so, not as rulers, but as simple members of the community. They may speak only according to the "analogy of faith" (Rom 12.6). Each prophet is subject to the judgment of others (1 Cor 14.29), especially those who have the grace of discernment of spirits (1 Cor 12.10). Like other Christian believers, they must submit to the norms of Christian orthodoxy (1 Jn 4.2–3) and to the authority of the apostles (1 Cor 14.37–38). Merely charismatic speakers, therefore, are no longer prophets in the strongest sense of the term. They are not organs of revelation independent of the Catholic hierarchy.

History gives many instances of prophetically inspired men who, preferring their own lights to the authoritative guidance of the magisterium, have fallen into sad delusions. The prophet who obstinately rejects the divinely established authorities in the Church automatically forfeits his supernatural mission, and ends by tearing down the Church which he was sent to edify.[76]

These observations apply to non-Catholic prophets as well as to Catholics. Even if they are not aware of the divine authority of the Church, Protestant charismatics are not completely independent of it. If their message departs from Catholic teaching or leads men away from the true Church, their witness is, to that extent, inauthentic, and their prophetic charism itself becomes suspect.

There is always something problematic about prophecy as exercised within dissidence. The prophet being in error on many essential points, his testimony will have limited value. Some Catholic theologians have suggested that the dissident prophet who is invincibly ignorant of the true Church can have a real prophetic mission, not as regards the universal Church, but as regards those of his own obedience who are linked to the *Ecclesia Catholica* by their good faith.[77] We should prefer to say that his utterances, while offering inadequate guidance, may contain insights of value, both for his coreligionists, and for the Church of God.

Since charisms are always given for the edification of the Mystical Body (Eph 4.12; 1 Cor 14.4; etc.), they will not be given outside the Church except with a view to leading men toward the Church, but men do not become Catholics in an instant. The conversion of a great Protestant leader, such as Newman, will be the result of a whole series of charismatic graces by which he and his followers have been brought progressively closer to Catholicism. Even if Newman had died before his conversion, it could hardly be denied that he already exercised an important prophetic ministry within the Oxford Movement.

One could think of many Protestants who seem to have played a genuinely prophetic role while remaining Protestants. Bouyer, in his work on conversion from Protestantism, makes frequent mention of Wesley, Kierkegaard, Grundtvig, Wilhelm Löhe, Adolphe Monod, and Louis Meyer in terms that would seem to place them in this category.[78] Congar, in his discussion of prophecy among dissidents, dwells particularly on Karl Barth. In his profound sense of the divine transcendence, in his insistence on the divinity of Jesus Christ, and in his forthright rejection of Modernism and of Nazism, Barth, according to Congar, cuts a prophetic figure.[79]

The spirit of prophecy, wherever it appears, testifies in favor of the true faith. Thus, Barth in his prophetic utterances reaffirms as a private person what the Catholic hierarchy has proclaimed as a prophetic organ—e.g., in its condemnation of Modernism under Pius X or of National Socialism under Pius XI. It is also true, as Bouyer remarks,[80] that the most fruitful revivals in Protestant Christianity have regularly been attended by a rediscovery of lost Catholic values. The Catholic will find in such a recuperative tendency a potent sign of the leading of the Holy Spirit.

It is not impossible, then, that a Protestant minister may have an authentic prophetic mission. This mission will not confer the public authority which would be required to constitute him a "preacher" in the full ecclesiological sense. But it will involve a certain *gratia sermonis* over and above that given to each and every Christian believer. Prophetic charisms doubtless play a role in accounting for the spiritual efficacy with which some Protestant leaders have proclaimed the word of God.

PROTESTANT MINISTRIES: INSTITUTIONAL ASPECTS

Because of the great weight which Protestantism has traditionally laid on the common priesthood of the faithful, and on the uncovenanted gifts of the Spirit, one might think that our survey of Protestant preaching would be substantially complete at this point. But in actual fact the laity—whether the ordinary faithful or the charismatic leaders—have borne no greater share of the apostolate in conservative Protestantism than in Catholicism. In Anglo-American "dissenting" Churches and in the Pietist sects spontaneous initiative from below has been an important factor, but in traditional Lutheranism and Calvinism the constituted ministers have kept almost complete control. The "pure preaching of the word" and the "right administration of the Sacraments"—the two cardinal functions of the Church—have been the almost exclusive prerogative of a professional class of "legitimately called" and ordained ministers.[81] As Hendrik Kraemer observes with regard to early Reformation Christianity, "the 'standing' and 'apartness' of the new-born 'ministry' were, in many respects, similar to those of the former 'clergy.'"[82]

Because of the primary role played by regularly constituted ministers in confessional Protestantism, we must say something about the theological significance of the Protestant ordination and *vocatio externa* in relation to the preaching of the word. The significance will, of course, vary considerably according to the theory of ordination professed by the particular ecclesiastical group involved, and we cannot discuss all the individual differences. We can, however, set forth here some of the Catholic theological principles which would be relevant to this question.

Negatively, certain things are clear. (1) Speaking of Anglican orders, Leo XIII wrote in *Apostolicae curae* (1896): "We pronounce and declare that ordinations carried out according to the Anglican rite have been and are absolutely null and utterly void."[83] We have no such authoritative decision regarding Lutheran or Calvinist ordinations, but it is difficult, generally speaking, to judge their situation more favorably. We may, therefore, take it for granted that Protestant ministers, by and large, do not have valid orders. Their ordinations are not, in the technical sense, Sacraments; they confer no sacerdotal character. This means that Protestant ministers, unlike Catholic priests, are not members of a special caste or "order" having the exclusive *potestas physica* to perform specifically hierarchical actions, such as, most importantly, the consecration of the Eucharistic elements. The Decree on Ecumenism (n. 22) reaffirms this traditional position. (2) The Protestant minister, even though he be lawfully appointed to office according to the constitutions of his Church, does not have an apostolic mandate. Being neither a bishop, himself, nor authoritatively sent by a bishop having jurisdiction in the Church of Christ, he cannot preach with such authority that others are bound, in the name of religious obedience, to accept his teaching. In the technical language of traditional theology, Protestant ministers lack both *postestas ordinis* and *potestas jurisdictionis*.

There should be no particular controversy about either of these negative observations. Protestants themselves (with negligible exceptions) do not look upon their ordination as a Sacrament in the Catholic sense, nor do they teach that their pastors wield jurisdictional power.

These negative judgments, however, do not exhaust all that may be said about the external call and ordination in a Protestant Church. Even without a sacramental character, hierarchical powers, or jurisdiction, there is still room for some positive significance. As Sartory puts it: "Lack of validity does not mean complete inefficacy. Hence we believe that a *vestigium ecclesiae* must be admitted also for the ministry." [84]

Sartory himself sees the significance of Protestant ministries in the line of the prophetic as opposed to the apostolic. The prophet, he says, is not ordained as the priest is; but he, too, has an office in the Church, his chief function being the proclamation of the gospel. Thus, the public ministry of the word in Protestant Churches, according to Sartory, involves a certain charism of proclamation, although this charism is defective to the extent that the minister does not consciously subject himself to the guidance of the Catholic hierarchy. [85]

Dom Gribomont speaks in much the same terms as Sartory. Protestant ecclesiastical offices, he maintains, are "nicht nichts." More precisely, they can effectually "serve as instruments of God's grace, being rendered fruitful through the charisms of prophecy and teaching, and thus contribute to the edification of the Church." [86]

We agree that, as these authors point out, Protestant ministries tend to be conjoined with various *gratiae gratis datae* for the heralding of the faith. But the exact connection between the office and the charisms deserves fuller study than Catholic theologians have yet devoted to it. Furthermore, it seems doubtful whether the significance of Protestant ministries, even from the standpoint of preaching, can be reduced to the charismatic alone. Without any pretense to completeness, we submit that the following five factors must be taken into account.

(1) In the first place, the ordination, or external call, to office is a visible and social recognition of certain interior qualities which the subject is believed to possess. In the opinion of others, he meets certain standards of natural talent, theological knowledge, and "orthodoxy" according to the standards of the group. He is, moreover, judged to show signs of an interior vocation. The liberal branches of Protestantism especially emphasize the primacy of the "interior gifts of grace"—gifts which come to the individual directly from God.

(2) The recognition of which we have spoken is not a simple acknowledgment of what has already occurred. It has positive results. In the first place, it clothes the subject with a certain prestige. Because of the group's approval he becomes an authorized spokesman. His activities take on a public significance, and this in a double sense: (1) he becomes able to address his own community as a trusted teacher; (2) he is able to speak to the world in the name of the religious group.

The failure of Protestantism to recognize the *potestus ordinis* and *potestas jurisdictionis* does not, then, totally deprive its regularly constituted ministers of special status. They are the official teachers and leaders of the group; they possess what the group recognizes as the *officium docendi et praedicandi*.[87]

The official status of the Protestant minister should not be taken too lightly. He is not a mere counterpart of the director of a club or professional association or of the functionary of a civil government. Vatican Council II, in the texts cited at the beginning of this chapter, has made it clear that Protestant communities have a genuinely ecclesial character. By reason of their visible and invisible Christian endowments, they have a kind of corporate life in Christ, and their public ministries must be understood in the context of this supernatural corporate existence. The various Churches obviously differ from one another in their respective fidelity to the total Christian heritage, but even where there are deviations, they do not simply cancel out the ecclesial character of Protestant ministries.

(3) The ordained minister or pastor is more than a functionary of the group, however. He represents not merely the Church, but, to some extent, Christ Himself in the eyes of his congregation. [88] Whether or not the group officially teaches that its ministers have special authority from God, the faithful will apply to their pastors the biblical words, "He who hears you hears me" (Lk 10.16). They will look upon their clergy as sacred persons, calling them "Reverend" (even though not "Father"). The ministers will consequently be in a position to do considerable spiritual good or harm, according to the type of leadership they supply.

(4) Will the special standing of the minister in his religious group entitle him to expect a sort of "grace of state"? In moral and ascetical theology the term "state" is currently employed in a wide sense to designate a person's place in society and the function which he habitually exercises. [89] Accordingly, the term "grace of state" may be used to mean "the graces needed to fulfil the duties imposed by the situation in which a person finds himself by reason of circumstances." [90] In the ordinary course of His providence God accommodates His graces to the dispositions and responsibilities of the recipient, as well as the spiritual needs of those who depend on Him.

From what we have said in the preceding paragraphs, there can be no doubt but that the Protestant pastor is in a special situation. Where there is good faith in the minister, and, speaking generally, in the congregation, it seems proper to suppose that the former will receive special helps to lead those who depend on him toward the truth. While this "grace of state" cannot be expected to result in miracles and may be partly offset by special temptations, it should not be dismissed as unimportant. In some cases, no doubt, this grace will even lead the minister or his subjects to a deeper affinity with the full Catholic heritage.

The objection might be made that since Protestant Churches exist contrary to the will of God, there is no reason to believe that spiritual ministries can be fruitfully conducted within them. This objection, however, reflects an unacceptable ecclesiological rigorism similar to that shown by Cyprian in the baptismal controversy. Its unsoundness is evident, since the Church has solemnly affirmed that the Sacraments can be efficacious within dissidence. While Protestantism is undoubtedly displeasing to God in so far as it diverges from Catholic truth and unity, it by no means follows that God does not wish there to be salutary ministries within Protestantism. Granted the fact of dissidence (of which He disapproves), God may will, *sub hypothesi dissidentiae*, that the Word and Sacraments should be administered as fruitfully as the situation of dissidence permits. No other view of the matter seems to do justice to God's universal salvific will.

(5) The supposition that Protestant ministers may receive special graces corresponding to their situation is reinforced by a consideration of their rite of ordination. This rite, as stated above, is not a Sacrament; it does not confer grace *ex opere operato*, but this does not mean that it can confer no grace. Of the sacraments of the Old Law, St. Thomas says that although they did not contain grace or confer it by their own power, they could nevertheless be efficacious as protestations of faith in the power of Christ's passion.[91] Something similar, *mutatis mutandis*, seems to be true of Protestant "quasi sacraments," including their ordination. More specifically:

(*a*) Even independently of its relation to the Sacrament, the Protestant rite of ordination may be a protestation of faith in the power of the Christian ministry and a fervent prayer for grace to fulfil it in a manner truly pleasing to God. The provisions of the Westminster Assembly of 1645 will illustrate what we have in mind. It is here prescribed that on the day of ordination "a solemn fast shall be kept by the congregation." The ordaining ministers are enjoined to say a prayer at the moment of the laying on of hands, in which they thank God "for fitting and inclining this man to this great work" and further "entreat Him [God] to fill him with His Spirit, to give him (whom in his name we thus set apart to this holy service) to fulfill the work of his ministry in all things, that he may both save himself and the people committed to his charge."[92]

When Protestants sincerely offer up official and communal prayers of this nature for their ministers, there is no reason to think that God will be deaf to their petitions.

(*b*) The Protestant ordination rite takes on an even fuller significance when considered in relation to the *sacramentum ordinis*. Externally and objectively, the rite points to the Sacrament, of which it is a *vestigium*, much as the ceremonies of the Old Law pointed forward to the Christian Sacraments, of which they were figures.[93] Because of this objective connection the rite is apt to arouse and express a sincere personal desire for the Sacrament.

Can one speak in this connection of a reception of the Sacrament *in voto*? The Catholic doctrine of the *votum*, very commonly applied to Baptism, Confession, and the Eucharist, may surely be extended to the other Sacraments. According to this doctrine, one who desires a Sacrament, but is physically or morally impeded from having physical access to it may, in proportion to the intensity and supernatural qualities of his desire, receive some of its fruits (*res sacramenti*).[94] As the Holy See has recently pointed out with regard to the *votum ecclesiae*, there must be an actual, though not necessarily explicit, desire for the reality in question.[95]

It seems meaningful to speak of an "ordination in desire" on the part of persons who, within a community, in good faith desire and intend to receive *priestly* ordination, but are not in fact ordained owing to a lack of power in the officiating prelate. Such might be the case, for example, with certain High Church ministers, who believe that their bishops have valid orders. The desire would not, of course, confer the sacramental character,[96] but it might give certain other graces corresponding to the priestly state.

In orthodox Protestantism, however, the ordaining officers and the candidate for ordination do not normally have an explicit desire for an essential effect of the Sacrament of Order, namely, the sacrificial function of the priest.[97] Will the desire, then, be sufficiently determinate to be called a longing for that Sacrament? While the question requires further study, we are of the opinion that such a person may actually desire properly sacerdotal graces, such as those of being a qualified herald of the Word of God and a director and shepherd of souls. He may also, as Thijssen suggests,[98] earnestly wish to unite men about the one table of the Lord. An intention of this sort, vague though it be, might be sufficiently oriented toward the Sacrament of Order so that the ensuing graces would take on a sacramental quality. The minister would in consequence be able to proclaim the word of God with something of the power corresponding to the priestly office. The Protestant rite of ordination, in so far as it fosters or expresses such a *votum sacramenti*, would itself deserve to be called a "quasi sacrament."[99]

It may even happen that what a Protestant perceives as an inner call to the ministry will, in fact, be the early stage of a vocation to the Catholic priesthood. In concrete cases, however, it is difficult to tell whether this is the case. If the minister eventually becomes a Catholic priest, we can reason retroactively that his assumption of the Reformation ministry was an initial response to an incipient sacerdotal vocation. But in most cases we must be content to leave the judgment to God, who alone sees His own graces and the motives of men's hearts.

In view of the preceding five considerations, it seems clear that the efficacy of the word among Protestant Christians need not be explained solely in terms of the common priesthood of all the faithful, nor even in terms of a merely charismatic vocation which comes *senkrecht von oben* to a few privileged individuals. The institutional structure of the Protestant Church, notwithstanding its defects, tends to foster, up to a point, the ministerial vocation. Thus the Protestant pastor, through his external vocation and ordination, may have a greater share than the layman in that *gratia sermonis* which we have shown to be requisite for the fruitful heralding of the Christian Gospel.

As we learn to take the ecclesial reality of the Protestant churches more seriously, we shall probably tend to think less exclusively in terms of a direct relationship between the

Protestant ordination and the Catholic priesthood. The Protestant ordination derives its primary value and significance from its connection with the Protestant ecclesial community, which in turn is related as a whole—with all its ministries and sacred actions—to the *Catholica*. This relationship is grounded, not only in the past, inasmuch as every Christian community stems from the apostolic community of the New Testament, but also in the future, inasmuch as organized Christianity is essentially oriented toward the eschatological community of salvation. Catholic theology can discern, in the various Protestant ministries, a kind of "extraordinary" and *de facto* efficacy, corresponding to the type and degree of ecclesial reality which is to be attributed to the Protestant community in question.[100] The traditional categories of "valid" and "invalid" are too crude to take care of the subtleties of the situation. The Protestant minister who is permanently called and ordained in a regular way, according to the prescriptions of his own church, is theologically something more than a layman, and, in view of his will to be a faithful shepherd, he can by no means be classified as a usurper of sacred authority.

THE TEST OF FRUITFULNESS

Dr. Asmussen, as we have seen, claims that the validity of Protestant ministries is proved by their fruitfulness. Referring to Mk 16.17–18, he holds that the New Testament recognizes the test of power. "We cannot, and will not, deny what Christ has done for us and through us. Any attempt to persuade us that our ministries are a nullity would be for us a denial of the deeds of God."[101]

As Thijssen has remarked, Asmussen here reverses the normal order of evidence.[102] Ordination and hierarchical mission are ordinarily the credentials whereby a man establishes his authenticity as a minister, rather than his ministry being a proof of his mission. In the first generation of Christian history the divine authority of the apostles was certainly manifested by the extraordinary fecundity of their preaching, attended by physical miracles, but God does not commonly give this extraordinary kind of attestation, especially not in lands where the faith has already been planted. In any case, one may question whether Protestant ministers can show the kind of signs referred to in the closing verses of Mark.

The test of fruitfulness has frequently been urged by non-Catholics against Catholics, by Evangelicals against Anglicans, and by sectarians against conservative Protestants. Newman, as an Anglican, had to answer the Wesleyans' claims to a valid ministry, and as a Catholic he had to reply to the Anglicans.[103] In each case he pointed out the extreme complexity of the argument which his adversaries were seeking to use. The chain of reasoning can be attacked at many points. How can it be proved, asks Newman, that preachers are really doing the work of God if they do not point the way to the true Church? Or if they do convert man to a salutary faith in Christ, is it really they who do so, or rather the Church which works before them? And if real effects of grace are attributable to their ministrations, does this prove the validity of the ordinances themselves?

In our opinion, the comparative fruitfulness of Protestant ministries is very well explained by the indications we have given. Those fruits are not so imposing as to warrant the claim of an objectively valid apostolic mission. The confessions of Protestant Christendom are too various, vague, and shifting to be the product of a fully authorized ministry. We gladly acknowledge that the Protestant proclamation of the Gospel often arouses a genuine and salutary, though doctrinally imperfect, Christian faith. But this can be accounted for without assuming that they have a public ministry which is *de facto* on a par with the Catholic priesthood. As believers, Protestants can give testimony. Their testimony may be fortified by an inner urge from the Holy Spirit to communicate their faith. That inner impulse, moreover, can be confirmed by an exterior call from the ecclesial community to the ministry of the word. This exterior call, in turn, may be attended with communal prayers and reverent ceremonies; in some cases it may be conjoined with a supernatural longing for the priesthood, or at least for some share in the authentic Christian apostolate. All of these factors can lend spiritual power to the Protestant witness, but none of them alone, nor all of them taken together, amount to a fully valid apostolic ministry according to the full intention of Christ.

On the other hand, it would be a mistake for Catholics, relying on traditional, juridical conceptions of the ministry, to ignore or disparage what the Holy Spirit may be accomplishing through the preaching of Protestants. Since Vatican II the whole question of ministries, both Catholic and Protestant, is beginning to appear in a new perspective, the precise implications of which have yet to be worked out. We are all forced to take more seriously the fact that in a tragically divided Christendom, juridically extraordinary ministries may be factually ordinary. The lines between the charismatic and the institutional are unclear, since charismatic graces tend of their own weight to find institutional expressions. It is increasingly obvious, moreover, that the ecclesial reality of Protestant Churches cannot be adequately judged by comparison with what Roman Catholicism claims for itself. Finally, as we become more conscious of the servant character of the Church, we shall come to look upon its ministries less in terms of power and privilege than in terms of function and service, both toward the Church and toward the world. In a renewed ecclesiology, more appropriate to the "pilgrim Church," it may prove possible at length to transcend some of the ancient dilemmas which have stood in the way of an ecumenical theory of ministries.

For the present it is clear, at least, that the Catholic preacher, looking upon his Protestant counterpart, cannot complacently appeal to the greater institutional regularity of his own situation. Lest he be found unworthy of his calling, he must exert himself so as to "stir up" the grace which has been given to him through the laying on of hands (2 Tim 1.6).

PART THREE

THE ECUMENICAL DIALOGUE

8

The Orthodox Churches and the Ecumenical Movement

Until recently it was commonly believed, by Catholics and non-Catholics alike, that the Roman Catholic claim to be the "one true Church" of Christ precluded membership in an organization such as the World Council of Churches. The teaching of Vatican II, in the Constitution on the Church, and the Decree on Ecumenism, has reduced, and perhaps even removed, this obstacle. The Church, without abandoning its claim to have remained substantially faithful to the full revelation of Christ, can advantageously participate in the give-and-take of ecumenical dialogue, and listen respectfully to the witness of other Christian traditions. While responsible theologians are not recommending immediate full membership of the Catholic Church in the World Council, many feel that the barriers are, today, practical and prudential rather than strictly dogmatic.[1] It seems evident that, with the passage of time, the Church will become more closely related to this and other ecumenical organizations. In the light of this probability, it is more pertinent than ever for Catholics to study the experience of the Orthodox Churches in their dealings with the Ecumenical Movement, and, in particular, with the World Council of Churches. In many ways, the Orthodox Churches have been deterred by the very elements in the Ecumenical Movement which have been distressing to Catholics. Insisting that Orthodoxy alone has retained the fullness of the Christian patrimony, the Eastern churches have consistently opposed those Protestant groups which have conceived of Christian unity as something to be newly constructed through a merger of existing denominations.

The Eastern Orthodox have generally been quite explicit in holding that their own communion—namely, Orthodoxy—is the sole true Church. Although some liberal Orthodox theologians have been influenced by the Protestant notion that the true Church is not visible, the opposite view is so generally accepted that we may take it as an essential note of Orthodoxy. Like Catholics, therefore, the Orthodox have found themselves faced by a serious question of conscience whether, and if so how far, they ought to join in the Protestant-sponsored Ecumenical Movement. As we shall see, they have never come to a clear and unanimous position on this question, but some Orthodox representatives have been present at each of the great meetings of the Ecumenical Movement. A Catholic is naturally prompted to ask whether such a course is consistent with the doctrine of the Orthodox themselves on the nature of the Church, and further, whether their participation in the movement is, by Catholic standards, desirable. In order to cast some light on these questions we shall briefly scan the history of Orthodox participation in the Ecumenical Movement.

FIRST APPROACHES TO ECUMENISM

Throughout the nineteenth century, the Anglicans and Old Catholics made a series of efforts to effect some sort of union with the Orthodox. These approaches stimulated considerable discussion among the Orthodox regarding the status of the non-Orthodox in general, and of these denominations in particular. Some, following Khomiakov, took the "Cyprianic" view that outside the true Church (viz., the Orthodox) there simply was no grace; all non-Orthodox sacraments were therefore null and void. The Protestants and Catholics of the West were in the same condition as pagans. Other theologians, following Philaret, adopted a more liberal position, and were inclined to admit that persons not formally and juridically incorporated in the true Church might nevertheless have grace and be, in a real sense, Christians.[2] Members of the latter school of thought were more inclined to seek a *rapprochement* with other denominations, and to admit that Baptism and even Orders might validly be conferred outside the Orthodox Church.

Partly as a result of this new interest in relations with the Western Churches, Joachim III, the Ecumenical Patriarch of Constantinople, made in 1902 a move which later proved to have been of prophetic import. He wrote an Encyclical Letter to all the Orthodox Churches, asking for their views on means for establishing greater unity among themselves and likewise on the question of contacts with the non-Orthodox Churches. Specifically, he put the question, "Does the present moment seem propitious for a preparatory study of the question, in order to prepare a common ground of friendly mutual relations, and to determine by common agreement among the members of the universal Orthodox Church, the bases, measures, and methods which will seem best?"[3]

As a matter of fact, the response of the Churches proved disappointing. The reply of Moscow was typical. In a long point-by-point discussion, the Holy Synod expressed resentment at Western proselytism, and called attention to the "religious exclusivism and even fanaticism, mixed with scornful arrogance, with regard to Orthodoxy" which "distinguishes the Protestants, it may be said, even more than the Catholics." As a result, "it is our task, at the present moment, less to sweeten our relations with the Western Christians and lovingly to draw their communities toward union with ourselves, than to defend tirelessly and vigilantly the spiritual flock which has been committed to us against the aggressions and manifold seductions on the part of the Latins and the Protestants."[4]

Despite this negative attitude on the part of the Holy Synod, the Russian Church received, in 1915, an invitation to take part in the opening conference on Faith and Order. Their reply, written by Metropolitan Anthony Khrapovitski, is significant in the light of subsequent history. It is definitely "Cyprianic" in tone. Outside the Orthodox Church, the author declares, there is no grace; there is merely "this world, foreign to Christ's redemption and possessed by the devil." Such an attitude, however, by no means precluded participation in the proposed conference. On the contrary, the Orthodox would be glad to attend. "We are not going to concelebrate there, but we shall have to search together for a true teaching on the controversial points of faith."[5]

The end of World War I was favorable to further progress along ecumenical lines, especially in the Balkan sector. The break-up of the Turkish Empire in Europe had led to the formation of autocephalous Churches in the Balkan States, and to a corresponding reduction of the authority of the Ecumenical Patriarch. The Moscow Patriarchate was temporarily beset with difficulties caused by the Bolshevik Revolution, thus leaving the initiative to Constantinople. Finally, the founding of the League of Nations, born amid the highest expectations, seemed to suggest that a similarly international League of Churches might be attempted.[6]

Under these circumstances the Ecumenical Patriarchate, acting through its *locum tenens*, issued in January 1920 an Encyclical to all the Churches of the World, which remains today the Magna Charta of Orthodox ecumenism, at least in its Greek form. The opening paragraph indicates the spirit of the document:

> Our Church is of the opinion that a closer intercourse with each other and a mutual understanding between the several Christian Churches is not prevented by the doctrinal differences existing between them, and that such an understanding is highly desirable and necessary, and in many ways useful in the well-conceived interest of each one of the Churches taken separately, and as a whole Christian body, as also for preparing and facilitating the complete and blessed union which may someday with God's help be attained.[7]

The present hour, the Ecumenical Patriarchate then declares, is particularly propitious for such an endeavor, for it would enable the *rapprochement* of Churches to coincide with the establishment of the League of Nations, whose inauguration had recently been celebrated under such favorable auspices. As a preliminary measure, it is insisted, the Western Churches must desist from the proselytism whereby they continually trouble the inner peace of the Eastern Churches. Once mutual confidence has thereby been re-established, it will be possible to reawaken mutual love and charity, and to collaborate in solidarity. An eleven-point program, largely practical in scope, is then set forth. It includes such measures as unification of the Church calendar, regulation of mixed marriages, burial ceremonies of Christians who die in territories where their own Church is not organized, mutual assistance between Churches in humanitarian works, etc. It is further proposed that dogmatic controversies be "impartially studied," especially from a historical point of view.[8]

The Encyclical of 1920 was a spontaneous move in which the Ecumenical Patriarchate showed courageous and far-sighted leadership. The emphasis on practical measures, as opposed to theoretical discussions, indicates the approach which, in years to come, would be characteristic of the Greek and Constantinopolitan Churches as contrasted with the Slavic.

RELATIONS WITH FAITH AND ORDER (1920–1937)

In the same year, following a visit to Constantinople by a delegation of the Faith and Order Movement, it was arranged for a group of eighteen Orthodox delegates to be sent to Geneva that August for the Preparatory Conference on Faith and Order. These delegates represented the Patriarchates of Constantinople and Alexandria, the Churches of Greece, Bulgaria, Rumania, and Serbia, and included, also, an archbishop of the Church of Russia who was in exile.[9] On behalf of the delegation, Professor Alivisatos of the Greek Church submitted an eight-point program, largely based on the Encyclical of 1920, and predominantly practical in scope.[10] It called for the suppression of proselytism, an accord on missions to the infidels, and collaboration against immoral and unchristian principles in society. A more or less academic study of differences concerning faith and order "in a spirit of friendship" was also proposed. The question of proselytism was a very serious issue at the Geneva Conference, and was anxiously discussed in unofficial meetings between Orthodox and Anglicans, and between Anglicans and Evangelicals. The difficulty of reaching any agreement on this problem seemed to constitute the greatest threat to continued Orthodox participation in the Faith and Order Movement.[11]

The Geneva meeting was significant from another point of view as well. It gave Bishop Söderblom, who was in the city at the time, an opportunity to interest the Orthodox in the Life and Work Movement, which was based on objectives somewhat akin to those enunciated in the Encyclical of 1920. Orthodox affiliation with the Life and Work Movement, which began at this time, never labored under the dogmatic difficulties which constantly arose in Faith and Order meetings. The accreditation of delegates to the Stockholm Conference on Life and Work in 1925 was the first official participation of Orthodox in the Ecumenical Movement. They were again represented at the Oxford Conference in 1937. But social thought and action has traditionally played a much smaller part in the Orthodox Churches than in Protestantism, and for this reason, among others, they were less able to make an outstanding contribution to the Life and Work Movement than to Faith and Order. We may therefore concentrate our attention on the latter aspect of Orthodox ecumenism.[12]

The first Conference of the Faith and Order Movement was held at Lausanne in 1927. Twenty-two delegates from the Orthodox and "Lesser" Eastern Churches were present. Metropolitan Germanos of Thyateira (who had been Exarch of Western Europe since 1922) made a distinguished contribution to the conference. In his opening address he insisted that in the Orthodox view "unity in faith constitutes a primary condition of reunion of the Churches," and that "the teaching of the ancient, undivided Church of the first eight centuries . . . must, to-day, also constitute the basis of the reunion of the Churches."[13]

In the course of the conference, the Orthodox effectively counteracted the influence of those liberal Protestants who naively conceived of union in terms of some "common denominator" currently accepted by all the member Churches. They insisted on the essential importance of certain doctrines and devotions which had been all but forgotten in the Protestant West. Bishop Velimirovic of Ochrida in Serbia gave a remarkable speech on the Sacraments, and Prof. Bulgakov, of the Orthodox Theological Institute in Paris, pointed out that reunion would presuppose an agreement on the meaning and importance of devotion to the Mother of God, since she is "the head of mankind in the Church . . . joined with all the saints and angels in the worship and life of the Church." The liberal Protestants objected that the question of our Lady was outside the scope of the Conference, and when they were sustained by the chair in this objection, Professor Bulgakov refused to accept this adverse ruling.[14]

At the close of the Conference, the Orthodox delegation abstained from voting on any of the reports except one on "the Church's Message to the World." Archbishop Germanos made a declaration in the name of the Eastern Orthodox explaining the reasons for this abstention. "The principles adopted as a basis for the declarations," he asserted, "are not compatible with those of the Orthodox Church which we represent." In particular, he objected to the two declarations on the Nature of the Church and the Common Confession of the Church.

> The drafting of these two latter was carried out on a basis of compromise between what in our understanding are conflicting ideas and meanings, in order to arrive at an external agreement in the letter alone; whereas, as has often at other times been emphasized in statements by representatives of the Orthodox Church, in matters of faith and conscience there is no room for compromise . . . .
>
> This being so, we cannot entertain the idea of a reunion which is confined to a few points of verbal statement; for according to the Orthodox Church, where the totality of the faith is absent there can be no *communio in sacris*.[15]

The Orthodox statement closed with the assertion that "We, the undersigned Orthodox representatives . . . wish to declare that in our opinion the most we can do at present is to enter into collaboration with other Churches in the social and moral sphere on the basis of Christian charity."

Lausanne marks an important stage in the development of Orthodox ecumenism. Here for the first time the Eastern Churches began to perform what has since become their great mission in the Ecumenical Movement—that of bearing witness to a fuller and richer faith than is possessed by the Protestant members, and insisting on points of view which are too often neglected in the Protestant West. In the presence of Western Liberalism and Evangelicism, the Eastern Churches came to understand, as never before, the riches of their own heritage, and consequently bore themselves with dignity and distinction. While they steadfastly refused to compromise with regard to essentials, their contribution was by no means entirely negative. The ideas of Father Bulgakov on the nature of the Church, the Communion of Saints, and even on Mariology, while they did not prevail at Lausanne, were placed on the agenda for further study, and actually became the subject of theological discussions subsequently held at Edinburgh and Lund.

At the Second World Conference on Faith and Order, held at Edinburgh in 1937, the Orthodox played a part similar to that which they had played at Lausanne ten years before. Once more they were led by Archbishop Germanos; and once more they found it necessary to submit a dissenting report, protesting against "vague" and "ambiguous" declarations of faith and attempts to achieve intercommunion without previous agreement in the realms of faith and order.[16] Regarding the Communion of Saints and the veneration due to the Mother of God, the Orthodox were pleased to note some progress over Lausanne, but regretted that essential points of difference remained. They likewise protested that the Church on earth is essentially visible; that the Church is more fundamental than the Scriptures, which have been divinely committed to it as an instrument of sanctification; and that the human will plays an active role in the process of salvation, aptly designated "co-operation." All these points, they asserted, were overlooked or denied in the official statements of the Conference. Once again, as at Lausanne, the Orthodox showed no tendency to be sucked into Protestantism. On the contrary, they were stimulated to achieve a greater awareness of the riches of their own tradition, and to express their own faith more articulately than before.

RELATIONS AMONG ORTHODOX CHURCHES

The encounters with the Protestants at Lausanne and Edin-burgh gave rise to different views among the Orthodox them-selves as to the extent and manner in which they should take part in the Ecumenical Movement. In particular, there was a diver-gence of views on the advisability of entering into dogmatic discussions with the West. The Greeks generally took the view that there was nothing to be gained from such discussions; even if all undesirable compromises were avoided, the only result would be bitterness and misunderstanding. It would therefore be better to collaborate only in the field of social and practical action. The Russians and Bulgarians, on the other hand, were keenly interested in theological debate. They felt that it was in this field that the Orthodox could make their greatest impression on, and contribution to, the Ecumenical Movement.[17]

In order to achieve greater internal unity, the Orthodox held a series of conferences among themselves beginning in 1933. The most important of these was the Pan-Orthodox Congress of Theologians held at Athens late in 1936, as part of the work of preparation for the Oxford and Edinburgh Conferences of 1937. In the opening allocution, Prof. Alivisatos clearly summarized the reasons for the Athens meeting:

> In these international meetings [of the Ecumenical Movement], which have for the first time become possible in this new era, Orthodox theologians have for the first time met and come to know each other . . . Finding themselves in a strange environment, they spontaneously came together to defend Orthodox points of view, and presented themselves as a united Orthodox group . . . [The

question therefore arose] would it not then be possible to organize an exclusively Orthodox meeting in order to group and relate our own forces more directly in a single organized effort, so as to present Orthodoxy as a united and truly Christian force—as indeed it actually is—from which we ourselves and those who are not of us expect so much?[18]

The Athens Conference was, in general, a marked success for the forces favoring ecumenical ties. At its close, the delegates adopted a cautiously worded resolution to the effect that the Ecumenical Movement was a "happy manifestation of the present general renewal of interest in the Church and in theology" and that the Orthodox Congress "welcomes this movement and is prepared to collaborate with it in an Orthodox spirit."[19]

The Athens Conference, however, by no means overcame all opposition to ecumenism among the Orthodox. In 1938, for example, the local Synod of Karlovtzy in Yugoslavia, representing the Russian Church in Emigration under the jurisdiction of Metropolitan Anastasius, showed itself rather hostile. The Council observed that some of the leaders of the Ecumenical Movement were members of Anti-Christian Masonic societies, and that Orthodox attendance at these gatherings, instead of effectively bearing witness to the Orthodox faith, tended rather to obscure its unique position. Such participation, however, might be justified "for missionary ends" if carried out "in obedience to ecclesiastical authorities," and under certain very definite conditions: Orthodox doctrines should be explained without any kind of compromise, and no part should be taken by Orthodox delegates in proposing resolutions, in voting, or in common religious services.[20]

The Churches recognizing Anastasius' jurisdiction took an even more antagonistic position to the Ecumenical Movement at Brussels in October 1948, where they asserted that the danger of Communistic infiltration, among other things, made it advisable to avoid all participation.[21] But the importance of this declaration is overshadowed by the momentous decisions taken at Moscow in July 1948. The Moscow Consultation was held to commemorate the fifth centenary of the autocephalous existence of the Russian Church. The Patriarchs of Rumania and Yugoslavia, and representatives of all the Orthodox Churches, except the Patriarchate of Jerusalem and the Churches of Cyprus and Finland, were present. Representatives of the Churches of Constantinople and of Greece took part in the celebrations, but did not collaborate in the work of the Conference, and consequently were not affected by its declarations. These declarations amounted to a round condemnation of the Ecumenical Movement in its present form. Dominated by the Slavic theologians, the Consultation took the view that the Movement had given excessive attention to social and political questions, and had shelved the quest for dogmatic unity. The fusion of the Faith and Order Movement with the Life and Work Movement was taken as evidence of this regrettable trend.

> Impelled by a concern to preserve its own existence, and choosing the path of least resistance, Protestantism is intent upon achieving an abstract union on social, economic, and even political grounds. In its projects for future action, the Ecumenical Movement takes its stand on the theoretical idea of creating a new external apparatus, a "World Council," an institution within the State, which would be linked in some way to the state and exert temporal influence.[22]

The declaration concluded with an affirmation that none of the Churches taking part in the Moscow Conference would become members of the Ecumenical Movement as presently constituted.

These decisions, taken at Moscow on the eve of the First Assembly of the World Council of Churches, came to Orthodox ecumenists as a "heavy and unexpected blow," in the words of Professor Zander of the Paris Institute of Theology.[23] It was the first definite condemnation of the Ecumenical Movement to emanate from the Orthodox hierarchy, which had hitherto showed itself generally favorable. The Moscow pronouncements were not due merely to political considerations, although these of course played their part. "As a matter of fact," Professor Zander acknowledges, "ecumenism was never popular among the

Orthodox and its champions were comparatively few, although officially everything was working smoothly."[24]

As a result of the Moscow Consultation, the Orthodox Churches had but forty of the 589 official representatives at the Amsterdam meeting of 1948. Of these forty, only half were regularly accredited delegates. Altogether absent were the Churches from behind the Iron Curtain—those of Russia, Georgia, Serbia, Rumania, Bulgaria, and Poland. The Patriarchates of Antioch and Alexandria and the Churches of Albania and Armenia, as parties to the Moscow declarations, likewise sent no representatives. Except for one representative from the Rumanian Orthodox Diocese of North America, Orthodoxy was represented at Amsterdam by the Greek Church alone. This Church, however, was present under three of its aspects—Constantinople, Athens, and Paris (i.e., the Russian *emigrés* under the jurisdiction of the Ecumenical Patriarch).[25]

The Orthodox contingent at Amsterdam, besides being depleted in numbers, suffered the further indignity of being placed on the same footing with the various Protestant denominations—including the Quakers and the Salvation Army, whom the Orthodox did not even recognize as Christians. They could hardly be enthusiastic at the report on the Universal Church, which exhorted all the member Churches to "begin our labors in the World Council of Churches in a spirit of penitence for what we have been and in a spirit of hope for what we shall become."[26] The general conduct of the Assembly seemed to take no cognizance of the Orthodox claim to be the one, true, visible Church of Christ. Nevertheless, the delegation at Amsterdam did not submit a dissenting report as had been done at Lausanne and Edinburgh. They acknowledged that they were "receiving" the message of the Conference, and would transmit it to their Churches for further study and decision as to what practical measures should be taken.[27]

The results of Amsterdam met with a mixed reception in the

Greek-speaking Churches. Monsignor Michael, the Metropolitan of Corinth, considered that the delegates at Amsterdam ought to have filed a serious protest of the official statements, and that the Orthodox Churches should refrain from any further participation in the dogmatic aspects of the World Council. The Amsterdam delegates, however, replied in defense of their role that they had not accepted the decisions of the Assembly, but merely passed them on for consideration. They pointed out also that the World Council was not a union of Churches, as some seemed to imagine, but a consultative council for the realization of practical aims not unlike those which had been outlined in the 1920 Encyclical of the Patriarchate of Constantinople. The World Council, of course, was defective on certain counts, for it defined Christianity too broadly, and admitted as members, religious bodies which did not deserve to be called Christian; on points such as these revision should be sought.[28]

A new crisis confronted the Orthodox Churches when the time approached for the Third Conference on Faith and Order at Lund. The Ecumenical Patriarchate sent an Encyclical Letter in January 1952, asking for the views of the other Orthodox Churches on the question whether and how to take part in the Lund meeting.[29] The Patriarch submitted his own views that the World Council of Churches was primarily practical in scope, that Orthodox representatives could not profitably take part in the discussions and voting of the Faith and Order Commission, and that, if present, they should carefully avoid participation in interconfessional worship. In deliberations occasioned by this Encyclical, the Church of Greece decided not to send the delegation which it had already designated for the Lund Conference. The Ecumenical Patriarchate, on the other hand, sent a delegation headed by Athenagoras, Metropolitan of Thyateira, and including a number of Russian theologians from the Russian Church in emigration, who were subjects of the Patriarchate of Constantinople.[30]

Archbishop Athenagoras, in his opening address at Lund, made the limitations of his powers quite clear:

... the Hierarchy of the entire Greek Orthodox Church reserves for itself only the right to decide on what is wrong in religious matters and to pronounce what is compatible or incompatible with her faith.

That is why she allows her theologians, professors of theology in the Orthodox theological schools and above all her representatives at conferences to make only positive and definite statements about our faith without being involved in sterile disputes or voting for resolutions on matters of faith, worship and order, which cannot be settled in this way.[31]

In theory, therefore, the Orthodox were present at Lund merely as witnesses to the true and ancient faith of their own Church. In testifying to that faith, however, they took a lively part in the discussions, and exerted an influence which, if not large, was out of proportion to their numbers. They did not vote on the resolutions, nor did they submit any final statement of their own.

In August 1954 the Second Assembly of the World Council was held at Evanston, Ill. Since the discussion here, unlike that at Lund, was not restricted to doctrinal matters, it was easier for the Churches under Constantinople's jurisdiction to find reasons for attending. But their delegation was rather small. Altogether there were twenty-nine delegates and seventeen non-delegates from the various Orthodox Churches. Of the delegates, eleven were from the Ecumenical Patriarchate, six of them being metropolitans or bishops. The Church of Greece likewise sent eleven delegates, including one archimandrite and ten professors. None of the three metropolitans who were named as delegates by the Church of Greece actually attended.[32]

In an important speech at the Assembly, Professor Florovsky, a delegate of the Russian Orthodox Greek-Catholic Church of North America, called attention to the ambiguities latent in the theme of the Faith and Order Section, "Our Unity in Christ and Our Disunity as Churches." Was there here, he asked, any implication that the unity was real, and the disunity only apparent? If so, the very theme was misleading, for the discord of opinions was all too evident. No progress, he noted, had yet been made in healing the disagreements which had been apparent ever since the beginning of the Faith and Order Movement. "In our ecumenical conversation we have reached a stage at which it is becoming increasingly difficult to speak with a common voice, or to make agreed statements, or to engage in united action." The comparison of agreements and disagreements, he submitted, had reached a dead end, where no further discussion could be profitable. As an alternative he suggested that this "ecumenicism in space" might profitably be supplemented by an "ecumenicism in time"—that is, by a common return to the Christian tradition in an effort to find where the true path had been lost. Only thus could one hope to recover a right sense of direction in carrying out the true mission of the Church on earth.[33]

At the close of the Evanston Assembly, the Orthodox did as they had done at Lausanne and Edinburgh. Instead of joining in the common declarations, they submitted dissenting statements of their own.[34] Their statement concerning the Report on Faith and Order was, as might be expected, particularly vigorous. "The whole approach to the problem of reunion," the delegates declared, "is entirely unacceptable from the standpoint of the Orthodox Church." *The Christian Century*, commenting on this statement, found that it exemplified "a general increase in confessionalism and even in sectarianism," and that "it left some people wondering why, if they held these views, they wished to continue in the Assembly."[35]

As a matter of fact, there were no signs of any tendency toward withdrawal on the part of the Orthodox representatives at Evanston. They came without high expectations, and were resigned to making but small progress. The Protestants, on the other hand, were by now accustomed to the singular position of the Orthodox in their midst, and were not surprised by their failure to subscribe to the general reports.

On the whole, the Orthodox delegates at Evanston were quite unenthusiastic in their comments after the Assembly had come to an end. Archimandrite Kotsonis, who acted as head of the delegation of the Church of Greece, observed that the Conference "though perfectly well organized, presented a tremendous lack of inspiration in the general meaning of the term."[36] Father Schmemann, who was present as a Youth Consultant, considered that the Assembly evidenced a grave need for theological consultations among the Orthodox themselves in order to overcome their provincialism and nationalism, and bear witness together to Orthodox truth, as demanded by the needs of the hour.[37]

A contrary reaction, however, came from a rather unexpected quarter. Monsignor Michael of Corinth, whose previous opposition to the results of the Amsterdam Conference has been noted above, reported that the Evanston meeting had totally changed his views on the desirability of dogmatic discussions:

> Did our participation at Evanston result in gain or loss? Beyond all doubt, in gain and even very great gain, prodigious for the prestige of our Mother, the ancient and most holy Orthodox Church. We were not there without being noticed. We did not mingle with the other representatives so as to lose our own colour and become agreeable to them. We were not afraid to proclaim to those present the whole truth on the subject of the faith of the Church. It is enough to take the trouble to read the two communications which we submitted to the Plenary Session, to be fully and absolutely persuaded that we spoke the truth. All the participants, as a result of our two communications, deeply felt the presence of the "one and holy" Church.[38]

SINCE EVANSTON

In the years between the second and third General Assemblies of the World Council of Churches (1954–61) the Orthodox continued to take part in important meetings of the Faith and Order Commission, and of the Central Committee of the World Council. At the Pan-orthodox conference which met at Rhodes in 1959 the Orthodox participation in the Ecumenical Movement was, in general terms, approved. The main efforts of the Orthodox during these years centered about two issues. In the first place, they were seeking a revision of the basis of the World Council of Churches. Following a nineteenth century formula devised for the Y.M.C.A., the Council of Churches had hitherto called itself "a fellowship of churches which accept Our Lord Jesus Christ as God and Saviour." The Orthodox generally felt that this formula failed to do justice to the Trinitarian faith of the early creeds. In the second place, most of the Orthodox Churches wished to head off the integration of the International Missionary Council with the World Council of Churches, mainly for two reasons. On the one hand, they felt that this would compel them, as members of the World Council, to support the proselytizing activities of Protestant groups, some of whom were seeking to convert Orthodox Christians to Protestantism. On the other hand, they felt that the merger would invest the World Council with missionary responsibilities, thus inevitably giving it some of the attributes of a "superchurch."

The third General Assembly of the World Council, meeting at New Delhi from Nov. 18 to Dec. 6, 1961, inaugurated a new era in the relationship of the Orthodox Churches to that body. The Orthodox were represented more numerously than ever before. There were delegations from the Patriarchates of Constantinople, Antioch, Jerusalem, Russia, Rumania, and Bulgaria, as well as from the Churches of Cyprus, Greece, Poland, and the Russians in exile in America. The Greeks came under instructions from the Holy Synod to insist—under the threat of possible withdrawal—on the adoption of a Trinitarian Basis, and to vote against the integration of the International Missionary Council into the World Council of Churches. Cordial messages of greeting were sent to the Assembly by the Ecumenical Patriarch, Athenagoras of Constantinople, and by the Patriarch Nikolai of Moscow.[39] Archbishop Iakovos, one of the five Council presidents, who had been selected to read the message from Athenagoras, also made a speech in which he announced that the Orthodox at this Assembly did not intend to submit any special declarations of their own positions unless absolutely necessary, but rather to participate actively, as full and responsible members of the Council, in all the discussions. While Iakovos made these remarks, as he explained, in a purely private capacity, many suspected that he was, in fact, reflecting the views of the Ecumenical Patriarch.

As a matter of fact, the Orthodox did submit a contribution of their own delegation in the Section on Unity, setting forth reservations about the Faith and Order Report on "The Nature of the Unity We Seek" which had been issued at St. Andrews, Scotland, in August 1960. This report, they maintained, reflected too much the Protestant idea of unity as something to be constructed through negotiation between different denominations acting as equals. According to the Orthodox view, they explained, unity should be sought through a common effort to recapture the ancient and apostolic tradition of the Church—in other words, through "ecumenism in time." The Orthodox, however, found great satisfaction in the proposed statement that unity was to be achieved "with the whole Christian fellowship in all places and all ages." By and large, the New Delhi report on the nature of Unity came closer to Orthodox positions than previous World Council statements on the same subject.

One of the main addresses at the New Delhi assembly was that of the Greek lay theologian, Nikos Nissiotis, on "The Witness and Service of Eastern Orthodoxy to the One Undivided Church."[40] This statement was surprisingly liberal in tone; it called upon Orthodoxy to "give up its defensive confessional-apologetic attitude" and to abandon slogans such as "come back to us." The speech, as one might expect, was sharply criticized by some Orthodox spokesmen, one of whom found it smacking of "ecclesiological Docetism."

From the point of view of the Orthodox, the New Delhi Assembly was marked by three developments of immense importance, with which we may conclude the present survey.

In conformity with the longstanding wishes of the Orthodox, a new Trinitarian Basis was adopted. The Council resolved to substitute for the exclusively Christological formula quoted above, the following: "The World Council of Churches is a fellowship of churches which confess the Lord Jesus Christ as God and Saviour according to the Scriptures and therefore seek to fulfil together their common calling to the glory of the one God, Father, Son, and Holy Spirit."[41] The recommendation to adopt this formula was appropriately presented by Archbishop Iakovos.[42]

The second major development was contrary to what most of the Orthodox would have wished. The International Missionary Council was integrated into the World Council in such wise as to constitute a new "Division of World Mission and Evangelism." Many of the Orthodox were reconciled to this change, partly through repeated asseverations on the highest level that the Council had no intention of becoming a "superchurch," and even more because they became convinced that the integration would have the effect of restraining the offensive proselytism of certain groups who were seeking to win converts from other Christian bodies. By simultaneously adopting a statement on "Christian Witness, Proselytism, and Religious Liberty," the New Delhi meeting took a decisive step in this direction. As a matter of fact, the Greek delegates, in spite of their instructions from the Holy Synod, did not speak or vote against the incorporation of the I.M.C. into the World Council.

Thirdly, the New Delhi meeting was signalized by the admission of four Slavic Orthodox Churches into the World Council—those of Russia, Rumania, Bulgaria, and Poland. Archbishop Athenagoras of Thyateira, in an address of November 20, enthusiastically welcomed the new Orthodox member churches in his own name, and on behalf of the Ecumenical Patriarchate and its Holy Synod, declaring that "Their participation . . . will undoubtedly increase the contribution of Eastern Orthodoxy to the Ecumenical Movement, and the message of Orthodoxy will be heard more emphatically throughout the Christian world—its legacy and heritage will be appreciated and shared by all."[43] As the Evangelical Protestant, Carl Henry, ruefully noted in an editorial on New Delhi in *Christianity Today*, "The Protestant character of the Anglo-Saxon ecumenical thrust is now influenced in a major way by the Orthodox sacramentarian-ritualistic emphasis. . .The 17 members of Eastern Orthodox churches (five from the newly admitted Russian Orthodox Church) now comprise the largest single bloc in the WCC's 100-member central committee."[44]

APPRAISAL OF RESULTS

Glancing back over the 40 or more years of Orthodox involvement in the Ecumenical Movement, one cannot but be struck by the fact that they have made their chief contribution in the area of faith and order, which is the precise area which the Ecumenical Patriarchate of Constantinople, in the Encyclical of 1920, advised them to shun, whereas they have made no significant impression in the social and practical field, which had been specially recommended to them. But as the Greek theologian Demosthenes Savramis points out, this reversal of emphasis was practically inevitable, since the Orthodox Church possesses no systematic social doctrine or social ethics, and lacks any specialized theological talent in this area. "Only the dogmatic field was open for the collaboration of the Orthodox, and there they did labor very positively and fruitfully, as, for example, the broadening of the Basis of the World Council proves."[45]

The ecumenical experience of the Orthodox in the World Council of Churches is, for many reasons, important for Catholics in their own dialogue with the Orthodox. Catholics can feel only grateful for the way in which the Eastern churches have been emerging from their previous isolation, and developing a sincere concern for the total interests of Christianity. Through the World Council, the Orthodox have, to a great extent, overcome their tendency to suspect and distrust all things Western. They have been stimulated to recognize their own weaknesses—their excessive nationalism, their lack of social concern, their organizational weaknesses, and the insufficient education of their clergy. They have discovered the possibilities of inner renewal through living contact with other Christian traditions. Finally, they have acquired a deeper realization of the unique and distinctive value of their own liturgical and dogmatic heritage, which has been so much appreciated by many Protestants who lack anything similar.

Far from being undermined by Protestant influences, the Orthodox have come to a deeper sense of their confessional identity as something to be shared with others. To a surprising degree they have helped to rescue the World Council from any tendency to become an Anglo-Saxon Pan-Protestant alliance and to transform it into a truly ecumenical body. With a loyalty which has, at times, bordered on stubbornness, they have clung to many values which the Catholic holds dear, such as the abiding truth of the ancient creeds and dogmas, the sacredness of tradition, the visibility of the Church, the Apostolic succession, the seven Sacraments, the veneration of saints and images. So long as the Catholic Church remains absent from the deliberations of the World Council, the Orthodox Churches are the most powerful representatives of many accepted Catholic positions which might otherwise fail to win a hearing in that body.

The relationships of the Orthodox Churches to the World Council have been various, and, at times, strained. They are still complex and ambivalent, but on the whole the story has been an encouraging one. The Catholic, seeking to reflect on how his own Church might relate itself to that body, will find many useful lessons in the experience of the Orthodox. Apparently insuperable obstacles have, at times, been overcome, and unexpected blessings have been received by the Orthodox themselves and by the World Council as a whole.

9

The Ecumenical Perspectives of Popes John and Paul

In the course of the ages Christianity seems to pass through alternating phases of centrifugal and centripetal motion. From 1500 to 1900 the dominant trend was centrifugal. Christendom seemed to be breaking up into smaller and smaller units. The nineteenth century was the age of maximum sectarianism. In a spirit of rugged individualism each believer blazed his own independent trail to God, and often found a God whom no one else had previously discovered.

Since 1900 a kind of sociological miracle has been occurring. The segments of fragmented Christianity have been coming together again as if to show that, in spite of all apparent separation, they are animated by a common Spirit. Christians seem conscious as never before that to find God as He truly is they must find one another in Christ. Believers in one Lord, enlivened by the one Spirit, they must practice one baptism, profess one faith, and dwell together in one body as sons of one and the same Father (see Eph 4.6–6). This religious unity is what one might call the final goal, or at least the hope, of the ecumenical movement.

Whether Christians want to be united or divided is not just a matter of personal preference or current fashion. Behind the whole ecumenical endeavor, energizing and inspiring it, is the prayer of Christ that all his disciples may be manifestly one; "that the world may know that thou hast sent me, and that thou hast loved them. . ." (Jn 17.23).

During the first third of the twentieth century the ecumenical movement was primarily a Protestant operation (or more accurately Protestant and Anglican), but by the late 30's Catholics began to take an active interest. For at least 20 years before John XXIII became pope, prominent Catholic theologians had been working for better relations with the separated communities, in the hope of eventual reunion. The Holy See took cognizance of the movement, and did not disapprove, but Rome seemed to feel that its main task was to be vigilant that Catholics were not lured into heresy; that they did not do anything to compromise the purity and integrity of the faith; that they did not grow impatient with doctrinal difficulties, and fall into indifferentism. Occasionally Rome had an encouraging word for those engaged in the apostolate of reunion, as in the famous instruction of the Holy Office (Dec. 20, 1949),[1] but I think it is fair to say that the dominant attitude of the Vatican toward the Ecumenical Movement until 1958 was one of prudent reserve, and this was the attitude of Catholics in general. When we thought of Christians not in union with Rome, the first thing that came to our minds was the negative point that they were non-Catholics, that they were in error, that they needed to be converted. Until very recently we found it rather hard to look upon Protestants and Eastern Orthodox as believers, as fellow-Christians living an authentic religious life based on revelation and grace.

THE VISION OF JOHN XXIII

It was given to Pope John XXIII to change all this. To be sure, he invented no new theory of Christian unity. The least theological pope of recent times, he was no theoretician at all. He was, in his own words, a humble priest on whom God had bestowed some good insipirations, and these inspirations opened up a new era in Catholic ecumenism.

Pope John's first step was to state very plainly what he had seen with his own eyes. His close contacts with Orthodox Christians in Bulgaria, Greece, and Turkey, and with Protestants in Paris and elsewhere, had taught him that Catholics are not the only believing Christians. In his first Christmas message as Pope, he expressed this thought. "They too bear the name of Christ upon their foreheads, they read his holy and blessed Gospel, and they are not unreceptive to the stirrings of religious devotion and of active, beneficent love of their neighbor."[2]

This fact involved stringent practical lessons for Catholics. We must learn to look upon these other Christians with esteem and affection. We must cultivate, as Pope John put it,

> a real understanding of those brethren who, while bearing the name of Christ on their foreheads and indeed in their hearts, are yet separated from the Catholic Church. We must bestir ourselves and not rest until we have overcome our old habits of thought, our prejudices and the use of expressions which are anything but courteous, so as to create a climate favorable to the reconciliation we look forward to . . .[3]

Pope John's most striking contribution to the ecumenical problem was, no doubt, the charity of his own heart. He obviously felt strong fraternal ties with all who worshipped the name of Christ. This made it possible for him to speak with sincerity and tact, and from the heart. He avoided terms such as "heretics," "schismatics," and even "dissidents"; the term "separated brethren" itself seemed to stick in his throat as sounding too harsh. Quite characteristically he called them, on one occasion, "brothers who deserve every respect even though they are separated, as it is said." The main point was that they are our brothers, and this Pope John could never forget. "Whether they wish it or not," he quoted from St. Augustine, "they are our brothers, and will not cease to be such until they cease to pray, 'Our Father'."[4] Later, in the same message, he described his relationship to the separated brethren by applying to himself the moving text from the Old Testament, "I am Joseph your brother."[5] Such affectionate words coming from the Roman pontiff could not fail to find a way into the heart of the other Christians.

Until the time of Pope John, Catholic ecumenism had seemed to be rather complacent. We seemed to admit, with reluctance, the survival of certain Christian vestiges outside the Church while insisting that we ourselves lacked nothing. In loyalty to the Church we felt obliged to deny that Catholics were in any way responsible for the divisions in Christendom. We spoke of the others as straying sheep as though the biblical verdict, "all we like sheep have gone astray," had no application to Catholics. We spoke of the Church as possessing the fullness of truth and grace, as though we had nothing more to learn and no need to receive from God. We seemed to be caught in a posture of proud immobility, in unbending self-approbation, requiring all others to come round to our position, to submit to Roman claims with an unconditional surrender, while we ourselves took no blame for the past and adopted no positive measures to make reconciliation possible.

The entire pontificate of Pope John, if I may speak so generally, was dedicated to breaking down this illusion. With regard to the past, he showed not the slightest interest in demonstrating that the chief blame for disunity must fall on those who had broken away from the Church. "We do not wish to conduct a trial of the past," he declared; "We shall not seek to establish who was right and who was wrong. Responsibility is divided. We only want to say, 'Let us come together; let us make an end of our divisions.'"[6]

In his estimate of the Church today, John XXIII said quite plainly that vast improvements must be made. Without inordinate breast-beating, he made it clear that we must set to work to restore the purity and fervor of our Christian life. This was not simply a matter of personal reform on the part of individuals but a task confronting the Church at large. Before we can expect others to desire reunion with the Church, we Catholics must mirror in our whole corporate existence the joy and holiness of the Gospel. With this in mind Pope John took the bold and unexpected step of summoning a general Council and this decision he himself ascribed not to human reasoning but to a sudden inspiration from on high.

I cannot resist quoting one or two of Pope John's statements on the aims of the Council. One of his most characteristic declarations may be found in his sermon at the Byzantine-Slavic Mass at which he officiated on November 13, 1960:

> Everything that the new Ecumenical Council is to do is really aimed at restoring to full splendor the simple and pure lines that the face of the Church of Jesus had at its birth, and at presenting it as its divine Founder made it: without blemish or wrinkle.[7]

And in the same sermon he said, a little later, that the "highest and noblest aim of the Ecumenical Council" is "to pause a little in a loving study of the Church and to try to rediscover the lines of her more fervent youth." In a magnificent address to the diocesan presidents of the Italian Catholic Action the previous year, Pope John clearly explained the connection between this self-reform of the Church and the restoration of Christian unity:

> By God's grace, then, we shall hold this Council; we shall prepare for it by working hard at whatever on the Catholic side most needs to be healed and strengthened according to the teaching of the Lord. When we have carried out this strenuous task, eliminated everything which could at a human level hinder our rapid progress, then we shall point to the Church in all her splendor, *sine macula et ruga*, and say to all those who are separated from us, Orthodox, Protestants, and the rest: Look, brothers, this is the Church of Christ. We have striven to be true to her, to ask the Lord for grace that she may remain forever what he willed. Come: here the way lies open for meeting and homecoming: come, take, or resume, that place which is yours, which for many of you was your fathers' place. O what joy, what a flowering even in civil and social life, may be looked for by the whole world if we once have religious peace and the reestablishment of the family of Christendom.[8]

From these and many other statements of like tenor it can be seen that John XXIII gave a new tone to the call for Christian unity which had been issued by many popes before his time. On his lips that call did not sound like a condemnation, a threat, or a demand for submission. He showed the utmost respect for the liberty of consciences, and for the gradual working of grace in the hearts of Christian believers. He did not want those outside the Church to abandon anything good which they had found in their own traditions, but to grow in the truth under the promptings of the Holy Spirit. He issued no commands, but only a gentle invitation for all to gather, not in a strange and unfamiliar household, but in the home of our common Father, in which the other Christians, by their faith and baptism, had always retained a right of patrimony. He, of course, took it for granted that the final meeting place of Christians would be the Catholic Church; but there could be no question of merely returning to the past or even of a general reunion with the Church as it appears today. The vision of Pope John looked forward to the Church of tomorrow—to a Church, that is, not radically different, but refurbished, renewed, more fervent and devoted. As he was personally humble, so was he also free from any taint of collective pride. His longing for Christian unity was not marred by any thirst for domination. He acted out of the most pure affection, desiring nothing but the peace and joy of seeing the reassembly of God's family according to the most holy prayer of Christ.

John XXIII was a man of long vision. He did not harbor any illusions that the unity of Christians would be quickly reestablished. "In ecumenical work," he once told the Anglican Canon Rea, "we must be patient and know how to await God's hour."[9] When his pontificate was ended by his noble death, his work had scarcely begun.

ELECTION OF PAUL VI

What would happen now to the Johannine reform? As soon as he died the question was on everybody's mind: would there be a reaction to more conservative ways of thinking? Would the new pontiff be a man of entirely different interests and ideas? Or would the conclave elect a cardinal who had squarely identified himself with the Johannine program? Giovanni Battista Montini was generally regarded as the man for continuity. The first cardinal appointed by John XXIII, he became an ardent supporter of the same open and pastoral approach. As Archbishop of Milan he did not content himself with ministering to loyal Catholics; he went out and won back to Christ great segments of the dechristianized working classes. His pastoral letters were progressive and inspiring. One of them, his Lenten Pastoral of 1962, explained the goals of the Council in terms strikingly similar to those which Pope John was to use in his opening allocution to the first session on October 11 of the same year. This marked similarity has made some suspect that the late pope was, in part, inspired by the ideas of the Archbishop of Milan.

In the first session, Cardinal Montini gave an important speech expressing dissatisfaction with the unprogressive and over-juridical project on the Church which had been offered for the Fathers' consideration. Without causing needless offense to anyone, he made it clear that he shared the view that the schema on the Church would have to be entirely reworked on different principles—as was, in fact, done before the second session.

Also, during the first session, Montini wrote a series of reports on the Council for the archdiocesan newspaper of Milan, *L'Italia*, the last of which (Dec. 2, 1962), pointed out that the work of the Council was being excessively delayed by practically endless debating, and that the draft decrees were too lengthy and involved. The projects, he said, should be drastically streamlined so as to deal only with issues of general and urgent import for the pastoral mission of the Church. After the death of Pope John, Cardinal Montini gave a eulogy in the Cathedral of Milan in which he maintained that the Church could not afford to turn aside from the course which the late pope had marked out for it.

Could we ever abandon the paths which John XXIII has shown us so brilliantly, even at some future date? We must believe that we cannot! It will be fidelity to the broad directives of his pontificate which will perpetuate his memory and his glory, and which will keep him ever before us as a father, and as one who is near to us.[10]

The early election of Montini at the conclave of June 1963 showed that the majority of Cardinals were pleased with the progressive measures of the previous pontificate and wanted continued leadership in the same direction.

It is still too early to summarize the ideas and achievements of Pope Paul in the ecumenical sphere. Until the end of 1965 the Council was still in session, and he was reluctant to do or say anything which might seem to curtail the Council's freedom. But from the beginning he made it clear that he shared Pope John's concern for Christian reunion. In his coronation homily of June 30, 1963, he announced that this quest would be a dominant theme of his reign. "In this regard," he added, "we embrace the heritage of our unforgettable predecessor Pope John XXIII. Moved by the Holy Spirit, he brought into being in this domain great hopes which we consider it a duty and an honor not to disappoint."[11]

Pope Paul has given impetus to the Ecumenical Movement, not only by words, but even more powerfully by actions of great symbolic import. Among these must be listed his pilgrimage to the Holy Land in January 1964, his initiative in the establishment of the Ecumenical Institute for Advanced Theological Studies at Jerusalem (which is expected to open in the near future), and the reciprocal action by which he and Patriarch Athenagoras I of Constantinople on Dec. 7, 1965, voided the excommunication decrees which each Church had launched against the other's spiritual head in 1054.

In addition to the Encyclical *Ecclesiam Suam* of August 6, 1964, of which we shall speak in the next chapter, three early documents of Pope Paul's pontificate are particularly expressive of his ecumenical doctrine: his opening allocution at the second session of the Council (Sept. 29, 1963), his address to the observer delegates at the second session (Oct. 17, 1963), and his Epiphany sermon at the Grotto of the Nativity at Bethlehem

(Jan. 6, 1964). From sources such as these we can construct a good general picture of his views on Christian unity.

ECUMENICAL DOCTRINE OF PAUL VI

In the way in which he speaks about the separated communions as groups, Pope Paul adheres closely to the terminology of his predecessors since Leo XIII. He calls them "communities," "denominations," or "confessions"—traditional terms to which no special significance can be attached. The Eastern communions he calls "venerable communities" or even "churches," here, again, following the precedent set by earlier pontiffs.

When speaking of individual members, however, Pope Paul has been unusually positive in his language. He habitually avoids the term "non-Catholic," which would seem to emphasize what they lack; instead he calls them the "other Christians" or more precisely, "those who believe in Christ but are not perfectly in communion with us."

Even here note the word "perfectly." Paul does not deny all communion between them and us. On the contrary, he frequently points out that we are bound to them by the precious and important ties of sacramental Baptism, faith in Christ, esteem for the Scriptures, and other authentic Christian elements. In his coronation address he used very flattering terms, saluting "those who, while not adherents of the Catholic Church, are united to us by faith in, and love of, the Lord Jesus, and who are marked by the seal of the one true Baptism."[12] For reasons such as these, said Pope Paul, we should esteem them. "We look with reverence upon the true religious patrimony which we share in common."[13] Not only have they preserved this intact, but, as Pope Paul mentioned in his opening allocution at the Council, they have, in some ways, soundly developed their heritage. He did not specify what developments he had in mind, but one could think here of Protestant biblical scholarship or of the liturgical worship of the Eastern Orthodox.

With regard to the causes of present disunion, Pope Paul

has continued along the lines of his predecessor. He feels that it is unprofitable for theologians to debate the question of historical responsibility. Discussions of this sort, he told the observers, are likely to reopen old wounds which are not yet fully healed. In his opening speech at the Council, he publicly begged pardon of God and of the separated brethren for such offense as Catholics may have given them, and on behalf of the Church he gladly forgave them for all injuries committed against Catholics.

He did not wish, however, to dwell on the past. It is best, he said, to look to the present and especially to the future. In speaking to the observers[14] he quoted very aptly from the letter to the Philippians: "Forgetting what I have left behind, intent on what lies before me, I press on with the goal in view, eager for the prize, God's heavenly summons in Christ Jesus" (3. 13f). For Pope Paul these words give, not simply a program of personal spirituality, but a mandate for the whole Church. He looks upon the Church by preference as God's pilgrim people, still voyaging in the desert, and as yet far from the goal of total union with the risen Lord. To the observer delegates, Pope Paul quoted the saying of St. Augustine, "Seek in order to find, and find in order to seek still further." Reflecting on this point he added: "A true Christian is a stranger to immobility." This is something which we Catholics would do well to ponder deeply. If the Church is heir to the full revelation of Christ, as we cannot doubt, still we shall never sound its depths. The God of revelation still remains veiled in mystery. Only gradually, and with faltering steps, do we arrive at a better realization of what the revelation really means. For this reason Pope Paul has said: we have not yet reached our destination. The Council itself, as he sees it, must seek to open new horizons and "channel over the earth the new and untapped spring waters of Christ our Lord's doctrine and grace."[15]

For Pope Paul, as for Pope John, Christian unity can never take the form of a mere return to the past. We cannot ask the other Christians to retrace their steps and to reenter by the same door by which their ancestors left the Church. Christian unity must be a creative achievement. It will be, as Paul VI has said, "the birth of something new, the realization of a dream. . . Hope is our guide, prayer our strength, charity our way in the service of divine truth which is our faith and our salvation."[16] All Christians therefore are called to go forward in Christ by a deeper penetration of the Gospel which they acknowledge as the basis of their religious lives. This common heritage furnishes a sound basis for a fruitful dialogue and for a measure of communion in prayer. Of this prayer for unity Pope Paul has said: "We shall put our trust in prayer which, even though it is not yet united prayer, rises up from ourselves and from Christians separated from us like two parallel columns which meet on high to form an arch in the God of unity."[17]

Regarding the nature of the unity to be sought, Pope Paul has not swerved from the perennial doctrine of the Church. Like previous popes from Pius IX to John XXIII, he firmly asserts that the true Church of Christ is one alone, and necessarily unique. The full unity of the Church rests, not simply upon interior thoughts and sentiments, but also upon external, visible signs—including the threefold bond of identity of faith, participation in the same Sacraments, and "the organic harmony of a single ecclesiastical direction. [18] But unity, he explains, is not uniformity. The essential unity of the Church can embrace a great variety of verbal expressions, modes of worship, laws and customs, as is quite evident from the diversities between Catholics of the Latin and Oriental rites.

Concerned as he is with the unity of Christians, Pope Paul does not limit his ecumenism to the Christian family. Stretching beyond the confines of the Christian horizon, his affectionate longing reaches out to those of other religions. From Bethlehem in January 1964, he sent his good wishes to those of other faiths, "especially those who profess monotheism and who worship, as we do, the one true God, the supreme and living God, the God of Abraham, the God all high."[19] Following up an intention announced early in his pontificate, he established, on May 19, 1964, a new secretariat, patterned on the Secretariat for Promoting Christian Unity, aimed to foster understanding of, and respectful dialogue with, the non-Christian religions. Not content with extending ecumenical principles to the other religions, Pope Paul has repeatedly stressed that the Church wishes to engage in fraternal conversation with all those sincerely concerned with human welfare. To this end he established on April 8, 1965, a secretariat for non-believers. Thus Pope Paul has supplemented the notion of ecumenical dialogue, in the strict sense, with that of a "missionary dialogue" which must include all men of good will.

PAUL VI'S CONCEPTION OF THE CHURCH

For a better grasp of the motives and principles behind Paul VI's views on Christian unity, it will be helpful to add a few words on his conception of the Church. His views on ecclesiology are, in some ways, more significant for the future of ecumenism than his statements bearing directly on Christian unity, since a man's vision of the Church inevitably conditions his thinking about the unity which God wills for his people.

Over the past century and especially since Vatican Council I, non-Catholics have repeatedly voiced certain standard complaints about the Catholic conception of the Church. Catholics, they protest, have absolutized the Church, setting it in place of Christ himself; second, they have conceived of it too much along the lines of other visible, juridical societies, such as the secular state; third, they have immoderately exalted the powers and prerogatives of the Roman pontiff; fourth, they have unduly depressed the position and dignity of the other bishops; and finally, they have reduced the laity to a passive status in the Church with no positive or creative function. Without mentioning any of these criticisms, and apparently without any direct intention to meet them, Pope Paul's opening discourse at the second session of the Council laid down the main lines of a Catholic answer.

In this address Pope Paul eloquently explained that the Church is by no means equal to Christ, but lives in total and incessant dependence upon Him "from whom we come, by whom we live, and toward whom we go."[20] From Christ the Church must receive everything. It is not an autonomous earthly society, but a mysterious community, vivified by the invisible power of the Holy Spirit. For this reason, the Church is not clearly definable in human language. Its essence must be approached asymptotically—we might say—by a counterbalancing of contrary images. Among these images drawn from the Bible, Pope Paul listed: the building raised up by Christ, the house of God, the temple and tabernacle of God, His people, His flock, His vine, His field, His city, the pillar or truth, the Bride of Christ, and His Mystical Body.[21]

As regards the organization of the Church, Pope Paul praised his predecessor for having banished the false assumption that just because the Roman Pontiff had supreme governing power, he must therefore be able to do all things without the help of ecumenical councils.[22] Paul VI has repeatedly called for a more effective and responsible cooperation of the entire episcopate in the direction of the Church. On Holy Thursday 1964, he said that it would be a principal aim of the Council to give "to episcopal collegiality the significance and value which Christ intended to confer on His apostles in the communion and reverence of the first of them, Peter."[23] In giving due scope to corporate functions of the episcopate, Vatican Council II later gave substance to this hope and thus complemented the work of Vatican I, which defined the powers of the pope as successor of Peter.

This stress upon mutual collaboration among the bishops promises to make the Catholic doctrine of the Church more intelligible and acceptable to the Eastern Orthodox, who have always maintained a somewhat similar theory of communion among the bishops. Anglicans, too, will be pleased by this upgrading of the episcopate, but Protestants will be particularly struck by the new emphasis on the role of the laity in the Church. In this movement, too, Pope Paul has long been a leader. In an introduction to a work by Cardinal Suenens, which he wrote as Archbishop of Milan, Montini declared: "The greatest and most remarkable effort is being put forward today by those members of the Church who, in past times, were passive rather than active, namely the laity. And this is the new note which is struck: the laity are also called upon to collaborate in the work of the apostolate."[24] Under Pope Paul's leadership, the Council put an end to the illusion that the Church consists essentially of the papacy, the hierarchy, or priesthood alone. All of these offices exist in the service of, and, in a sense, for the sake of, the whole Catholic people, who constitute a priestly nation, the flock of Christ. Pope Paul's vision of the Church, which unquestionably harmonized with that of most of the Council Fathers, has done much to correct the narrow papalism and clericalism found in certain theological manuals, and has thereby reduced the barriers of misunderstanding between us and other Christians.

PILGRIMAGE TO JERUSALEM

The most dramatic manifestation of Pope Paul's ecumenical spirit was undoubtedly his lightning trip to the Holy Land in the first week of January 1964. This sudden pilgrimage of the Roman pontiff to the cradle of Christianity, to celebrate the solemn feast of the Epiphany, was a powerful symbol of the future possibilities of Christian reunion. The pope's journey seemed to say: in the last analysis it is not the city of Rome that counts, nor the Latin language, nor European culture, nor scholastic terminology: it is Christ the Saviour and His Gospel. He is the bond of union and only in Him can we hope to find each other.

In Jerusalem, it will be recalled, Pope Paul had two meetings with the remarkable patriarch of Constantinople, Athenagoras, whose role in Eastern Orthodoxy has sometimes been compared to that of John XXIII in Roman Catholicism. The two spiritual leaders, Athenagoras and Paul, met, embraced, and exchanged the kiss of peace. At their first conference they read Christ's high priestly prayer for unity from the 17th chapter of John, alternately, verse by verse, in Greek and Latin. At their second conference they recited together the Our Father, first in Latin, then in Greek. In order that the Protestants might in some way be spiritually included in this encounter, the Pope and Patriarch read these prayers from a Protestant edition of the New Testament (Nestle).

Neither of the churchmen made any effort to conceal his own profound emotion. Athenagoras later declared that Pope Paul had impressed him "as a brother in the same Christ. . . . His embrace, his gentleness, his words, and all his gestures made me feel the great fraternity which should unite the Church, the one Church which has the same Gospel, the same Christ, the same Sacraments, the Church which must remain faithful to the will of the Lord."[25] And the Pope on his return to Rome said that "what remained most deeply etched on his soul (of the events of the pilgrimage) was . . . his conversations with the Ecumenical Patriarch of Constantinople." He liked to look upon these meetings, he said, as "the first fruits of perfect unity in the one Church of Christ, even though that unity is still very distant."[26]

This pilgrimage, carried out in a spirit of prayer and penitence, underscores a decisive attribute of Pope Paul's entire pontificate—humility. He has definitely broken with any kind of baroque triumphalism, which would depict the Church as a resplendent sovereign or as a conquering army. In his opening homily at the Council,[27] the Holy Father described a famous mosaic of Christ in the basilica of St. Paul's at Rome. He recognized himself, he said, in the diminutive figure of Pope Honorius, who is portrayed prostrate, kissing the feet of a Christ of gigantic proportions, blessing the Church. In his desire to share his supreme authority with the other bishops, Paul has given proof of his personal humility. He wants the Church too to be humble. He refers to it as an entity which has no value in itself, but draws all its virtue and merit from Christ. The Church is in the world as the servant of mankind, thus imitating its Master who came, not to be served, but to serve. Individually and collectively, we Catholics, whether we be priests or laymen, teachers or taught, must look upon ourselves as useless servants, who have been unfaithful in many things, and have much to beg pardon for. Only through such a recognition of our own failings, which greatly hinder the high mission entrusted to us, can we be fully honest with God and with ourselves. Only by striving ceaselessly to imitate the divine Servant can we hope to make others recognize in us the Church of Christ.

The names of John and Paul are inseparably linked in the New Testament. Angelo Roncalli chose his papal name, as he himself declared, because he wished to imitate John the Baptist, whose role was to summon the people of God to repentance and renewal, and John the Evangelist, the apostle of Christian love. In like manner our present holy Father undoubtedly wished to put his ministry under the protection of the great missionary apostle who called himself the least of all the saints, the last and most unworthy of the apostles. In his personal self-effacement, his apostolic zeal, his worldwide perspectives, and his total reliance on the grace of Christ, Pope Paul shows himself a faithful follower of the Apostle of the Gentiles. The relationship between John and Paul has been admirably summed up in a sentence which I borrow from the French Assumptionist, Father Wenger: "After John XXIII, the pope of love, God has given us Paul VI, the pope of humility. This being granted, all things become possible."[28]

10

Ecumenical Dialogue and Apostolic Renewal

Vatican II, in its *Constitution on the Church*, emphatically restates the constant doctrine of the Catholic Church regarding Christ's missionary mandate. Referring to Mt 28.18–20 and Acts 1.8 the Council declares: "The Church has received from the apostles as a task to be discharged even to the ends of the earth this solemn mandate of Christ to proclaim the saving truth."[1] The motive of this universal missionary activity is not simply the precept of Christ, but also the inner impulse of the Holy Spirit, which urges the Church to labor so that Christ may effectively be "the source of salvation for the whole world." The ultimate goal of the apostolate is that "the entire world may become the People of God, the Body of the Lord and the Temple of the Holy Spirit, and that in Christ, the Head of all, there may be rendered to the Creator and Father of the Universe all honor and glory."[2]

This insistence on the worldwide apostolate of the Church is quite traditional, but the development given to the theme in the Vatican II documents is remarkably original. Until very recently the apostolate was conceived in terms that were predominantly doctrinal and institutional, rather than personal and spiritual. The apostle was pictured as one who handed on to others that which he possessed and they lacked—the doctrine and the law of Christ. Vatican II, without rejecting these ideas, reflects a much more nuanced view. The Church is conceived of as a pilgrim people, pressing forward through the desert amid many infirmities and persecutions. She is in perpetual need of renewal and enlightenment, in order that she may not waver in perfect fidelity to her mission. Involved in the contingencies of history, she is continually forced to seek anew the truth which she has to proclaim. And those outside, often enough, in some sense already grasp the truth which they seek. Thus the dividing lines between those within and those without are fluid and ambiguous. Following St. Augustine, the Constitution recognizes that many who are inside according to the body are outside according to the heart, whereas others apparently outside are, by will and intention, joined to the Church. Even among the unevangelized some are closely united to the Kingdom inasmuch as they sincerely seek God and strive by the help of grace to do His will. The Jewish and Moslem peoples, thanks to their faith in the God of Abraham, enjoy a very special relationship to the Church. Far more is this true of baptized Christians who, even though they lack the fullness of Catholic communion, "lovingly believe in God the Father Almighty and in Christ, Son of God and Savior."[3]

Because the Church is in constant need of inner renewal, and because those who do not formally belong to her may yet share in her blessings, the apostolic relationship between Catholics and the rest of mankind cannot simply be described as a matter of having and lacking, of giving and receiving. We can no longer equate Catholics in an unqualified and exclusive sense with the "faithful," as if those outside the visible limits of the Church were incapable of a living faith. The apostolic mandate of the Church no longer evokes the complacent feeling of having everything to say and nothing to learn. On the contrary the apostolic relationship between Catholics and others—and especially other Christians—is reciprocal, or dialogical. The notion of apostleship, therefore, is being intrinsically modified by that of ecumenical dialogue.

THE NOTION OF DIALOGUE

Dialogue in a wide sense is equivalent to conversation, but in contemporary usage it has come to mean a conversation in which there is mutual respect and a genuine reciprocal relationship between parties who address and respond to one another.

In the third section of his first encyclical, *Ecclesiam suam*, Paul VI luminously explores the nature of dialogue. Using as his prime analogate the divine-human conversation which consists in the exchange of revelation and faith, the Pope points out that God has not disdained to enter into dialogue with men. By a spontaneous and free initiative, proceeding entirely from charity, God has spoken to men, and adapted his speech to our capacity for hearing. In imitation of Him we should seek to prolong the dialogue of salvation, addressing others clearly, patiently, meekly, trustingly, respecting their sensitivities and adapting our approaches to the ways in which they respond.

If some non-Catholic ecumenists have expressed dissatisfaction with Paul VI's presentation of dialogue, this is doubtless because, in his concern to develop a very wide and profound conception of dialogue, he did not attend in detail to the specific features which have come to characterize the interconfessional dialogue in our century. He did not emphasize the elements of mutuality, of equality, and of co-operative discovery which enter largely into the current ecumenical notion. But *Ecclesiam suam* in no way excludes these further specifications which, as we shall see, are provided for in the conciliar documents.

The kind of dialogue in which there is two-way communication and reception has been excellently described by an Episcopalian expert on pastoral theology, Reuel Howe. "Dialogue," he writes, "is a reciprocal relationship in which each party 'experiences the other side' so that their communication becomes a true address and response in which each informs and learns."[4] The fact that such dialogue is taking place between the Protestant and Roman Catholic Churches is, Howe believes, one of the most hopeful signs of our times:

Until a few years ago the rigid language, concepts, and images of both produced only monological approaches. Each considered the other as an object to be misrepresented and proselytized. Now, however, the situation is beginning to change and mutual respect is appearing. To some extent, each is beginning to regard the other as a partner, someone to be taken seriously, whose point of view must be understood and whose meanings must be examined; both are aware of the possibility that the meanings of one may cause those of the other to be revised. Language and concepts are being brought under the greater judgment of truths. Images are being broken through and displaced by the efforts to meet and see the other as it really is. This diminishes the anxieties, makes defenses less necessary, and leaves both sides open for a reconsideration of their respective purposes. We are witnessing a resumption of dialogue between Protestants and Roman Catholics which may very well produce miracles that a hundred years ago seemed impossible.[5]

It will be our contention that the *Decree on Ecumenism* of Vatican II lays a solid doctrinal basis for the type of dialogue here described, but before directly discussing this point, it may be helpful to give some indications of how the use of dialogue has gradually developed with the rise of the ecumenical movement.

PRE-DIALOGUE CONTROVERSY

Until the present century the verbal exchange between separated Christian groups lacked that element of reciprocity which is basic to the contemporary understanding of dialogue. Instead, one had controversy—at worst, polemic and at best, irenic.

Polemical controversy is as ancient as heresy itself. From the time of Irenaeus it has been common for theologians to write treatises *Adversus Haereses*. After the split between East and West, the Eastern theologians wrote innumerable tracts *Kata Latinōn*, to which the Western church replied with works *De haeresibus et praevaricationibus Graecorum*. Thus it is not surprising that in the sixteenth and seventeenth centuries the same techniques were used by Protestants and Catholics for mutual refutation.

At the risk of engaging in a polemic against polemics, one may point out certain defects in this style of confrontation. Polemical theology, as many contemporary critics have shown, is based on the hidden presupposition that theological truth is achieved by accurate deduction from authoritative texts—a highly rationalistic assumption. In its exclusive concern with defending established positions, polemics tends to suppress the spirit of inquiry which is the very soul of theology. The structural balance of theology, moreover, is upset because in polemics the content and emphasis are dictated by the supposed errors of the adversary, rather than by the inherent importance of the matter. Oppositions are stressed beyond measure; real difficulties against one's own stand are glossed over; and in many cases the "adversaries" are unjustly caricatured. Theology becomes infected by an unhealthy spirit of pride, disdain, and coldness. Little light is thrown upon the actual sources of disagreement, since no real effort is made to enter into the mentality of the adversary. As Congar remarks, "John Eck, in 1530, arrived at the Diet of Augsburg with a list of four hundred and four errors which he had discovered in the works of Luther. No one asked what Luther had in mind or what causes had brought about the Reformation. The internal coherence and spiritual meaning of the Reformation were ignored."[6]

Polemical literature, while intended as a service to the cause of truth, frequently falls into a kind of dishonesty. As Baum has said with regard to the tracts against Reformation Christianity, such literature

seeks to point to the weaknesses of the Protestant position and to defend the superior claims of Catholic truth. In order to convince more readily, this kind of literature is willing to understand Protestantism through its weakest elements and to produce an abundance of arguments for the Catholic Church, even when this means oversimplification and neglect of the real problems. The tracts of convert-makers often willingly sacrifice depth to greater polemical impact.[7]

Not all anti-Protestant controversy fell into these errors. Some polemicists, such as Bellarmine, succeeded in being remarkably fair. Francis de Sales, Bossuet, and others introduced a milder form of controversy which attempted to present each side in its inner consistency. This "irenic" method came to full flower in the nineteenth century with the new science of comparative dogmatics or "symbolics." Johann Adam Moehler, the greatest representative of this movement, saw that it was not enough to catalogue resemblances and differences, but that one must go back to first principles and find the leading idea or intention behind a whole confessional pattern. By showing that Protestantism moves in a different "spiritual world" than Catholicism, this pacific style of controversy prepared the way for the ecumenical dialogue characteristic of our century.

THEOLOGICAL DIALOGUE IN THE ECUMENICAL MOVEMENT

In the early stages of the Ecumenical Movement the theological encounter was heavily preoccupied with sifting agreements and disagreements among the various church-groups. The objective of the First World Conference on Faith and Order held at Lausanne in 1927 was thus described in the official report: "To register the apparent level of fundamental agreements within the Conference and the grave points of disagreements remaining; also to suggest certain lines of thought which may in the future tend to a fuller measure of agreement."[8]

This method of comparative doctrinal confrontation has obvious advantages. On the one hand, it brings out the large measure of unanimity among the "separated" communions—such as their Trinitarian faith, their dedication to the same Lord and Savior, their acceptance of the Scriptures of the Old and New Testaments, and their liturgical life stemming from Sacramental Baptism. On the other hand, by its careful attention to disagreements, this method precludes any tendency to reduce Christianity to some common denominator acceptable to all. But as Canon Thils remarks, the procedure is too abstract and formalistic. The statistical enumeration of points of agreement and difference is often superficial and scarcely more than verbal; it fails to penetrate the genuine thought and existential attitudes behind the terminology.[9]

Many speakers at Amsterdam in 1948, and at Lund in 1952, expressed the feeling that this method had failed to point the way to any real reconciliation. As the Lund report stated, with respect to ecclesiology, "We have seen clearly that we can make no real advance toward unity if we only compare our several conceptions of the nature of the Church and the traditions in which they are embodied."[10]

At Amsterdam approaches were made toward a new method, which seemed more promising. Karl Barth, in his dialectical theology, had insisted on the necessity of retaining, in paradoxical confrontation, the apparently contradictory aspects of revelation—Christ both divine and human, man both guilty and justified, both condemned and forgiven, etc. Only by preserving both thesis and antithesis in undiluted contrast, according to Barth, could one be faithful to the plenitude of the word of God, which refuses to be imprisoned in the categories of human conceptual thought. Could not a similar method, some asked, be applied to the conflicts among the separated Christian communities? An attempt was made to illuminate the theology of the Church by "dialectical confrontation." The "deepest difference" was found to consist in the divergence between a "Protestant" mentality which would accent the direct relationship of the individual believer to God and a "Catholic" mentality which would stress the horizontal relationship between man and man in a historically continuous Church. Florovsky (for the "Catholic" side) and Barth (for the "Protestant") set forth in sharpest opposition the two poles, but the confrontation, while it exposed certain hidden agreements within the polar opposition, failed to dispel the "hard core of disagreement" noted in the official report.[11]

A third method of dialogue, currently most in use in

the Ecumenical Movement, emerged in full clarity at Lund. Two years later at Evanston (1954) Bishop Nygren described it succinctly: "In their conversations the churches are moving from the periphery to the center. Instead of registering our various conceptions—with eventual agreement or disagreement—we are led to the center of Christian faith and required, not to present the peculiar conceptions of our denominations, but together to learn from the divine word."[12] Throughout the past decade, in the discussions of Faith and Order, the participants have been seeking to turn their attention away from the immediate issues by which they are divided, and to seek to penetrate together the more fundamental truths which do not seem to be directly in dispute. The theology of the Church, for instance, is being pondered in relation to Christology and Pneumatology. In this way it is hoped that each party to the dialogue may find a new point of view and that all alike may transcend the limitations of their previous positions. The goal may perhaps be described as a creative synthesis which, without simply negating the traditional stand of any one confession, enables them to fit within a common framework of discourse in which there is hope of greater mutual understanding and agreement.

THE CATHOLIC CHURCH AND ECUMENICAL DIALOGUE

The present stand of the Catholic Church with regard to inter-confessional dialogue is most authoritatively set forth in the conciliar *Decree on Ecumenism*.[13]

On the negative side, the Decree repudiates the old-style polemical controversy. Theology, it declares, must be taught, not polemically but "from an ecumenical point of view";[14] the positions of non-Catholics must be presented with justice and truth;[15] every effort must be made "to eliminate words, judgments, and actions which do not respond to the condition of the separated brethren with truth and fairness and so make mutual relations with them more difficult."[16]

On the positive side, Catholics are admonished to acquaint themselves by diligent study with the "distinctive doctrines of our separated brethren, their history, their spiritual and liturgical life, their religious psychology and cultural background."[17] Competent experts are urged to engage in a mutual interchange of ideas which will give each side an accurate knowledge and appreciation of the other's true position.[18] Catholic doctrines are to be explained in a way that others can readily understand, so that terminology may no longer raise unnecessary barriers.[19] Through dialogue of this sort all should be in a better position to recognize the common heritage which still survives among the separated Christian groups.[20] At the same time, care must be taken to present our doctrine completely, not suppressing points of difference in a false spirit of irenicism, which would be entirely foreign to the genuine ecumenical spirit.[21] The distinctive features of each position must be clearly brought out, so that the discrepancies, as well as the points of agreement, will be evident.[22]

As thus far described, the method would seem to correspond closely with that of the Ecumenical Movement prior to Amsterdam, but there are also suggestions of the new approach to dialogue which became current at Lund. The Council recommends collaborative theological work in depth as a means of transcending present difficulties. Catholics are exhorted to proceed with love of truth, charity, and moderation in "investigating the divine mysteries with the separated brethren." Particular doctrines on which there is disagreement are to be studied in their relationship to the fundamental Christian faith (*nexus cum fundamento fidei christianae*) with the result that "the way will be opened for a kind of fraternal rivalry to incite all to a deeper realization and a clearer expression of the unfathomable riches of Christ."[23]

We have already mentioned the frequent complaint that the Catholic Church, claiming infallibility for herself, cannot enter into genuinely dialogic relationships with other Christians. She can only preach to them; she cannot be really disposed to hear. The Decree implicitly answers this objection by declaring that, in the interconfessional dialogue, representatives of the various groups may "deal with each other on an equal footing."[24]

Catholics, without fearing that the Church has allowed the substance of the faith to be corrupted, may frankly acknowledge that the understanding and presentation of revelation in any given age has left much to be desired.[25] The idea of corporate humility is stressed, both in the *Constitution on the Church*, and in the *Decree on Ecumenism*. In the Constitution we are told that the pilgrim Church, "is at the same time holy and always in need of being purified, and incessantly pursues the path of penance and renewal."[26] The Decree explicitly states that "Christ summons the Church to continual reformation," and that the Church is always in need of this, "insofar as she is an institution of men here on earth."[27] This theme of renewal in the Church, we are reminded, has "notable ecumenical importance."[28]

To this "reformability" of the Church on the plane of theological understanding, doctrinal formulation, and moral conduct, corresponds, on the part of non-Catholic communities, a capacity to communicate authentic Christian insights. It would be false to imagine that everything possessed by the other Christians has already been achieved in explicit form within the Catholic Church. The separated churches have distinctive traditions of their own which are worthy of all esteem. Chapter III of the *Decree on Ecumenism* emphasizes the value for Latin Catholics of the spiritual and liturgical traditions of the dissident Eastern Churches.[29] Their theological traditions, likewise, are said to be, in many cases, complementary rather than opposed to those of the Latin West.[30] Being based on the living tradition of the Apostles and the orthodox Fathers, these doctrines promote the "right ordering of Christian life and, indeed, pave the way to a full contemplation of Christian truth."[31] It stands to reason, then, that the Latin West can benefit from assimilating the riches which subsist in these other communions. The barriers caused by present divisions make it difficult for the Church "to express in actual life her full catholicity in all its aspects."[32]

In speaking of the separated communities of the West, the Council is more reserved, but the Decree makes it clear that Christians of the Reformation tradition, as well as others, can have "the life of grace, faith, hope, and charity, along with other interior gifts of the Holy Spirit."[33] Thanks to these super-natural endowments, they are evidently in a position to meditate fruitfully on the word of God and on the mysteries of the Christian faith. Catholics should resist any temptation to deny or belittle the effects of grace in these communities. "Nor should we forget that whatever is wrought by the grace of the Holy Spirit in the hearts of our separated brethren can be a help to our own edification. Whatever is truly Christian never conflicts with the genuine interest of the faith; indeed it can always result in a deeper realization of the mystery of Christ and the Church."[34] This implies that Catholics ought to be care-fully attentive to all that these other Christians have to offer by way of positive insight. The need of reformation in the Church, on the other hand, makes it clear that we should listen to the criticisms offered by non-Catholic Christians. The importance attached to the presence of the observer-delegates at the Council lends emphasis to this point. It illustrates how, by the practice of dialogue, "all are led to examine their own faithfulness to Christ's will for the Church and, wherever necessary, to under-take with vigor the task of renewal and reform."[35]

The Council affirms a mutually beneficial relationship between ecumenical action and self-renewal. On the one hand, as we have just seen, dialogue stimulates all parties to reexamine their previous positions, and to submit to the renewing inspira-tions of the Holy Spirit. On the other hand, interior conversion and self-renewal are prerequisites of a successful dialogue. "For it is from renewal of the inner life of our minds, from self-denial and an unstinted love that desires of unity take their rise and develop in a mature way."[36] The Ecumenical Movement, like every other renewal in the Church, is "essentially grounded in an increase of fidelity to her own calling."[37]

In the last analysis, therefore, the ecumenical dialogue is inseparably intertwined with spiritual progress within the Church. It is never a purely academic exercise. It demands, not only serious study, but, even more urgently, a conversion of heart and holiness of life (*cordis conversio vitaeque sanctitas*).[38] Unless we are individually and corporately humble, open to new insights, and willing to learn from our separated brethren, we shall not be disposed to hear what God wishes to tell us through their agency. Such deafness on our part would impede, not only the reunion of Christians, but the theological and apostolic renewal to which God is summoning the Church in our time.

The reunion of Christians is presented by the Council in very fluid and dynamic terms. Unlike previous documents of the Holy See, the *Decree on Ecumenism* carefully refrains from summoning the separated Christians to "return to their Father's house." There can be no question of a regression to the parting of the ways which occurred centuries ago. The Decree recognizes, of course, that individual Christians may, by God's grace, perceive that full communion with the true Church of Christ can be had only through full incorporation in the Catholic community.[39] In such a case the individual will be, not merely permitted, but, generally speaking, strictly obliged to join the Church. As the Constitution expresses it: "Whosoever . . . knowing that the Catholic Church was made necessary by God through Jesus Christ, would refuse to enter it or to remain in it, could not be saved."[40] But the reconciliation of dissident groups as such with the Catholic Church is not proposed as a present imperative. Rather, the Vatican documents seem to envisage it as the result of a long-term historical process. Even in the case of the Eastern Churches, which are institutionally closest to Catholicism, the *Decree on Ecumenism* urges "that every effort should be made toward the *gradual* realization of this goal" of unity.[41]

In order to prepare for the desired reconciliation, the Catholic Church must energetically rejuvenate herself under the renewing breath of the Holy Spirit. She cannot remain passive and expect others to do all the changing. "This most sacred Synod urgently desires that the initiatives of the sons of the Catholic Church, joined with those of the separated brethren, go forward without obstructing the ways of divine Providence and without prejudging the future inspiration of the Holy Spirit."[42] Since he is the Spirit of Christ, the measures which he inspires will, of course, be "in harmony with the faith which the Catholic

Church has always professed, and at the same time directed toward that fullness with which our Lord wants His body to be endowed in the course of time."[43] Thus the ultimate reunion to which the Council looks forward will involve a reconciliation of the separated brethren, not with the Church as she now appears, but with a purified and revitalized Catholicism.

ECUMENISM AND APOSTOLATE

For purposes of analysis we may conveniently divide the apostolate of Catholics, as set forth by Vatican II, into three areas—that directed to Catholics themselves, to non-Catholic Christians, and to non-Christians. In each of these areas the success of the apostolate depends heavily upon ecumenical action and upon the spiritual renewal which must attend this.

The apostolate of Catholics to the Catholic community, as set forth in the Decree, appears as an inseparable element of true ecumenism. "In their ecumenical work, Catholics must assuredly be concerned for their separated brethren. . . . But their primary duty is to make an honest and careful appraisal of whatever needs to be renewed and achieved in the Catholic household itself. . . ."[44] The mission of the Church, as Tavard has said, "is primarily a mission of the Church to herself. . . . The Church constantly calls to herself to be faithful to her Lord."[45]

The apostolate to the Catholic community is directly related to the second field of apostolic endeavor—the ecumenical impact of the Church on non-Catholic Christianity. "Let all Christ's faithful remember that the more purely they strive to live according to the gospel, the more they are fostering and even practicing Christian unity."[46] Christian reunion, the supreme goal of the apostolate toward the separated Christians, is likewise the ultimate objective of ecumenism. The term "ecumenical movement," as defined by the Decree, "means those activities and enterprises which, according to the various needs of the Church and opportune occasions, are started and organized for the fostering of unity among Christians."[47] But even short of the goal of formal reunion there are many collateral and intermediate benefits which can accrue to all the Churches and communities engaged in the ecumenical dialogue. Their mutual strengthening in the Gospel is a major apostolic concern.

Both the inner regeneration of Catholicism and the progressive restoration of Christian unity have an obvious bearing on the third field of the apostolate—the evangelization of the non-Christian world. Each of these two aspects is stressed in the Decree. When Catholics fail to make fervent use of the means of grace available within the Church, "the radiance of Christ's image" is impaired, with the result that "the growth of God's kingdom is retarded."[48] A divided Christianity, moreover, can scarcely herald the Gospel with full efficacy, for the disunity of Christians quite evidently "scandalizes the world and damages the holy cause of preaching the gospel to every creature."[49]

It would be erroneous to imagine that the three areas of the apostolate were in conflict, as though it were possible to make a choice between self-renewal, ecumenical work, and missionary activity. All three apostolates depend on one another. Ecumenism is needed for Catholic renewal and for Christian unity alike. Only a renewed and reintegrated Christianity, moreover, can measure up to the full missionary responsibility which Christ inalienably conferred upon the Church.

Turning now to the non-Catholic Christian communions, it may be asked whether they, too, have a share in the apostolate. Without using the term, the Decree seems to accord them a certain apostolic function toward the unevangelized, toward their own members, and even toward the Catholic communion. That the separated brethren can evangelize non-Christians is implied in the statement that they show forth the effects of grace in "bearing witness to Christ, sometimes even to the shedding of their blood."[50] Even more directly, the Decree reminds them of their duty to bear witness to the central truths of faith: "Before the whole world let all Christians profess their faith in the triune God and in the Incarnate Son of God, our Redeemer and Lord."[51] This capacity for common witness presupposes a share in the power to proclaim the Gospel. We may therefore apply to non-Catholic Christians, in some sense, the statement of the *Constitution on the Church*: "The obligation of spreading the faith is imposed on every disciple of Christ, according to his state."[52] While the conciliar documents, thus far, have not dealt specifically with the question of different states of life within non-Catholic Christianity, there seems to be no reason to doubt that some are called by the grace of God to dedicate themselves professionally to the spreading of the Gospel.

The Decree is generous in recognizing the salvific value of separated churches and communities with regard to their own members. They are said to be "by no means deprived of significance and importance in the mystery of salvation. For the Spirit of Christ has not refrained from using them as a means of salvation" by virtue of the authentic Christian elements they have retained.[53]

The apostolic responsibility of non-Catholic Christians toward the Catholic Church is a more delicate point, not directly discussed in the Vatican documents, but it seems that the principles set forth in the *Decree on Ecumenism* would require that such an apostolic function should be admitted. For these communities, as we have seen, have something authentically Christian to give; and the Catholic Church, in her actual historical condition, has much to receive. Christians, even as separated brothers, are one another's keepers. Mysteriously bound together in the communion of saints, they can share in one another's prayers and spiritual graces. They must likewise bear one another's burdens. Through the ecumenical dialogue they take part in a process of mutual giving and receiving, to the end that all may advance toward the fullness of what the Church should be, and in this way converge also toward one another.

The possibilities of mutual enrichment through this dialogic apostolate are by no means limited to the reciprocal communication of the spiritual capital which the several parties already have on hand. Dialogue is a creative process which mysteriously yields greater treasures than are brought to it by any one participant, or even all together. As Reuel Howe profoundly observes:

The dialogical person must be prepared to participate in the discipline of great dialogue, out of which true creativity is born. Have we not all had the experience of finally submitting our question or thought to a group of peers and then seeing emerge from the painful yet exciting wrestling with the truth an insight or understanding that was greater and more profound than that offered by any single contributor? So tremendous is this experience that we find it easy to believe that God was in the midst and that through our dialogue he made us participants in his revelations.[54]

The "discipline" of great dialogue, to which Howe advisedly refers, imposes heavy demands. "Ecumenism," as Congar has said, "seeks a reform within ourselves, for we are full of aggressiveness, clannishness and arrogance of distrust and rivalry. We must be converted by detachment from all this and from ourselves, and acceptance of a humble submissiveness to what the Lord expects of us."[55] At this perplexing moment of history, when all Christianity is confronted by the turmoil of an ebullient secularity, we can no longer afford to immure ourselves within the castle of our cherished habits of thought. Nor is it enough to become friendly and garrulous. If the dialogue is to succeed, we must engage in serious mutual questioning and criticism, prayerfully seeking together for the message we are to proclaim. Only in faithful and wholehearted response to their ecumenical vocation can the churches hope to find a word capable of renewing the face of the earth. Through ecumenical dialogue, according to the principles of the Vatican Decree, the Christian communities can jointly perform an invaluable apostolic service. They can dispose themselves and one another for this creative discovery.

PART FOUR

REVELATION IN CONTEMPORARY
PROTESTANT THEOLOGY

11

Paul Tillich and the Bible

Under the stimulus of recent progress in linguistics and archaeology, biblical studies have flourished remarkably in the present century. Advances on the technical level have been attended by a renewal of interest in the Bible from a theological point of view. Catholic and Protestant theologians alike have been seeking to make use of the new information and to assimilate it harmoniously into their respective systems.

Unlike many other Protestant theologians of our day—the names of Eichrodt, Bultmann, and Cullmann come immediately to mind—Paul Tillich is not outstanding as a biblical scholar. He is primarily a systematic theologian, but his system has, with some justification, been called biblical, on the ground that it is "wholly and finally determined by the revelation of God recorded in the Bible."[1] In his theological writings he tried to work out a general theory of what the Bible should mean to the contemporary Protestant believer and theologian. As has been pointed out in a number of recent studies, Tillich's system holds exceptional interest for the Catholic theologian.[2] His views on the Bible are, perhaps, especially interesting, since they exhibit some startling approaches toward the Catholic position, and at the same time some fundamental divergences.

The Bible, in Tillich's view, is a uniquely important collection of source documents. He sees in it the primary source of

God's final revelation to mankind, the original record of man's response to that revelation, and the basic font of Christian theology. We may conveniently consider Tillich's biblical doctrine under each of these three heads, and then conclude our study with a brief critical appraisal.

THE BIBLE AND REVELATION

In order to understand Tillich's biblical doctrine, one must begin with a clear conception of what he means by "revelation."[3] His theory of revelation is basic to his system, and is quite different from that familiar to Catholics. Like most Catholic theologians, he avoids the term "natural revelation" as confusing, if not contradictory. Revelation is, for him, a special and extraordinary type of knowledge. It is the apprehension of the mysterious—of that which lies beyond the grasp of man's natural powers. In revelation, indeed, God manifests Himself; the human intellect is brought face to face with the transcendent God. Now man, in his present existential state—the condition of fallen nature—is estranged from his true self, and consequently from God also. This is indicated by the evident fact that our ordinary knowledge bears on finite beings, which are grasped as "objects" in opposition to ourselves. But God is neither a finite being nor an object. He is the transcendent ground of all being, including our own. Hence he cannot be reached by ordinary human knowledge. In order to acquire any genuine knowledge of God it is therefore necessary for the mind to overleap all finite categories and transcend the ordinary distinctions between subject and object. Extraordinary knowledge of this sort is what Tillich means by revelation.

Revelation has two aspects, objective and subjective. In the objective order, something really happens which manifests the mysterious ground of being. As is evident from the history of religion, revelatory events have always been described as "shaking, transforming, demanding, significant in an ultimate way."[4] Occurrences of this kind are, in Tillich's terminology, called "miracles." The subjective apprehension of revelation, wherein the mind rises above its ordinary limits, is technically called "ecstasy." Revelation may therefore be described as the self-manifestation of God through miracle and ecstasy.

The terms "ecstasy" and "miracle" must be understood in the technical sense which Tillich gives them. Ecstasy, in his terminology, is not emotional overexcitement, nor is it a state of demonic possession destroying the rational structure of the mind. Rather, it is an elevation of the mind whereby it experiences union with the mysterious ground of being. By miracle, on the other hand, he does not mean a supernatural intervention of God in the order of nature. Such an interposition of God in the chain of created cause-effect relationships would, in Tillich's philosophy, be incompatible with the divine transcendence. By a miracle he, therefore, means an unusual event—extraordinary either in its regularity or its irregularity—which somehow points to the ultimate source of reality and of meaning. While Tillich's ontology does not directly concern us in this study, it is important to note, at the outset, that he denies all supernatural interventions of God in the world.

That which is revealed, as we have said, is strict mystery. It cannot be apprehended by ordinary thought, and, for the same reason, it cannot be expressed in ordinary language. Propositions about revelations are not themselves revelatory. This point will be of pivotal importance in Tillich's analysis of the Bible.

On the basis of these observations about Tillich's general view of revelation, we may inquire how he conceives of revelation in the concrete.[5] In the Christian view, he asserts, there is but one final revelation—the manifestation of God in Jesus as the Christ. This revelation was originally made through Jesus to His disciples, but the final revelation has not ceased. It goes on in the Church, and will go on to the end of time. The original revelation, and its reception by the first disciples, is the primary source from which all subsequent Christian revelation derives. The latter may, therefore, be called dependent, as contrasted with original, revelation. In opposition to the Evangelicals, who would maintain that the Spirit gives new revelations to individuals reading the

Bible, Tillich maintains that the Christian revelation has been given, once for all, in its fulness, and that subsequent revelations within the Christian economy can add nothing substantially new.

Christian revelation, however, is not the only revelation. Tillich differs sharply from Barth, who would maintain that the final revelation is cast "like a stone" into the human situation, without any previous conditioning on the part of man. Man cannot receive a revelation which does not answer to a felt need. Hence the human mind must be disposed for final revelation by revelations of a preparatory character. Preparatory revelation, according to Tillich, may be called universal, not in the sense that everyone receives it, but in the sense that it can occur at any place or time.

The concrete revelations which directly prepared the Jewish people for the final revelation are recorded in the Old Testament. The New Testament contains the basic documents of the final revelation itself. The Bible, therefore, is a record of divine revelation.

But the Bible is not merely a collection of documents about revelation; it is also itself revelatory. The biblical writers were, themselves, involved in the revelatory events they described; they wrote as witnesses to revelation. It is even true to say that they were inspired writers. In speaking of inspiration, Tillich is careful to exclude any suggestion of supernaturalism. He explicitly rejects the notion that the Bible was divinely "dictated," or that God in any way intervened to shape the thoughts and intentions of the human authors. Inspiration, in Tillich's vocabulary, is the cognitive aspect of ecstasy. "The inspiration of the writers of the New Testament is their acceptance of Jesus as the Christ, and with him, of the New Being, of which they became witnesses." By literary inspiration Tillich understands simply the vital and creative response of an author to a revelation which he has received.[6]

As a revelatory document, the Bible transmits to us God's self-disclosure in ancient Jewish history and particularly His final manifestation in Jesus as the Christ. That message, in its revelatory dimension, cannot be set down in ordinary human language. Propositions can express contingent facts, abstract doctrines, or ethical precepts, but they cannot convey revelation. For revelation, in Tillich's view, is not scientific or factual or even practical information. It adds no new content to human knowledge, but gives it a new dimension of ultimate meaning. It manifests the ground of being, that which concerns us ultimately.[7]

While human language, in its ordinary propositional use, cannot serve as a vehicle of revelation, there is a peculiar kind of speech which is appropriate to the task. This is symbolism, which Tillich defines as the use of finite materials in order to create a revelatory situation.[8] Symbolic speech might be described as the miracle of language. Words are so used that their proper meaning is negated, and they point beyond themselves to the ultimate ground of being. The metaphors applied to God in the Old Testament are an excellent example of symbolic writing. Although often described as anthropomorphic, they are not really so; for they are charged with symbolic overtones and thereby communicate a vivid sense of God's transcendence. Not only metaphors and parables, but also myths and legends, according to Tillich, have value as symbols. The truth of a symbol, obviously has nothing to do with its literal verification. Symbols have a type of truth peculiar to themselves; they are true to the extent that they adequately reflect the revelatory situation which they are intended to express. In his attitude toward symbolism, Tillich takes great pains to dissociate himself from the Modernists. The latter, he charges, "have interpreted religious language symbolically in order to weaken its seriousness, its power, and its spiritual impact." He is also critical of Bultmann for unjustifiably equating myth with a merely primitive world-view which should be cast aside. For Tillich, on the contrary, myth and symbol are the only way in which revelation can be communicated.[9]

The biblical writers were the recipients of a unique series of revelations leading up to God's final self-manifestation in the person of Jesus. As inspired authors, they used language with singular revelatory power. The Bible is, therefore, a genuine source of revelation. When read by a person with the requisite dispositions, it enables him to enter into the revelatory events described, and to share in the ecstatic experience of the biblical writers. As a medium of revelation, the Bible possesses a certain sacramental quality. It is a holy book.

THE BIBLE AND HISTORY OF RELIGION

Thus far we have considered the Bible as a record and source of revelation, but there is more in the Bible than revelation. Revelation is an act of God which necessarily implies, as its correlative, a reception on the part of man. The human reception of and response to revelation are what Tillich means by the term "religion."[10]

Considered in the abstract, revelation and religion are very different. Revelation moves from God to man; religion moves from man to God. Revelation is divine and absolute; religion is human and contingent. In the concrete, however, revelation is not revelation except in so far as it is actually received; God's self-disclosure is proportioned to the receptive capacities of man. To see how imperfectly men have responded to divine revelation, there is no need to look beyond the Bible. It tells a constantly reiterated story of how men have resisted the word of God, distorted it by superstition, rejected it in favor of idolatry. In order to maintain the purity of revelation, the prophets raised an unceasing protest against these human perversions.

In so far as it gives an account of Jewish religion, the Bible is a historical work, but the biblical writers, quite evidently, are not historians in the same sense as a von Ranke or a Trevelyan. Their main interest is to bear witness to divine revelation. They sometimes write about historical facts which, by their miraculous character, have revelatory significance, but they also make use of myths and legends to convey their message. It is theologically unimportant, Tillich maintains, to know exactly where fact ends and fiction begins. The theologian, therefore, can be indifferent to the historical aspects of the Bible. "The truth of religious symbol has nothing to do with the truth of the empirical assertions involved in it, be they physical, psychological, or historical."[11]

Tillich's discussion of creation and the fall is illustrative of his symbolical method of interpretation. On philosophical grounds he denies that creation and the fall are two actual past events. They are symbols which aptly express man's existential predicament—the necessarily tragic state of finite freedom. "Finite freedom, when it becomes actual, disrupts the essential, uncontested, innocent unity between finitude and its infinite ground."[12] Through their apprehension of this truth, according to Tillich, philosophers of the stature of Plato and Origen, Kant and Schelling, were driven to invoke the myth of a transcendent, non-historical fall. Since the fall was not a historical event, "it is inadequate to ask questions concerning Adam's actual state before the fall, for example, whether he was mortal or immortal, or whether he was in a state of righteousness."[13]

One of Tillich's colleagues, Reinhold Niebuhr, has powerfully criticized his views on this point, alleging that they falsify "the picture of man as the Bible portrays it, and as we actually experience it."[14] "There is no myth of 'the transcendent fall' in the Bible, but only the myth of a historical fall."[15] Without violence to the clear intent of Scripture we cannot telescope the narratives of the creation and the fall. "There is significance in the fact that there are two stories, the one symbolizing the beginning of history and the other, the corruption of freedom in history. It is important that the two stories be separated," for that very separation shows that man's act of self-estrangement was a defection from a more ideal possibility. Biblical faith, according to Niebuhr, is distinguished from Platonistic and Oriental speculations by its strong insistence on the significance of history. Tillich, in his biblical exegesis, does not always do justice to the dimension of the historical.[16]

The problem of the relations between revelation and history arises most acutely in the realm of Christology. Does not the Christian faith essentially involve the factual occurrence in time of certain contingent events such as the Incarnation, the crucifixion, and the resurrection? If so, can Tillich sustain his contention that the truth of revelation has nothing to do with assertions of empirical fact? The thorough discussion of these points, in the second volume of Tillich's *Systematic Theology*, is little more than an application of the general principles regarding the relationship between revelation and history developed in his earlier writings. In view of the purposes of the present chapter, we may focus primarily on the latter.

The writers of the New Testament, he maintains, are interested in transmitting a religiously significant picture of Jesus, not in reporting merely factual data of a sort that could have been picked up by a sound-recording camera. The life of Jesus, as a revelatory event, has been recorded in revelatory language, that is to say, in symbolical and mythical expressions.[17] It would be erroneous to look to the Bible to give us a photographic picture of Jesus, conceived according to the principles of certain modern schools of historiography. "The original picture, which existed from the beginning, was of a numinous and interpreted character, and it was this which proved to have the power to conquer existence."[18] From the point of view of religion, there is no need to supplement this picture with one that is merely factual. If scientific history wishes to try to reconstruct a "historical Jesus" according to the principles of its own methodology, it is free to do so, but such a picture will neither add nor subtract anything of theological interest. The scientist can speak with precision about the documents of revelation, but he cannot speak as a witness of revelation, and hence cannot add to our revelatory knowledge. Using the techniques of his own science, he can nether confirm nor deny the revealed truth about Jesus; for revealed truth, according to Tillich, "lies within the dimension of revelatory knowledge" alone.[19] A. T. Mollegen, summarizing the views of Tillich, has put the matter well:

> This Biblical historical Christ is normative for Tillich. The quest of the historical Jesus which Schweitzer so brilliantly described in his book of the same name, and to which he added a revolutionary chapter, can neither replace nor support the Biblical portrait in as much as faith and theology are concerned. Conservative

criticism cannot give us a purely factual Jesus which guarantees the photographic details of the Biblical historical Christ's life, nor can theological liberalism by critical methods reconstruct a "historical Jesus" who becomes a new canonical scripture supplanting the New Testament portrait, nor can radical criticism destroy the human flesh and blood existence of "the Biblical Christ."[20]

Tillich is, therefore, quite unconcerned about the historicity of any particular details in the life of Jesus, but at the same time he is deeply convinced that the Christian revelation has a basis in actual fact. Even as a theologian, he can affirm that revelation always occurs in a constellation of ecstasy and miracle. Since we have revelatory writings, we can argue to the occurrence of revelation in and through Jesus. In the objective order, there unquestionably were miraculous events. Indeed, since the revelation given in Jesus as the Christ is the final revelation, the life of Jesus may be called the supreme and ecstatic moment of history. Tillich emphatically repudiates the suggestion that Christianity might have arisen out of some merely subjective experience:

> I may express the hope that one false view is excluded by every-thing I have tried to say: namely, the mistake of supposing that the picture of the New Being in Jesus as the Christ is the creation of existential thought or experience. If this were the case, it would be as distorted, tragic, and sinful as existence is itself, and would not be able to overcome existence. The religious picture of the New Being in Jesus is the result of a new being: it represents the victory over existence which has taken place, and thus created the picture.[21]

The final revelation expressed in the New Testament, then, presupposes as its foundation a human individual, whose life and character were such as to support the biblical picture. Our faith and salvation, in Tillich's view, do not depend merely on the inter-preted picture of Jesus, but equally on the events which that picture interprets. The miracle and the ecstasy are strictly correlative. Neither is salvific without the other. "The Christ is not the Christ without the church, and the church is not the church without the Christ."[22] Faith in the Christ is capable of giving us a New Being because, by accepting the revelatory picture, we participate in the reality of the Christ. "The church from its beginning through the present participates in a reality which is different from any other reality and which, therefore, is called the New Being."[23]

Thus Tillich accepts the reality of Jesus as a human individual. But he does not do so precisely on the authority of the biblical writers. He looks to them for the interpretation of the facts, but not for the facts which they interpret. He recognizes, of course, that the Gospels, like many other sections of the Bible, purport to relate actual events; they are not merely symbolic speech. Even though the Bible is not scientific history, there are factual assertions in the Bible. As a theologian, however, Tillich passes no judgment on the value of the Bible as history. When the biblical writers make historical or scientific affirmations, he would say, their statements are as reliable as the evidence on which those statements are based. There can be no such thing as revealed history or revealed science, for history and science, by their very nature, do not concern us ultimately. They are not the ground of our being, and hence are not matter for revelation. The question of factual truth falls within the province of the positive sciences and cannot be prejudged from a theological point of view. "That which concerns us ultimately is not linked with any special conclusion of historical and philological research. A theology which is dependent on predetermined results of the historical approach is bound to something conditional which claims to be unconditional, that is, with something demonic."[24]

Many theologians, according to Tillich, have failed to recognize that the Bible was written by human authors, who were fallible as witnesses of historical fact. There has thus arisen a sort of biblical "monophysitism." The practice of referring to the Bible as the "word of God" has been one source of this confusion. It has given support to supernaturalistic theories of inspiration and the dogma of the infallible book.[25] Great harm has come to religion from this type of thinking. Theologians, anxiously seeking to suppress elements of truth of which they were dimly aware, have become fanatical. In their efforts to reconcile the Bible with science, they have used "sacred dishonesty." After committing themselves to certain scientific theories on theological grounds, theologians have then sought to prevent the diffusion of new theories, only to capitulate ignominiously when further resistance became impossible. "This ill-conceived resistance of theologians, from the time of Galileo to the time of Darwin, was one of the causes of the split between religion and secular culture in the past centuries."[26]

Rightly understood, there can be no conflict between science and theology; they move in different dimensions. While scientific investigation cannot dissolve revelation, "it can undercut superstitious and demonic interpretations of revelation, ecstasy, and miracle."[27] Historical criticism, for example, protects us against an idolatrous fundamentalism in our interpretation of the Bible. By calling attention to the mythical elements in Scripture, it removes the false offense of pseudo-history and permits the Gospel to confront men with the true offense of the doctrine of the cross.[28] In such ways as this, the positive sciences are the allies of theology in its struggle against distortions of genuine revelation.

Tillich therefore distinguishes sharply between the revelatory value of the Bible, and its value as a historical document. In so far as it is revelatory, it manifests the ultimate ground of being and is not subject to error. In so far as it deals with historical facts, including religious history, it is neither inspired nor infallible. Even the religion of the biblical writers, Tillich would say, is imperfect. Religion, the reception of revelation, is always inadequate. As a human act, it belongs to the realm of history. Just as the Jews of Old Testament times were not immune from religious error, so too the biblical writers were capable of distorting the revelations which came their way. They were not exempt from the limitations of their own abilities and temperament, nor from the unhealthy influence of their secular and religious environment.[29] Thus the true message of the final revelation, the Christian kerygma, is not the arithmetical sum of the religious ideas which can be found in the Bible. The sacred writers did not receive the divine message in all its purity.

The Bible, Tillich insists, is not all of a piece. There is a higher level of revelation in the New Testament than in the Old, and even in the New Testament not all parts are of equal value. The high point is the religious picture of Jesus communicated through the interpreted events of the Gospel story, and the semi-mythological reflections of John and Paul. The Gospel, in its main lines, shows us the career of a man completely submissive to the divine demands, surrendering Himself even to the death of the cross. St. Paul expresses the significance of these events through the symbolism of a pre-existent spiritual being who takes on the form of a servant.[30] St. John, teaching the lesson of the crucifixion, presents Jesus as saying, "he who believes in me does not believe in *me*...."[31] In this vision of a man totally transparent to the divine we have, in Tillich's opinion, the final and unsurpassable revelation.

Even in the New Testament, Tillich would concede, the gold of revelation is mixed with dross. There is evidence of an idolatrous exaltation of Jesus to a semi-divine status. In the miracle narratives of the later New Testament traditions Tillich detects the incursions of a demonic supernaturalism.[32]

Tillich therefore finds it possible to use the Bible in so far as it is revelatory in order to criticize the Bible as a religious document. In virtue of what he calls the "Protestant principle"— that is, the refusal to exalt anything finite to the level of ultimate concern—he feels entitled to reject certain elements in the Bible itself. "Protestant theology protests in the name of the Protestant principle against the identification of our ultimate concern with any creation of the church, including the biblical writings insofar as their witness to what is really ultimate concern is also a conditioned expression of their own spirituality."[33]

THE BIBLE AND THEOLOGY

Theology, in Tillich's synthesis, is clearly distinguished from revelation. It is not revelation, but rather a particular form of man's religious response to revelation. The theologian's task is to construct an ordered body of knowledge concerning revelation.

The Christian message or kerygma is, in Tillich's view, identical with the final revelation. Christian theology, therefore, is not the Christian message, but only a reflection on that message. "While the message itself is beyond our grasp and never at our disposal (though it might grasp us and dispose of us), its theological interpretation is an act of the church and of individuals within the church."[34] Religious orthodoxy—of which American Fundamentalism is an instance—falls into the error of confusing a particular formulation of the message with the message itself. Such a confusion has "demonic" traits in so far as it ascribes eternal and infinite value to something which is by its very nature conditioned, finite, and temporal. Even the "neo-Orthodox" theologians—in spite of their principle that "God is in heaven and man on earth"—have committed the mistake of trying to create an unconditioned theology. Barth, while laudably attempting to focus attention on the eternal kerygma, has allowed his work to become tainted with what Tillich might call the heresy of orthodoxy.[35]

Theology, in so far as it is a reflection on revelation, must be based on revelation. The sources of Christian theology are the documents of the final revelation which occurred in Jesus as the Christ. In opposition to the neo-Orthodox, Tillich maintains that there are other Christian sources than the Bible, such as, for example, ecclesiastical tradition, but the Bible is the basic source, for it is the original document about the events upon which the Christian church is founded.[36]

In addition to sources, theology must have a norm, that is, a criterion in terms of which the sources are evaluated and interpreted.[37] The norm, as the formal element in theology, must itself be derived from the sources. If the norm were taken from philosophy or science, one could have a philosophy of religion, but not a genuine theology.

The Bible is not, never has been, and could not itself be the theological norm. For one thing, we cannot learn from the biblical books that they are canonical. The canon of the Bible must therefore be determined by something other than the Bible alone. The history of Christianity has shown certain variations of opinion about the limits of the biblical canon. These variations—which Tillich regards as a healthy sign of life and freedom—are due to varying conceptions of the theological norm. Even with respect to books acknowledged as canonical, they have never, in practice, been treated as all having equal authority. The Old Testament, Tillich observes, has never been directly normative; it has been measured by the New, and even the New Testament has never been equally influential in all its parts.[38]

Tillich is sharply critical of evangelicist biblicism, which attempts to erect the Bible into a self-sufficient norm. Such an attitude, he maintains, is sheer self-deception. The solitary reader of the Bible is more dependent on the church than he is usually aware. He has received the Bible as preserved by the church, as presented to him by the church, and as interpreted by the church, "even if this interpretation comes to him simply by way of the accepted translation into his own language."[39] It is quite impossible for the contemporary reader of the Bible to leap over two thousand years of church history and enter into the situation of Matthew or Paul. In point of fact, Tillich observes, the "biblical" theology of the evangelicals is heavily indebted to the dogmatic developments of post-Reformation theology. "Through historical scholarship the difference between the dogmatic teaching of most American evangelistic churches and the original meaning of the biblical texts can easily be shown."[40]

Thus the norm of theology, although primarily based on the Bible, is not the Bible, nor is it derived from the Bible alone. Historically, the theological norm has always been derived from an encounter between the Bible and the church. Ecclesiastical tradition, according to Tillich, plays an indispensable part in the establishment of the theological norm. He does not, however, admit the right of church authorities to dictate to theologians what their norm should be.[41]

In the concrete, what is the norm of theology? In answer to this question Tillich distinguishes between a negative norm, or critical principle, and a positive norm. We have already mentioned the critical principle in connection with Tillich's evaluation of Scripture; it is the axiom that no finite object should be identified with that which concerns us ultimately. This principle suffices to exclude false theologies, but does not give us the true one. The positive element in the norm is the particular way in which that which concerns us ultimately manifests itself. Since the final revelation is the manifestation of God in Jesus as the Christ, the appearance of Jesus as the Christ is the positive norm for Christian theology.

The total norm, taken in its positive and negative aspects, is the criterion for using all the sources of systematic theology. The norm for the use of Scripture is the final manifestation of what concerns us ultimately in the *biblical* picture of Jesus as the Christ.[42]

Every theologian, even the "biblical" theologian, must take cognizance of the theological norm. Biblical theology should not be treated as though it were a profane discipline. In its "material" aspect—if it be permissible to introduce a Scholastic term not found in Tillich's exposition—it is a historico-critical discipline, concerned with philological and exegetical problems. But the biblical theologian cannot stop on the scientific level. "Formally," as a theologian, he must unite philology with faith and devotion; he must give a genuinely theological appraisal and interpretation of biblical doctrine with reference to the norm of theology. It is exceedingly difficult to strike a proper balance between these two points of view, the critical and the pneumatic. But sound biblical theology is of inestimable importance. "Only such free historical work, united with the attitude of ultimate concern, can open the Bible up to the systematic theologian as his basic source."[43]

Just as biblical theology is dependent on philology and history for its contents, so systematic theology derives its material mainly from biblical theology. Systematic theology is the effort to construct a methodical synthesis of Christian doctrine appropriate to the needs of a given age and culture. The precise principles governing the theological synthesis will vary to some extent from century to century. For the purposes of his own system, Tillich formulates the theological norm in terms of the "New Being" which became manifest in Jesus as the Christ. This norm is basically biblical, since it is inspired by the Pauline concept of the "new creation." Thus formulated, the norm of systematic theology is adapted to the present state of culture and society. It points to the Christian message as the answer to the anxieties and needs of our age, which is haunted by the fear of self-estrangement, dissolution, and conflict.[44]

If it be objected that systematic theology, as he conceives and practices it, is not fully biblical, Tillich defends himself by calling attention to the precedent set by the biblical authors themselves. Textual criticism, he points out, makes it clear that they used and transformed the categories and symbols current in their own religious and cultural tradition.[45] The work of adaptation was continued by the primitive church—and quite properly so. Tillich repudiates the rigid biblicism expounded by Ritschl and Harnack, who accused the early church of having betrayed biblical religion by relating it positively to the concerns of Graeco-Roman culture. What Harnack called the Hellenization of the Gospel was a necessary step, both because the Gospel had to be introduced into the Hellenistic world and because the discovery of the ontological question by the Greek mind is universally relevant. "On this point, the early church was right, however questionable its concrete solutions may have been, and its nineteenth-century critics were wrong."[46]

This last observation brings us to a final criticism of biblicism with which we may conclude our summary of Tillich's views on the relations between the Bible and theology. The biblicists vainly seek to construct a theology which would avoid the ontological question. Such a theology, according to Tillich, is impossible. Since theology deals with our ultimate concern, it cannot escape the question of being, any more than can philosophy. Even the Bible, Tillich points out, describes the structure of experience in ontological terms. Not only the sapiential books and the theological meditations of John and Paul, but even the Synoptic Gospels abound in terms—such as time, law, life, love, and knowledge—pregnant with ontological significance.

> It is surprising how casually theological biblicists use a term like "history" when speaking of Christianity as a historical religion or of God as the "Lord of history." They forget that the meaning they connect with the word "history" has been formed by thousands of years of historiography and philosophy of history. They forget that historical being is one kind of being in addition to others and that, in order to distinguish it from the word "nature," for instance, a general vision of the structure of being is presupposed. They forget that the problem of history is tied up with the problems of time, freedom, accident, purpose, etc. . . . The theologian must take seriously the meaning of the terms he uses. . . . Therefore, the systematic theologian must be a philosopher in critical understanding even if not in creative power.[47]

Thus Tillich, while relying on the Bible as the basic source of the final revelation, directly opposes the narrow biblicism which has tended to stunt the growth of Protestant theology in the past. Against Pascal and many Protestant fideists he loudly proclaims that the God of Abraham, Isaac, and Jacob is the same as the God of the philosophers.[48] Tillich was bold enough to undertake a statement of the Christian message in fully ontological terms. However one may appraise the results of his efforts, he unquestionably made a great contribution to the revival of metaphysical thinking within Protestant circles in our day.

EVALUATION

For the Catholic reader the most disconcerting element in Tillich's treatment of the Bible, as in other areas of his thought, is his total rejection of the supernatural. His position in this regard radically affects his entire understanding of the Christian revelation. The Bible, for him, is not a supernaturally inspired book, nor does it contain revealed precepts, doctrines, or history. The biblical account of man's creation and fall is valid as symbolism, but tells us nothing about the prehistoric past. Even the Incarnation and the Redemption, which for classical Christianity constitute the central message of the Bible, are not, in Tillich's view, events which actually occurred. While admitting that these terms have mythical value in symbolizing the union of human existence with its creative ground, he refuses to accept them as properly descriptive of what objectively transpired. The notion of a unique ontological union between God and creature, such as underlies the traditional doctrines of the Incarnation, the Mystical Body, and sanctifying grace, is in Tillich's eyes idolatrous. His so-called Protestant principle is but one expression of his conviction that there can be no *communicatio idiomatum* between God and created natures.

Although Tillich continues to speak of the Christian revelation as "final," his conception of Christianity has little in common with what is usually understood by that term. In the words of a recent Protestant critic:

> If Tillich is right, the objective faith of the apostles and of the great company of Christian witnesses throughout the ages was wrong, and he plainly tells us so.... There is, for Tillich, no personal God who *objectively is*, who rules the nations and our lives, and who has judged us and saved us in Christ Jesus by his own coming into the world, being crucified, and being raised from the grave. Nor is there, for him, any life after death for us all, and thus no eventual solution to the tragedies and evils of our existence.[49]

To go into Tillich's reasons for excluding the supernatural would take us beyond the limits of the present study. In part they are philosophical. Since he does not admit the analogy of being as understood by Scholastic philosophers, he does not conceive of God as the Absolute Being, subsisting in Himself, fully distinct from creatures. Rather, God is for him the immanent-transcendent ground of finite being. For Tillich it therefore seems repugnant that God should act on creatures externally, as an efficient cause, or that He should preferentially unite Himself to some rather than others. To assert any such intervention, he maintains, is to degrade God to the status of a particular, finite being—one which acts upon, or unites with, others existing alongside of itself.

To many of his critics it has seemed that, in his rejection of the supernatural, Tillich inevitably falls into a sort of naturalism. This criticism has been made from the Catholic side by Gustave Weigel, S.J., and from the Protestant side by Nels Ferré. It has also been made from a non-theistic point of view by J. H. Randall, who shrewdly observes that "revelation" for Tillich "would seem to be a symbol for the power of reason to do what revelation notoriously does."[50] Sometimes Tillich himself refers to his system as "self-transcending or ecstatic naturalism,"[51] a term which suggests that he is basically a naturalist, though not of the reductionist stamp. But if Tillich is a naturalist, it is not because he wants to be. His constant endeavor was to find a middle path between naturalism and supernaturalism. On one occasion he affirmed: "My thinking is not naturalistic. Naturalism and supernaturalism provoke each other and should be removed together."[52]

While Tillich's blanket rejection of the supernatural order is doubtless rather too extreme, one may with confidence say that his critique of "supranaturalism" contains elements of great worth. It is true, for example, that naturalism tends to generate, by way of reaction, an unwholesome supernaturalism. Efforts to demonstrate the reality of the supernatural with quasi-mathematical exactitude from alleged violations of physical laws have all too often been based on an uncritical acceptance of rationalistic presuppositions. As Tillich puts it: "A kind of rationalist irrationalism develops in which the degree of absurdity in a miracle story becomes the measure of its religious value. The more impossible, the more revelatory!"[53] Tillich renders a valuable service in stressing that anti-naturalism of this sort does small honor to God, and that the prodigy-aspect of miracles should not be allowed to overshadow their function as religious signs. Thus far he is in line with biblical thinking. The notion of miracle, as found for example in Exodus, is hardly equivalent to the violation of a physical law. As G. E. Wright has said: "In the Bible a miracle is something quite different. It is any spectacular happening or 'wonder' which is a 'sign' of God's working."[54]

Beginning with the time of Newman, many Catholic authors have pointed out the inadequacy of defining miracles as though they were simply contraventions of the laws of nature, and the urgency of restoring the traditional emphasis on the religious and revelatory dimension.[55] Miracles, according to this conception, are astonishing events in which contingent causes are raised to a higher pitch of efficacy, producing effects which betoken the kingdom of God. Normally, at least, these wonders admit of a twofold interpretation—like the heavenly voice which the Jews explained as thunder (Jn 12.29). But the whole context of a miracle is such that the religious-minded inquirer is able to recognize the direct activity of God. Such a view of miracles embodies a supernaturalism which is the reverse of anti-naturalistic. It affirms that nature, instead of being a completely self-enclosed system, is open to the intervention of a higher Liberty, and that God can make use of created agencies to bestow gifts that are divine.

A similar critique may be made of Tillich's comments on inspiration. He rightly rejects the "supranaturalistic" view which would depict God as dictating the Bible or as substituting His own activity for the natural processes of the human mind. Inspiration is indeed—to use Tillich's own term—essentially ecstatic. That is to say, it implies that the rational structure of the mind is preserved and elevated, although transcended. It is quite true that some theologians, wishing to stress the divine authorship of the Bible, have pictured scriptural inspiration as a "demonic" possession of the mind by God. But no such charge can be made against official Catholic teaching or against the doctrine of St. Thomas. Aquinas ceaselessly emphasized the fact that God respects the freedom and rationality of the human author. Strictly scriptural inspiration, in the Thomistic view, does not involve any infusion of new information. It does not dispense the author from gathering his facts and forming his conceptions by natural methods, nor does it prevent him from expressing himself according to the thought-patterns and idioms of his own age and culture. For this reason, St. Thomas explains, the hagiographers "more commonly spoke about matters which could be known by human reason, and not as it were in the name of God, but in their own name (*ex persona propria*), although with the assistance of the divine light."[56]

Thus Tillich's attack on supernaturalism is directed less against the perennial Catholic doctrine than against the rationalistic distortions which tended to infect Christian apologetics in the era of Newtonian scientism. The same may be said of Tillich's biblical theology in general. He is mainly concerned with refuting errors and exaggerations which have arisen in the past few centuries, especially that radical biblicism which is distinctively Protestant. Catholics, who have never looked on the Bible as a self-sufficient source of revelation, can concur in many of Tillich's strictures on biblicism.

As regards the authorship of Scripture, the comments on inspiration in the preceding paragraphs indicate both the justice and the exaggeration in Tillich's views. He is on solid ground when he protests against a "monophysitism" which would ignore the role of the human author. He is right in insisting that the Bible did not drop down from heaven without any relation to the human situation, but that it reflects the patient pedagogy by which God gradually prepared mankind for the fulness of revelation in Christ. But Tillich goes to the opposite extreme and falls into a sort of inverse monophysitism. He tends to overlook the divine element in Holy Scipture, and in effect denies that it is the word of God. Thus he needlessly repudiates an article of faith as ancient and sacred as Christianity itself, and leaves the Christian believer without authoritative guidance.

Tillich does well, once again, in refusing to interpret the Bible with a literalism that would be sheerly verbalistic. The Catholic tradition has always recognized that Holy Scripture, in its literal meaning (*sensus litteralis*), is rich in imaginative, poetic, and figurative features. In recent years, moreover, the typical and secondary senses of Scripture have been made the object of intense theological study. As regards the historical sections of the Bible, every Catholic exegete would agree with

Tillich's assertion that they are not "pure history" as conceived in the secular tradition of post-Renaissance times. In order to ascertain the precise qualities of biblical history, one would have to make a more detailed analysis of the individual books than Tillich has done. As for the Gospels, there is no doubt that the evangelists wrote as witnesses to their faith, eager to convey the religious significance of the events they related. But it should also be noted that they attach great importance to the reality of some of these events. St. Paul, likewise, goes to great pains to establish that the resurrection was an objective occurrence, attested by competent witnesses. He even states that, if Jesus had not truly risen from the dead, the Christian's faith would be a miserable deception (1 Cor 15.1–19).

Tillich unduly minimizes the historical elements in the Bible. He even proclaims that "theology does not imply factual assertions," since particular occurrences do not concern us ultimately.[57] Yet he solemnly affirms, as we have seen, that there was a Jesus who lived on earth and spoke with His disciples. In making this assertion, is he not, in fact, relying somewhat on the results of modern biblical criticism, which generally affirms that there is a historical "core" to the Gospel story? Dorothy Emmet, who puts this question, remarks that Tillich seems to want "to have it both ways."[58] More fundamentally: does the question whether Jesus was a historical character fall within the province of theology? If so, Tillich must admit that theology and history can overlap, and that theologians and historians, operating within their own proper fields, might contradict each other. If not, he has no right to maintain as a theologian that Jesus was a real person. Logically, he is bound to admit that the Christian revelation could be a product of merely subjective experience. It does not seem that Tillich has succeeded in erecting a theology which is fully insulated from empirical fact. The relations between Christianity and history are better indicated by Cullmann's suggestive formula, "revelational history,"[59] or perhaps even by W. Pannenberg's programmatic slogan "revelation as history."

When he turns to the relations between the Bible and

theology, Tillich makes many observations with which Catholics will agree. He clearly demonstrates that the Bible is not the sole source of Christian theology, and that ecclesiastical tradition is a legitimate theological quarry. His assertion that "dependent revelation" continues to be given in the church through the power of the Spirit, inevitably reminds the Catholic of his own belief that there is a legitimate development of dogma.[60]

Catholics will agree also with Tillich's insistence that the Bible is not itself the theological norm. Neither the canon of Scripture nor a coherent interpretation of its contents can be arrived at without consulting ecclesiastical tradition.[61] Tillich even goes so far as to maintain that church decisions have a certain normative force, although he does not grant that they are binding on theologians. The Catholic, of course, accepts the Church's claim to teach with divine authority.

Tillich does well to emphasize that Christian doctrine cannot be a static thing. The radical biblicist, in his unwillingness to depart from the letter of the Bible, is unfaithful to its spirit. As Tillich points out, the Gospel cannot have its due impact unless it is presented in ways suitable to the needs and capacities of each successive generation. Although Tillich's conception of the kerygma does not quite coincide with the Catholic notion of the "data of revelation," his efforts to distinguish between the kerygma and theology will prove stimulating to many Catholic theologians. His emphasis on the "answering" function of systematic theology is in full accord with Catholic teaching on doctrinal development and adaptation. As Gustave Weigel said: "The Tillichian principle of correlation is not a new discovery but only an urgent exhortation to use efficiently the principle always functioning in the theological enterprise, though it often functions with less than desirable energy."[62]

Finally, Tillich gives a very sound exposition of the relations of biblical theology to scientific criticism on the one hand and to systematic theology on the other. Biblical theology, as he rightly holds, is an intermediate discipline, essentially ordered toward systematic theology. Catholics, accustomed to the dogmatic syntheses of the Scholastic doctors, generally recognize that theology cannot confine itself to merely biblical categories. The Christian message should be set forth, as far as possible, in genuinely metaphysical terms, answering to the ontologial hunger of the human mind.

Speculative theology, however, is a delicate enterprise, never entirely free from the risk of denaturing the gospel. One must be on guard against trying to squeeze divine revelation into any man-made framework of metaphysical speculation. The great Scholastic theologians recognized this. While making use of Platonic and Aristotelian conceptual schemes, they allowed the data of revelation to correct, enlarge, and inwardly transform their philosophical categories.[63] They saw likewise that every metaphysical transposition of Christian teaching must, of its very nature, fall short of the divine message, grasped in faith. They were therefore content that their theological systems should echo, faintly but not unfaithfully, the truths of revelation.

It is here, more than anywhere else, that Tillich is vulnerable. Like the Scholastic doctors, he sets out to achieve a Christian wisdom. He brings an impressive array of philosophical tools to the task. Familiar with nearly the whole range of Western philosophy, he makes particularly fruitful use of modern German speculation. The idealism of Schelling, the subjectivism of Schleiermacher, the phenomenalism of Otto, and the existentialism of Heidegger, all provide him with valuable insights. But he does not sufficiently purify his philosophical categories in the light of the revealed message. Instead, he lets the exigencies of his philosophical system determine in advance what God's revelation can and cannot be. The biblical message is reduced to the dimensions of an all-too-human philosophy.

While Tillich yields to no other theologian of our century in systematic rigor and synthetic power, it has been objected, not without reason, that he sacrificed the gospel to the system.[64] His "transpersonal" ground of being reminds one only distantly of the living God of Abraham and Isaac. Can one really address such a deity in the words of the Lord's Prayer or even make

Him—as Tillich urged—the object of one's ultimate concern? With a less rigid metaphysical framework, and with a stronger doctrine of analogy, Tillich might have been able to give fuller recognition to those divine deeds of love and mercy which have usually been regarded as the very heart of the biblical revelation.

12

Jesus as the Christ: Some Recent Protestant Positions

After approximately a century of vigorous debate, the relationship between the Jesus of history and the Christ of faith is as lively as issue as ever.[1] As new theories are concocted, defended, rebutted, and revised, the literature continues to swell at a rate that bewilders the novice and distresses the veteran scholar. The present essay is not intended to add to the complexity of the picture, but to provide a modest guide to the present state of the question. In view of the current ecumenical climate it seems pertinent to give a survey of Protestant positions as they appear from a Catholic point of view.

In concentrating on Protestant authors I do not mean to minimize the work of Catholic scholars who have shown unflagging interest in the problem. In the first quarter of this century M.-J. Lagrange, Léonce de Grandmaison, and others made notable contributions. A recent interconfessional symposium on "The Historical Jesus and the Kerygmatic Christ,"[2] containing articles by forty-eight scholars from twelve nations, includes a good representation of Catholic authors (Karl Adam, Jean Daniélou, Jean de Fraine, René Marlé, Béda Rigaux, Rudolf Schnackenburg, Heinz Schürmann). But in general it seems fair to say that scholars working within the Catholic tradition,

solid as their achievement has been, have shown a less venturesome spirit than their Protestant counterparts. They have been
more critical than creative; more a stabilizing influence than
initiators of new developments. With several important exceptions they have been content to follow the debate and comment
on it, rather than take a leading part. Perhaps this situation will
change in the near future, as the ecumenical dialogue progresses.
The instruction of the Biblical Commission "On the Historical
Truth of the Gospels" (April 21, 1964) furnishes wise and liberal
norms which will encourage Catholics to discuss the issues with
candor and sincerity.[3]

THE NINETEENTH CENTURY QUEST

The dichotomy between the "Jesus of history" and the "Christ of
faith" may sound strange and even scandalous on first hearing. It
seems to call into question a fundamental datum of Christian
faith, namely, that Jesus of Nazareth, who walked on this earth
in the flesh, was in sober truth identical with the Christ of the
Church's preaching. If the two are identical, how can there be any
room for debate among Christians as to their mutual relationship?

A partial answer is suggested by the very terms, "Jesus"
and "Christ." They designate the same individual under different
aspects. Jesus is His personal name, Christ His title. In the perspectives of Israelite expectation, the Christ is the Anointed One,
the Messiah, the promised King and Saviour. When we say "Jesus
Christ"—or, alternatively, "Christ Jesus"[4]—we are not simply
denoting a person; we are making a confession of faith. We are
declaring that the man, Jesus, who lived in Palestine more than
nineteen hundred years ago, really was and is Messiah and Lord.

Until the last century there was as yet no occasion for the
distinction between the historical Jesus and the Christ of faith.
The only available source of information about Jesus, for all
practical purposes, was the New Testament, which portrayed
Him as Messiah and Son of God. To know Jesus at all one had to
rely on the New Testament. Protestants and Catholics, while they
might dispute about later dogmatic developments, were agreed

in accepting the biblical testimony concerning Jesus. To challenge it would, they felt, be an act of historical skepticism, and a virtual rejection of Christianity as well.

In the mid-nineteenth century, however, a new avenue of approach was opened. Critical historiography began to develop as an independent discipline, somewhat on the pattern of the physical sciences. Aspiring to become, in the bold phrase of Renan, "an exact science of the things of the spirit," free from all subjective bias, the new history took as its domain the entire human past, including the various forms of man's religion. Inevitably, professional historians soon left the urge to practice their skills upon the Bible. More especially, they asked themselves how the figure of Jesus would appear if the Gospels were treated as ordinary human documents, irrespective of any confessional loyalty, and dissected under the cold light of rational criticism. Heinrich Julius Holtzmann, writing in 1863, gave classic formulation to the spirit of this enterprise:

> We are here simply concerned with *the* question, whether it is now still possible to describe the *historical* figure of the one from whom Christianity derives its very name and existence and whose person it has made the centre of its own particular religious view of the world, in such a way as to satisfy all just claims of a scrupulous historical-critical investigation. Is it possible to discover the character of the founder of our religion, the true, natural features of his person, by the application of the sole legitimate means of scientific historical criticism, or must we once and for all abandon any hope of achieving such a goal?[5]

Many Christians, both Protestant and Catholic, deplored this rational inquiry as an assault upon faith and as a profanation of the sacred books, but a number of Protestant scholars, including Holtzmann himself, welcomed the new quest. They were convinced that the subjection of the Gospels to severe critical scrutiny would ultimately serve to rectify and fill out the traditional picture of Jesus. What was this quest, they asked, except a continuation of the movement inaugurated by the Reformers themselves? Just as the sixteenth-century Reformation had aimed to cut through the accretions of the ages and recapture the original biblical faith, so now it seemed possible, on the same principle, to set aside the subjective interpretations of the early Church and to reconstruct the pure religion of Jesus Himself.

A vast progeny of lives of Jesus was spawned, most of them by pious Liberal Protestants. Rigidly excluding everything which might be due to the faith and theology of the believing community, these scholars relied chiefly on New Testament materials which they deemed acceptable by the canons of von Ranke and Bernheim. In substance, they rested their case on Mark and on a supposed sayings-document known as "Q," which was hypothetically reconstructed on the basis of certain traditions common to Matthew and Luke. These they regarded as the earliest and most factual reports on the life and message of Jesus. By a critical use of the Gospels according to contemporary standards of academic history, the Liberal Protestants thought it possible to put aside the numinous, supernatural traits previously ascribed to Jesus, and to unearth the image of a purely human, but supremely enlightened, ethical and religious teacher. Here was a figure whom the moralistic, scientifically minded European of the late nineteenth century could accept and admire. The triumph of the Liberal Protestant reconstruction of Jesus seemed definitive by the year 1900, when Adolf von Harnack published his famous Berlin lectures on the subject, *What is Christianity?* The main flaw in the picture was precisely its adaptation to the mentality of the age. As one critic ironically commented. "The Christ that Harnack sees, looking back through nineteen centuries of Catholic darkness, is only a reflection of a Liberal Protestant face seen at the bottom of a deep well."[6]

The assumptions and concerns behind the nineteenth-century "quest of the historical Jesus" were brilliantly exposed by Albert Schweitzer in his famous survey first published in 1906. "The historical investigation of the life of Jesus," he comments, "did not take its rise from a purely historical interest; it turned to the Jesus of history as an ally in the struggle against the tyranny of dogma."[7] The various scholars engaged in the enterprise, whether rationalists or idealists, liberals or skeptics, shared a common animus against dogma. Schweitzer himself commends this. "The dogma had first to be shattered before men could once more go out in quest of the historical Jesus, before they could even grasp the thought of his existence. That the historical Jesus is something different from the Jesus Christ of the doctrine of the two natures seems to us now self-evident."[8]

These assertions are typical of the rather complacent positivism of the era in which they were penned. They reflect what now appears as a naive overconfidence in the ultimate victory of scientific history over dogmatic tenets. The past fifty years have shown that it is far from easy to separate the Jesus of history from the Christ of faith and dogma; as a result many serious scholars now deny that there ever was such a being as the Jesus of pure history. To understand this change of perspectives we have only to consider some highlights of the history of the quest since 1900.

THE REACTION: FAITH WITHOUT HISTORY

As early as 1892 one farsighted Lutheran theologian protested against the direction being taken by the Liberal scholarship of his day. Martin Kähler gave a famous address, later printed as a brochure, contrasting two possible lines of access to the person of Jesus.[9] One route, he maintained, was through scientific, academic history, the other through the believing witness of the Bible. But the first approach, in Kähler's estimation, could never lead to a religiously significant picture of Jesus. For the real meaning of Jesus, as every Christian knows, is not perceptible to flesh and blood. It was never deduced from facts, but was revealed to the apostles through a special grace of God. The Gospels, charged as they are with the faith of the primitive Church, cannot be treated as profane historical documents. They do not, and were never intended to, provide the necessary materials for an accurate reconstruction of the objective facts of Jesus' career. The avenue of scientific history therefore turns out to be, religiously speaking, a dead end. The only fruitful starting point is the believing acceptance of the biblical Christ—that is, the Christ of faith heralded in the New Testament and preached in all churches which are faithful to the gospel.

Kähler's prophetic protest against a historical reconstruction that would by-pass the believing testimony of the Bible went practically unheeded in his own day, but the first two decades of the twentieth century lent unforeseen support to his thesis. The historical Jesus, like a mirage, seemed to recede further with every advance of scholarship. The biographers of Jesus became ever more sharply divided among themselves. Harnack had rejected the rationalistic views of H. E. G. Paulus and the idealistic reconstruction of David Friedrich Strauss in favor of his own portrait of Jesus as a rather stodgy Kantian moralist, teaching nothing but the Fatherhood of God and the brotherhood of man. In Harnack's own lifetime, however, men such as Johannes Weiss and Albert Schweitzer proposed a completely contrary view of Jesus as a fiery prophet who cared nothing for eternal moral principles, but was totally taken up in announcing the imminent end of the universe. Jesus, as portrayed by the "eschatological" school, was an apocalyptic visionary who expected the momentary arrival of the Son of Man riding on the clouds of heaven. Yet even this version failed to win anything like general acceptance. Other historians forged other images—such as Robert Eisler's picture of Jesus as a proletarian leader fomenting armed insurrection against the Romans. In this welter of confusion some scholars even began to question whether Jesus had ever existed.

About the time of World War I, it was widely felt that more rigorous methods of research were needed to prevent the proliferation of wild and arbitrary hypotheses. Some began to look hopefully to a new technique known as "form criticism" which Prof. Hermann Gunkel of Berlin had been applying with remarkable results to Genesis and Psalms. Two of Gunkel's former pupils, Martin Dibelius and Rudolf Bultmann, refined the method and applied it with great assiduity to the New Testament. The Gospels, they contended, are not unified literary works, but compilations of stories about Jesus which had been elaborated in the interests of the Christian community, and had circulated as independent units, gradually developing in accordance with the laws of popular oral tradition. These stories reflected the manifold concerns of the early Church—devotional, liturgical, apologetical, missionary, moral, and disciplinary—and gave many clues to the life of the primitive community. But they offered very little solid information about the life and teaching of Jesus Himself. In an oft-quoted sentence from his book, *Jesus and the Word*, first published in German in 1926, Bultmann declared: "I do indeed think that we can now know almost nothing concerning the life and personality of Jesus, since the early Christian sources show no interest in either, are moreover fragmentary and often legendary; and other sources about Jesus do not exist."[10]

Bultmann's negative conclusions regarding the historical reliability of the Gospels were disturbing to many believers, but he himself found them quite compatible with Christian faith. He took up with added emphasis Kähler's distinction between the Jesus of scientific history and the Christ of biblical proclamation. To designate the missionary preaching of the early community the New Testament uses the Greek term "kerygma." Adopting this terminology, Bultmann and his followers have contrasted the historical Jesus with the "kerygmatic" Christ—the Christ of Christian faith and preaching.

Historical research, according to Bultmann, is a purely secular discipline, which can neither confirm nor undermine Christian faith. Faith is a free commitment, in no way dependent on questions falling within the historian's province.[11] What the Church proclaims, and the believer accepts, is not, in Bultmann's opinion, a body of factual information about the remote past; rather, it is the redemptive significance of the Cross of Jesus as preached here and now. This saving power is expressed in the New Testament in what Bultmann regards as myths—for example, the miracle stories, the legend of the empty tomb, and the accounts of Jesus' return to bodily life. But these supernatural elements, in Bultmann's view, should not be taken at face value. The Christian kerygma, he maintains, can advantageously be cut loose from the primitive world-view of the biblical writers. Once the biblical myths are reinterpreted in forms which speak to the man of our day, the Christian faith will recover its credibility and dynamic power. It will appear that the true resurrection of Jesus is not His return to bodily life but His survival in the faith and preaching of the Church.[12] The message of the Cross, dynamically heralded as the word of God, has undying power to save men from selfishness and fear, and to bestow that inner liberty which goes with total surrender to God's demands. Thus the existential interpretation of the kerygma has validity independently of any particular historical reconstruction of the alleged facts concerning Jesus.

Bultmann's efforts to separate the provinces of history and faith have been seconded by a number of existentially minded Protestants. A few, such as the Swiss Fritz Buri and the American Schubert Ogden, outstripping Bultmann himself, call for a faith not necessarily dependent on the reality of God's action in Christ. Paul Tillich, while respecting history as a medium of revelation, reflects somewhat the same tendency. His various statements on the point do not lend themselves to any simple summary, but sometimes he seemed to say, quite logically on his own premises, that the Christian is not bound by faith itself to attribute any historical validity to the biblical portrait of Jesus.[13] What interested Tillich was the symbolic power of that portrait to manifest the appearance of the "New Being" as an answer to man's existential concern.

Tillich differs from Bultmann in his evaluation of myth and symbol. Instead of seeking to "demythologize" the New Testament, as Bultmann had proposed to do, he wished to restore and revitalize its religious symbolism. But he was at one with Bultmann in holding that Christian faith has no real interest in what Jesus of Nazareth actually was and said and did. For Bultmann, the Christian is one who accepts the demands of God embodied in the message of the Cross. For Tillich, the Christian is one who encounters the New Being in the biblical symbol of Jesus as the Christ. Neither of these theologians, of course, denies that Jesus really lived and inspired His followers by His words and deeds, but both of them look on the flesh-and-blood Jesus, with His concrete individual traits, as extrinsic to the Christian message of salvation.

This cleavage between faith and fact is unacceptable from a

Catholic point of view. The Church has always taught that the redemption of the world was accomplished by the real Passion, death, and exaltation of Jesus, the Second Person of the Blessed Trinity, Who actually became man in the womb of the Virgin Mary and left behind Him an empty sepulcher. These events really happened, independently of our knowing them. If this objective element were denied, Christianity might remain a beautiful and edifying story, a magnificent saga in the history of religions, but it would be powerless to unite man to God, and we Christians would be "of all men the most to be pitied" (cf. 1 Cor 15.19). Bultmann and Tillich have many brilliant insights on which the Catholic theologian would do well to meditate, but on this particular point their position seems basically irreconcilable with the Catholic vision of the Christian faith.

RENEWED CONCERN FOR THE JESUS OF HISTORY

Fortunately for the prospects of the ecumenical dialogue, not all Protestant theologians accept this radical dehistoricizing of the Christian message. During the past twenty years Protestant theology, generally speaking, has been taking an increasingly positive attitude toward the Jesus of history. In the remaining pages of this essay we may consider four main groups of Protestant theologians who have, from different points of view, emphasized the constitutive significance of the historical Jesus for Christian faith. In the interests of brevity I shall present these positions with some inevitable oversimplification, more for purposes of orientation than with any pretense to adequacy.

(1) An impressive number of Protestant biblical scholars are convinced that, while the nineteenth-century quest of the historical Jesus did not succeed, a more modest venture of the same order might be feasible in our own day. The distinguished Lutheran New Testament exegete, Joachim Jeremias, pointed out, several years ago, that we now have many research tools not available to our forebears.[14] For one thing, new techniques of literary analysis, including form criticism itself, have made it possible to identify the earliest strata of the Gospel tradition,

and thus to pick out many sayings and incidents which unquestionably embody memories of Jesus' first companions.
Furthermore, the discoveries of modern archaeology—including
very notably the recovery of the great Essene library at Qumran
on the Dead Sea—have vastly increased our knowledge about
Jesus' religious environment and the Palestinian customs of His
day. Then again, we now know enough Galilean Aramaic to re-
translate many of the Gospel sayings into Jesus' own mother
tongue, in which it becomes clearer why certain expressions of
His aroused the reactions described in the Gospels. We can see,
for instance, why men found it extraordinary that He should
address God by the intimate title *Abba* (Father). "The multipli-
cation of examples," concludes Jeremias, "yields ever the same
result: if, with the utmost zeal and conscientiousness, using the
critical resources at our disposal, we occupy ourselves with the
historical Jesus, the result is always the same. ... A man has
appeared; those who heard His message were indeed aware that
they had heard the word of God."[15]

In numerous studies of the Gospels—bearing such titles as
The Parables of Jesus, The Eucharistic Words of Jesus, and *The
Servant of God*—Jeremias has painstakingly applied his formi-
dable linguistic and historical erudition to distinguish between
the authentic sayings of Jesus and such secondary embellish-
ments as may plausibly be ascribed to the early Christian
community. These scholarly monographs have done much to
fortify the stand of historically minded Christians against the
negative conclusions of Bultmannian criticism.

One of Jeremias' compatriots, Ethelbert Stauffer, has at-
tracted attention by his recent efforts to make use of "neutral"
evidence in reconstructing the career of Jesus. In his fascinating
little study, *Jesus and His Story*, Stauffer makes extensive use of
archaeological data, pagan historians, and even hostile testimonies of rabbinic Judaism in order to ascertain the validity of
the Gospels. It is doubtless true, Stauffer admits, that we are in no
position to construct a *biography* of Jesus, in the sense of an inner
and outer description of His psychological development, but this
is not fatal. It is still in our power to write a *history* of Jesus, that

is, "the clear, strictly objective, statement of those facts which can still be actually discerned."[16] From this historical beachhead Stauffer swiftly penetrates into the bastions of theology if not those of creative literature. At the climax of his book he argues that Jesus, with His majestic "I am," decisively identified Himself with Yahweh, thus bringing to an unsurpassable culmination the series of theophanies which had been vouchsafed to Israel since the time of Abraham. For all its stimulating and dramatic qualities, Stauffer's work has not won the same scholarly approbation as that of Jeremias. Most critics feel that his detailed reconstruction of the facts and chronology of Jesus' life goes far beyond the evidence.[17]

Middle-of-the-road British scholarship has been marked by a similar interest in recovering, by conventional historical criticism, the outlines of Jesus' earthly career and ministry. The Presbyterian, T. W. Manson, an outstanding practitioner of this "common sense" approach, declared in 1956: "There is no escape from the historical inquiry. And there is no reason to be despondent about its prospects."[18] The noted Methodist exegete, Vincent Taylor, in his numerous works on the Gospels, has set forth ample grounds for such confidence. "The fact which emerges from the modern study of the Gospel tradition," he maintains, "is its trustworthiness, provided we do not make impossible demands upon it. Bultmann's claim that we must purge it of its mythical trappings and present its claims in terms of current existentialism rests upon a radical estimate of its contents which is not justified by the most fearless inquiry."[19] In connection with the canonical Passion narratives Taylor quite characteristically remarks: "The first narrators felt that it was enough to relate the events, without commenting upon them, and without making Jesus the mouthpiece of their doctrinal views. The result is that the reader is himself brought near to the events as they happened."[20]

Scholars of this category look upon history as a foundation for a reasoned and prudent faith. Scientific historiography, they contend, while it cannot produce faith, can prepare for and confirm it. "I doubt if we are justified in making the venture of faith," Taylor declares, "unless there are facts in the tradition which encourage us to make it."[21]

(2) Writers of a second school, without necessarily contradicting the group just considered, proceed rather in the inverse direction. For the Christian, they maintain, the essential question is not what profane academic history is able to unearth about Jesus, but what is implied in the acceptance of the Church's faith. Bultmann, according to these theologians, may very well be right in holding that scientific history can ascertain practically nothing about the career and personality of Jesus. If so, that should not distress us, for we have, in the biblical witness, a far surer mode of access to the events of salvation. The Swiss Calvinist, Karl Barth, objects that Bultmann makes an "illicit leap" when he argues that if an occurrence is not recoverable by modern historical science, with its postulates and rules of procedure, then it must be judged not to have taken place.[22] The French Lutheran, Oscar Cullmann, makes a similar criticism. The form critics are right, he concedes, in affirming that the Gospels are not documents of technical, objectivizing history, but believing testimonies of the primitive Church. But this does not mean that biblical history is a mythical representation of events. On the contrary, "this very witness of faith which comes to expression in the Gospel tradition has history itself as its object, since indeed it declares that Jesus of Nazareth is the Christ of Israel."[23] To accept the proclamation is therefore to acknowledge the reality of the events themselves.

The English Congregationalist, Prof. C. H. Dodd, has systematically inquired into the historical content of the earliest Christian preaching, as it would have been conducted by St. Peter or St. Paul.[24] From the first days of the Church, he contends, the kerygma already embodied a brief summary of the main facts concerning the life, death, and resurrection of Jesus. Since "gospel" means most fundamentally the "good news," neither the primitive Christians, nor we ourselves, could accept the religious message of Christianity without, at the same time, acknowledging the actual occurrence of the events which lie at the heart of that message. In the Gospel, writes Dodd, "is told the story of events that happened once for all, at a particular moment, whose particularity is a necessary part of what happened. If we lose hold upon that historical actuality, the Gospels are betrayed into the hands of the Gnostics, and we stand on the verge of a new Docetism."[25] In alluding to these heretical dangers Dodd would seem to have authors such as Bultmann in mind.

A number of Anglican writers might be mentioned here for their insistence on the essentially historical character of the Christian faith. To quote but one, we may reproduce the eloquent declaration of the late Dom Gregory Dix:

> Christianity is the revelation of Divine Truth from beyond all history and all time, but it is so only because it is the only fully historical religion. It is the only religion which actually *depends entirely upon* history. It is faith in the Incarnate God, it is Divine redemption given *from within* history, not by the promulgation of doctrines (even true doctrines) but by the wrenching of one Man's flesh and the spilling of His blood upon one particular square yard of ground, outside one particular city gate during three particular unrepeatable hours, which could have been measured on a clock. You cannot (and you never could) enter into the truth of Christianity apart from its history.[26]

Some prominent German Lutherans have likewise opposed Bultmann for his tendency to de-historicize the Christian kerygma. Ernst Kinder, at the end of an examination of Bultmann's program, pronounces the judgment: "There can be no compromise or peaceful agreement between the truth of the New Testament message of Christ and the 'pseudo-kerygma' of Bultmann."[27] Paul Althaus presses an analogous charge in his polemical booklet, significantly entitled *The So-Called Kerygma and the Historical Jesus*. The kerygma of the apostles and of the Church, he argues, has an essentially historical content, but in Bultmann's theology the person of Jesus and His concrete historical activity practically disappear behind the message. It is pointless, then, for Bultmann to declaim so impressively on the salvific power of the word. It has such power, Althaus maintains, precisely because of the unique reality of the past events which it proclaims. Cut off from the actuality of Jesus' personal existence, the preached word would lose its saving efficacy.[28]

Critics belonging to this second school show less interest in technical history than those previously mentioned. Their approach is more dogmatic or, in some cases, more charismatic, but like the members of our first class they emphatically hold that the Jesus described in the New Testament is, and must be, a real, concrete person. The kerygmatic preaching, so far from being indifferent to historical fact, depends totally for its truth and power on the unique quality of the life of the Incarnate Son of God. This is affirmed in direct opposition to the views of Bultmann and Tillich outlined above.

(3) A third group of Bultmann's critics, similarly pre-occupied with vindicating the dependability of the New Testament sources, comprises a number of eminent Scandinavian Lutherans, especially in Sweden. They belong to what is often called the traditio-historical school. In their opinion, none of the scholars so far named has done justice to the distinctive features of the Gospel tradition. The first group of Bultmann's critics, in their search for a solid historical nucleus, are too ready to pre-sume that whatever cannot be confirmed by philology and archaeology may appropriately be ascribed to creative imagina-tion. These critical historians ask us, in effect, to ferret out some tiny kernel of solid fact beneath the thick layers of imagina-tive wool. And the kerygmatic historians—those of the second group—while giving full faith and credit to the apostolic preaching, tend to look on the Gospel tradition as a late and dubious expansion of the central facts transmitted by the primi-tive kerygma. The Swedish school, in opposition to both these groups, holds that the true key to the Gospel tradition is to be found in a systematic study of the methods of oral transmission practiced by Palestinian Jews of the first century. While they are not the first scholars to have noted analogies between Jewish and Christian oral tradition, they have explored the question with un-precedented thoroughness.

Comparison with rabbinic usage, according to prominent representatives of the traditio-historical school, reveals the absurdity of supposing that the Gospels are contaminated by popular legends and empty myths. Jesus taught as a Jewish rabbi and His disciples came from rabbinic Judaism. He must therefore have instructed the disciples, as other rabbis did, by fixed verbal formulas and solemn symbolic actions, requiring them to take accurate note of all that He said and did, and even to repeat back His very words. He would presumably have followed this formal teaching by fuller explanations in which He unfolded to His intimate followers the deeper import of His sayings and conduct. The Gospels, in fact, give abundant evidence that this is just what Jesus did.

After Pentecost, in the view of the Scandinavian scholars, the apostles from their headquarters in Jerusalem gave primary attention to the task of building up a corps of skilled reciters to whom the ministry of the word could safely be entrusted. Our written Gospels are, in substance, a slightly edited version of the holy tradition first formulated by the Jerusalem Church under the vigilance of the Twelve. Harald Riesenfeld, one of the leading Swedish exegetes, surmises that, notwithstanding various redactional features, "the essential point is that the outlines, that is, the beginnings of the proper genus of the tradition of the words and deeds of Jesus, were memorized and recited as holy Word. We should be inclined to trace these outlines back to Jesus' activity as a teacher in the circle of his disciples."[29] In an abundantly documented study of rabbinic techniques Birger Gerhardsson, a disciple of Riesenfeld, has recently presented impressive evidence in favor of this theory that the Gospels rest on a body of sacred oral tradition.[30]

(4) A final group of Bultmann's critics includes a number of his own former pupils from Marburg—notably Ernst Käsemann, Ernst Fuchs, and Günther Bornkamm. The American Presbyterian, James M. Robinson, in a book entitled *A New Quest of the Historical Jesus*, gives an excellent sketch of the program of this school.[31] It is a serious error, according to these writers, to try to reconstruct from the Gospels the external facts of Jesus' life or the precise content of His words. Such an empiricist approach to history must

ultimately lead to the impression that the Gospels are second-rate sources. Rather, one must take into account the fundamental intention of the Gospels, which is not to convey factual data about Jesus, but to transmit His mind and message. The Evangelists exhibit Him in His existential impact upon His admirers and His enemies, His disciples and His critics. The contemporary reader may well doubt, in Bornkamm's opinion, whether Jesus used any of the messianic titles placed on His lips in the Gospel accounts. But the messianic import of Jesus' activity shines through every sentence written about Him. All that He said and did is charged with decisive significance as a sign of the reign of God which is already dawning in His very person.[32] Thus the historian today, if he opens himself to the religious significance of the Gospels, can find in them, as Bornkamm expresses it, "the person and work of Jesus in their unmistakable uniqueness and distinctiveness."[33] In this sense, the biblical accounts of Jesus are "brim full of history."

The old quest of the historical Jesus, according to the post-Bultmannians, was foredoomed to failure because it was committed to the presuppositions and methods of objective history, as canonized by the historico-critical school. The Gospels cannot, without violence, be reduced to these categories, but modern personalistic or existential history, which seeks an encounter with the true selfhood of other persons, is far better adapted to the New Testament materials. Contemporary man, in Robinson's opinion, has at his disposal two legitimate approaches to the person of Jesus. One is through the kerygma, the proclamation of the Church which authoritatively heralds the faith since Easter; the second is through existential history which examines the Gospels with openness to the inner meaning of Jesus' witness to Himself. Whether Jesus is encountered through the kerygma or through existential history, the result is essentially the same. Both confront us with the same urgent demand for personal decision. This proves, according to Robinson, "not that the *kerygma* is true but that the existential decision with regard to the *kerygma* is an existential decision with regard to Jesus."[34]

Bultmann has taken cognizance of this movement among his

former disciples. With characteristic incisiveness, he has criticized his critics.[35] The Gospels, he agrees, are not objective
historical sources, according to the ideals of the historico-critical
school, but this does not mean that they will yield their secret to
a new type of history which would seek to fathom their meaning
independently of the Christian kerygma. If the Gospels confront
us with God's gracious demands, Bultmann contends, it is
because they are shot through with the kerygma of the early
Church. They were wholly composed in the light of the Church's
Easter faith. It is almost impossible for us, today, to peel off the
contributions of the believing community, and to reconstruct the
original message of Jesus. Even if we could do so, Bultmann adds,
the effort would be largely futile. The teaching of Jesus, apart
from the kerygma, could never provide a sufficient basis for
Christian commitment. "If the proclamation of the historical
Jesus opens up this possibility," asks Bultmann, "why is not the
kerygma content to repeat the preaching of Jesus, how can it even
refrain from doing so, as Paul and John exhibit? Why does the
kerygma call for faith in Jesus as the Christ, thus substituting the
proclaimer for the proclaimed? And if a correct historical interpretation of the conduct of Jesus could, itself, lead to existential
decision, why should there be a kerygma at all?"[36] In Bultmann's
view, therefore, there is only one religiously meaningful approach
to the New Testament. We must seek out the Church's kerygma,
which is the saving word in which God comes to man. There is no
second approach to faith through scientific history, whether that
history be positivistically or existentially conceived.

CONCLUSIONS

In concluding this survey I cannot report any general consensus.
It may be safely affirmed that the great majority of Protestants in
our day feel that Bultmann and Tillich, not to mention Buri and
Ogden, make too sharp a cleft between faith and factual history.
But the authors who seek a positive relationship between the two
disciplines proceed in various ways, and to some degree contradict each other. If some of Bultmann's views are unacceptable,

it does not follow that all charges against him are valid, or that all his critics are right. In my opinion, all the schools we have examined have made useful observations on some points and have fallen short on others. I should like to close, then, with a kind of synthesis, indicating what views seem acceptable or unacceptable. A balanced appraisal which takes account of all the available evidence, in my opinion, leads to positions in full accord with Catholic doctrine.

(1) Negatively, the whole history of the problem, as it has been debated since the time of Kähler, shows the impossibility of constructing out of the Gospels a biography of Jesus according to the ideals of modern scientific research. The New Testament material, assembled from the point of view of faith, is not designed to give the kind of information which the pure historian would most like to have. While the Gospels provide many helpful bits of information, there can be no question of reconstructing the stages of Jesus' inner and outer development. In this sense we may apply the dictum of St. Paul that we no longer know Jesus according to the flesh (2 Cor 5.16).

(2) The kerygmatic theologians of both the Barthian and Bultmannian wings have done well in insisting that faith can never be a simple conclusion from historical scholarship. The believer is one who responds to the word of God—the same yesterday, today, and forever—as it is proclaimed for each generation by the living Church. The Church continually receives from on high the grace to preach the word with salvific power to those who listen in obedience. The faithful can rely on the word of the Church; they are not obliged to consult professional historians in order to be serene in their faith.

(3) Bultmann is justified, also, in maintaining that, since Easter, no religiously adequate relationship to Jesus can be achieved independently of the Church's preaching. The Church represents Christ in the world. Faith in Him, as Bultmann declares, inseparably involves faith in the Church as the bearer of the Gospel message. Any attempt by Christians to by-pass the interpretation which the Church, from the beginning, set on Jesus' career, and to substitute some "pure religion of Jesus" as

constructed by profane historical research, will inevitably end in a drastic impoverishment of God's word to man.

(4) Dodd and Cullmann, on the other hand, are correct in pointing out that the truth of the kerygma necessarily involves the antecedent reality of certain basic facts. The believer is committed by faith itself to various convictions about the past. Bultmann and his more radical disciples have deformed the biblical notion of the kerygma by virtually emptying it of historical content. They tend to propose, as the central object of Christian allegiance, a disembodied message or an abstract symbol, rather than an incarnate, personal Lord. The primary affirmation of Christianity is not that the Word became kerygma or symbol, but that He became a man of flesh and blood.

(5) With Taylor and Jeremias, moreover, we should acknowledge that conventional historiography, through its critical procedures, can make it evident that the Gospels are not sheer inventions; that they contain a solid nucleus of genuine fact. While the Christian need not build his spiritual life on the shifting sands of scientific history, he has no reason to fear that such inquiry will sweep away the foundations of his faith. The assured results of modern New Testament research have done nothing to cast doubt on the essential veracity of its witness. On the contrary, they have thrown new light on the value of the Gospels, and have helped us to understand them better. Critical scholarship can indirectly assist theology by reconstructing the religious, social, and cultural environment in which the New Testament took shape.

(6) A satisfactory historical appraisal of the Gospels, however, requires a more intensive study of the oral traditions behind the Gospels than has hitherto been made. The early form critics, who sought for analogies in popular legend and folklore, gave a false orientation to this quest. The Swedish traditio-historical school, with its concentration on "holy words," seems destined to make an important contribution, but the rabbinic analogy, exploited by Riesenfeld and Gerhardsson, represents only one line of approach. Other scholars attach greater weight to the Hebrew prophetic tradition or to the doctrinal tradition of the

Essene communities. In the last analysis, none of these comparisons is truly adequate, for Jesus was a unique figure with an utterly singular religious consciousness. Because He taught in the power of the Spirit, and could bestow the Spirit upon the community which He founded, He could rise above the limitations of scribal literalism.

(7) Finally, the existential and personalist historians, such as Günther Bornkamm and James M. Robinson, have quite properly protested against the tendency to measure the historical worth of the Gospels by the canons of nineteenth-century objectivizing historiography. The Gospels on every page confront us with the call of Jesus and solicit the response of faith. This existential analysis of the Gospels, however, is not really a new avenue, independent of the kerygmatic proclamation of the Church. Gospel and kerygma are not two separate realities, but two facets of a larger whole. If the Gospels confront us with the decision of faith, this is in part, as Bultmann remarks, because they, no less than the kerygma, embody the testimony of the believing Church. There is another reason, even more fundamental. The Jesus whom we encounter in the pages of the Gospels is the same person as the Christ of the Church's faith. The events of Easter merely brought to completion what He had already begun in His earthly career. The proclamation of Pentecost set forth, in all clarity, the message with which the preaching of Jesus was pregnant. The authentic recollections of Jesus' ministry, therefore, are by no means irrelevant to faith. They amplify, without essentially altering, the rather schematic formulas of the kerygma concerning the incarnate life of the Redeemer.

Against this background we may now draw up a summary reply to the central question about which this essay has revolved. Is the Christ of faith identical with the Jesus of history? A distinction is in order. If by "history" is meant a purely academic discipline which can be practiced by any reasonable and competent man, regardless of his religious dispositions, the Jesus of history is an unsubstantial and ambiguous entity without any existence outside the pages of scholarly books. He is emphatically not the Christ of faith. But if, by history, we mean the full reality of the past, with all its significance for weal and woe, including its decisive impact on the shape of things to come, then we must give a very different answer. The Christ of faith, and He alone, is the Jesus of history. The faith of the Church, conceived in the light of Easter and Pentecost, is alone capable of grasping the secret of this man. It lays hold of Jesus as He really was and is, because it recognizes Him as the Christ, the Son of God.[37]

13

The Death of God Theologies: Symptom and Challenge

The term "death of God theology" refers to the view of several American Protestants who accept Christianity, but deny the traditional Christian God, asserting that He is dead and will not revive. These writers sometimes call themselves radical theologians or Christian atheists. Those most prominently identified with the movement are all about forty to forty-five years old (as of 1967). Three should be specially mentioned:

Paul M. van Buren, an Episcopalian minister, now teaches in the Department of Religion at Temple University. His book, *The Secular Meaning of the Gospel* (1963) is best understood, I believe, as an attempt to investigate the meaning of the traditional Christian affirmation that Jesus is God. For contemporary secular man, who thinks in scientific terms, the word "God" has become problematical. By applying linguistic analysis, van Buren attempts to show that it is meaningless to affirm that God is a being, or that He does certain things. But if we reinterpret the Christian statements about the divinity and lordship of Jesus as assertions about our perspective on life, they can still be accepted. In van Buren's words: "The man who says, 'Jesus is Lord,' is saying that the history of Jesus, and of what happened on Easter, has exercised a liberating effect upon him, and that he has been so grasped by it that it has become the historical norm of his perspective upon life."[1]

Van Buren does not say that God is dead; in fact, he rejects the proposition as meaningless and absurd. His problem is that the *word* God has died in our language. Modern secular man, he thinks, cannot accept God as some kind of entity or agent, but can still find in the history of Jesus a universal and definitive norm of human life (p. 139).

William Hamilton, an ordained Baptist minister, teaches at New College, Sarasota, Florida. Until recently he has been saying in various ways that in our age we can no longer experience God as present, but that we do experience Him as absent—that is, "as a kind of pressure or wounding from which we would love to be free."[2] During this time of the absence of God, when it seems as though God were dead, we must devote ourselves to the service of our neighbor according to the Gospel. As we seek to find Christ in our fellow men, we can trust that God will eventually show Himself again.

In the past year or two, Hamilton seems to have shifted his position. He now speaks of the "death of God" as a real, irreversible, historical event. Perhaps this change of opinion is due to the influence of Altizer.

Thomas J. J. Altizer, an Episcopalian layman, teaches at Emory University in Atlanta. Following the metaphysics of Hegel, he holds that the divine passes from a state of essential or primordial being to actual existence by a process of self-negation, or estrangement, which may be called death. This descent of the divine into history occurred most dramatically at the Incarnation, when the Word literally became flesh in the humanity of Jesus, and was destined to be crucified. Since Christ, the process of redemption continues to occur as the Spirit embodies itself in new historical situations. Even after the death of Christ, therefore, God continues to exert a vital impact upon history. This impact takes the form of death insofar as God cannot enter history except under alienated, finite forms. The transcendent collapses into the immanent; the grain of wheat falls into the ground and dies, but in so doing, it impregnates the universe with a divine principle which will emerge again in manifest clarity at the end of time. In the final consummation, God, as St. Paul expresses it, will become all in all.

Besides these three thinkers there are several others whose names are often associated, less properly, with the movement. Gabriel Vahanian, for instance, has written about the death of God in modern culture. He holds that the name "God" no longer has any real meaning for modern man, and attributes this to the perversity of Christians who have domesticated God and set up idols in His place. Unlike the "death of God" theologians we have considered, Vahanian strongly insists that the living God is utterly transcendent, and must, in no case, be identified with any being in the world.

All the "death of God" theologians, especially van Buren and Hamilton, have been heavily influenced by the German Lutheran Dietrich Bonhoeffer, who was executed by the Nazis in 1945. Bonhoeffer was certainly not a "death of God" theologian, but his keen observations on the necessity of reinterpreting the gospel for our modern secular culture have been a powerful inspiration to the new radical theology.

The positions of van Buren, Hamilton, and Altizer differ greatly from one another, and cannot be criticized in general. Each of them has its own strengths and weaknesses, which deserve to be discussed in detail, but since others have given excellent critiques, I should prefer to concentrate here on the significance of the movement as a whole.[3]

SOURCES OF THE NEW ATHEISM

Notwithstanding the important divergences among them, it is astonishing to find even a few Christian theologians attempting to dispense with God. The question therefore arises: why has it happened in our generation—for the first time, I suppose, in history—that some Christian theologians feel they can be atheists? This new direction in theology must be symptomatic of something. Even more symptomatic is the international furor which the movement has aroused. When we hear it said that God has died in our time, or that His body is decomposing, or that the churches are His tombs and monuments, we cannot help feeling that these statements symbolize some great event in man's spiritual history. Nietzsche, the nineteenth-century prophet of the "God is dead" movement, perceived the tremendous mythical power of the slogan. By exploiting Nietzsche's myth the radical theologians have focused the spotlight of Christian concern where it has not been for centuries, that is, on the problem of God.

In the Enlightenment we became accustomed to belief in God without belief in Christ (deism), and began to take it for granted that the existence of God must come first, and Christianity second. Today, however, we find the opposite phenomenon— Christianity without theism. We must therefore ask why, in our time, men find atheism acceptable and, secondly, why some atheists feel that they can still be Christians.

Atheism is commonly defended on the ground that God has become inaccessible, superfluous, and degrading to man. Each of these three charges requires some explanation.

Modern man finds God inaccessible because all the traditional routes to Him seem to be blocked. Our ancestors used to find God in the Bible, in philosophy, in religious experience, and in the community in which they lived. Our contemporaries do not easily find God in any of these four places.

It used to be possible to read the Bible with the impression that it was a very simple, direct account of exactly what God had said and done, but under the influence of modern scholarship educated Christians now know that it is a very complicated book written by a primitive people whose patterns of life and thought were totally different from ours. As a result, we find it hard to interpret the Bible. We can no longer casually assume, as our ancestors did, that God spoke to Moses on Mount Sinai, or that angels came to explain the visions of Daniel. The historical reliability of the Bible can no longer be taken for granted, and its meaning very often seems to elude us. It is hard, therefore, to find God speaking to us in the Bible.

Until rather recently it was common to hold that philosophy could show beyond doubt that there must be an eternal, necessary, personal being at the origin of all things, that is, a God. Today it is widely admitted that the so-called proofs for the existence of God depend upon prior commitment to a view of reality which practically settles the question in advance. The view of reality that the proofs presuppose does not impose itself upon all men, but depends upon a personal interpretation of life and experience. God is regarded as a hypothesis which serves to solve certain problems, but which seems to raise other problems which defy solution. Many students, seeing how divided the philosophers are about the existence of God, feel that the philosophical road to Him is no longer viable.

The road of religious experience was much travelled by our predecessors, but many men today are not conscious of having any such thing as religious experience, and even if they seem to have it they distrust it as a source of knowledge. As late as Kant's time, people still found it possible to gaze with numinous awe upon "the starry skies above and the moral law within." But today the heavens, instead of reflecting the majesty of the eternal God, appear to be just a confused mass of material for man to explore and subdue. The moral law seems to be, in most cases, a product of human convention or perhaps some kind of projection from the unconscious. And if anyone comes claiming to have had a direct conversation with God, as the mystics used to claim, our spontaneous reaction is to send him to a psychiatrist.

Perhaps the most important support of faith in God, so far as the mass of men is concerned, has been the consent of the community. Until recently practically everyone in Europe and America accepted the existence of God. Normal sociable people believed, and went to church, at least occasionally. Young people as they grew up absorbed faith by a kind of osmosis from their social environment. But in our day the social pressures in favor of religion are rapidly diminishing. In some circles the situation has almost reversed itself; the convinced believer rather than the agnostic is the non-conformist, the independent thinker.

For all these reasons, God seems remote and inaccessible. Even with the best will, many find it almost impossible to get into contact with the divine. The only world in which they can believe is this world, the finite world of everyday experience.

Even if God's existence were to be admitted, many of our contemporaries feel that it would be irrelevant. What difference does it make, they ask, whether we acknowledge such a God or not? He seems infinitely distant, silent, impassive, inscrutable. Being perfectly happy in Himself, He presumably needs nothing that we can give him, and He seems to do nothing for us. For the biblical peoples, and for biblically minded Christians, the Lord was a living God. When it pleased Him He spoke to men; He made His will and His law known; He interfered in history to save His people from defeat, or captivity, and when they suffered, He let them know that He was punishing them for their sins.

Modern man no longer seems to enjoy such a living relationship with God. We can praise Him, and He does not give us tangible rewards. We can blaspheme Him, and the earth does not swallow us up; no thunderbolts come down from heaven. He seems to have left us completely on our own. If we want to learn something we have to find it out by our own efforts, or else it simply remains unknown. Instead of obtaining knowledge, as the ancients did, by prophecy and divination, we do so by observation, experiment, and rational inference. And so likewise, if we want something done we cannot expect God to do it for us. Whatever may have happened in the past, it seems clear that He no longer feeds the hungry in the desert by raining down manna from heaven; He does not cast the horse and rider of the enemy into the deep. As Napoleon cynically put it, God is on the side of the big battalions.

In other words, we no longer feel that we can turn to God as a solver of problems or as a filler of needs. In Bonhoeffer's often quoted words: "There is no longer any need for God as a working hypothesis, whether in morals, politics, or science. Nor is there any need for such a God in religion or philosophy (Feuerbach). . . . The only way to be honest is to recognize that we have to live in the world *etsi deus non daretur.*"[4]

Once this is admitted, it is but a short step further to say that the God of traditional Christianity is not merely useless, but positively harmful. "If God did exist," some would say, "we should have to abolish Him."[5] The reason for this attitude is the conviction that every notion of God which is not completely empty and meaningless is, in fact, an obstacle to human progress. God is invoked in order to make men accept social injustices; people are told to bear their lot because they will be fully compensated in heaven. Or God is invoked in order to give some divine sanction to a particular theory of government, science, or ethical conduct. The record of history seems to show that social and scientific progress, far from being assisted by supposed revelations, have usually been achieved in spite of them. The mere mention of Galileo and Darwin makes further argument unnecessary.

Modern atheism is intimately connected with the progress of science and technology, which has convinced man that he himself is master of the universe, not the slave of some higher power. Instead of standing in reverent awe before the order of the universe, conceived as something which manifests the divine, he feels that it is his function to impose order on the universe, and to establish his own rules of conduct. Belief in God, it is objected, keeps man passive and dependent when the times call for boldness and creativity.

Altizer maintains that the only God in whom contemporary man can believe is an alien, oppressive God, one who lays down restrictive laws, and stands against man as a vindictive judge. And nobody will bend his knee to such a God unless he is a masochist, one who takes pleasure in demeaning himself in order to escape the responsibility of freedom. Is it not obvious that some neurotic types multiply taboos, and derive a sense of holy satisfaction from observing them with pharisaical punctiliousness? Antichristian atheists, such as Sartre and

Camus, as well as Christian atheists, like Hamilton and Altizer, wish to liberate man from slavery to this repressive God. God must die, they proclaim, in order that man may live.

CHRIST WITHOUT GOD

We have seen some of the reasons why the new radicals do not accept the God of traditional theism. In this they agree with non-Christian theists in the tradition of Feuerbach and Nietzsche, but what is new about them is that they are Christian atheists. We must therefore ask how it has become possible in our time for a Christian believer to be godless.

According to the radical theologians the reasons for rejecting God do not tell against Jesus. God is a strange ethereal being, totally different from ourselves, but Jesus is a man like us, one who even felt abandoned by God in his agony. The idea of God seems to enslave and dehumanize man, but the image of Jesus sets them free for the service of their brothers. Van Buren, Hamilton, and Altizer, in their several ways, all maintain that, for the radical Christian, Jesus takes the place of God.

Jesus, according to van Buren, was a man uniquely free for his neighbor. Detached from selfish interests, He was fully open to the concerns of others. Jesus' freedom, moreover, has proved contagious; it grasps the Christian, and shapes his view of life and the universe. Thus Jesus, rather than God, becomes for the believer "the way, the truth, and the life." If we know Jesus, van Buren maintains, we have all we need. "Whatever men were looking for in looking for God is to be found by finding Jesus of Nazareth."[6]

Hamilton likewise holds that Jesus performs, at least in part, the functions which the classical tradition assigned to God. "If by God you mean the focus of obedience, the object of trust and loyalty, the meaning that I give to love, my center, my meaning— then these meanings are given not to men in general but to Jesus, the *man*, in his life, his way with others and his death."[7]

Altizer is less concerned with the ethical meaning of Jesus, but he makes much of Jesus as the one in whom the death of

God began to take place in history. Since, in Him, the Word was made flesh, it may be said that God, dying to himself, has become Jesus. Jesus, according to Altizer, witnessed the demise of the God of the Old Testament, and thus the *dawning* of God's kingdom on earth. He made Himself and his disciples free from the prohibitions of the Mosaic law. Just as Paul could claim that Christians were free because the Law had died in Christ, so, Altizer argues, we are free because, through the mediation of Jesus, the death of God is now a realized fact of history. For Altizer therefore: "A Christian proclamation of the love of God is a proclamation that God has negated himself in becoming flesh, his Word is now the opposite or the intrinsic otherness of his primordial Being, and God himself has ceased to exist in his original mode as transcendent or discarnate Spirit: God *is* Jesus."[8]

Christian atheists must, of course, face the objection that Jesus spoke constantly of his Father as the God whom he served, and whose will he proclaimed. When asked about this matter, Hamilton recently replied:

> Radicals must, of course, not only acknowledge but face directly the centrality of Jesus' own filial dependence on the Father. Can there be an attention to Jesus, a genuine obedience and discipleship to him, that is not at the same time an obedience to the one to whom he was obedient? I assume that a full theological analysis of this question would entail asking about the meaning of Jesus' demonology, of his cosmology, indeed, his eschatology, as first-century thought-forms that Christians need not feel obliged to "believe in" as he did. Might it not be possible to show that his dependence on the Father is of the same character—appropriate then, but not automatically transferrable to us?[9]

Generally speaking, the "death of God" theologians agree that the Bible, like any other document from ancient times, cannot be taken at face value as normative for us. We cannot accept the mythological world view of the biblical writers— the radical Christian argues—and it is useless to pretend that, while their scientific ideas were erroneous, their religious ideas were always correct. They thought as men of their times, and we must think as men of ours. If Christianity is to survive as a vital faith in our times, it must be presented, these theologians say, in a radically new way which modern man can understand and accept. What these theologians find authoritative in Jesus is not the ideas he taught but rather the intention or direction of his life—his freedom, openness, devotion to others. They find it possible to look on Him as the supreme ideal of what it means to be a man, and at the same time to repudiate his own ideas about God.

In summary, then, we may say that the new Christian atheism is symptomatic of many assumptions and attitudes which pervade the air we breathe. It reveals the modern antipathy to abstract metaphysical thinking, the prevailing distrust of traditional doctrines, the contemporary concern for relevance and pragmatic results, and the new accent on human freedom.

THE MOVEMENT AS A CHALLENGE

What now is Christian theism to make of this movement? Those of us who believe that God still lives can, if we like, make fun of the movement, for it is vulnerable to all kinds of ridicule. Or we can become angry and attack it as heretical and destructive. Or we can simply ignore it on the theory that, if we do not so much as mention it, the storm will blow over and things will return to normal. But personally I believe that things will not return to normal because there are elements in the contemporary religious situation which make some such movement almost inevitable.

Every time the Church has failed to meet the crucial questions of a given age, it has lost influence. For example, the Catholic Church in the sixteenth century, instead of facing the real questions raised by the Protestant Reformation, tried to handle the situation with disciplinary measures. The problems remained, as is shown by the fact that Vatican Council II has belatedly conceded some of the Reformers' main points. We should not repeat this mistake with regard to the radical theologians of our day. In the remainder of this chapter, therefore, I shall address myself to the challenge of the "God is dead" theology. We must ask what valid insights lie behind the movement, and make room for these insights, if room does not already exist, in our own theology. Theology grows and rejuvenates itself by meeting the problems which others put to it; it declines and becomes senile when it withdraws into its own private world, and concentrates on its favorite problems, as happened in the late middle ages.

To begin with, let me say that I do not regard biblical fundamentalism, or any other kind of blind conservatism, as the answer. When we are dealing with the Bible or ancient church documents we have to sift out what is conditioned by an antiquated culture, and translate the meaning into terms that speak to us. In the last analysis, each age has to find the divine in the light of its own primary concerns and presuppositions. With this frame of mind we must honestly ask whether the idea of God is itself obsolete, and if so, whether we can cling to Jesus alone, as the radical theologians do. We have seen why these authors think that God is inaccessible, superfluous, and positively dehumanizing. What validity is there in these assertions?

THE INACCESSIBILITY OF GOD

We may admit that in our time God is not easily accessible. With our exact scientific methods we are more sensitive than our ancestors were to the differences between statements about wordly objects and statements about God.[10] This is partly a gain, because we are not so likely to slip into the error of imagining that God is an object which can be grasped and contained within our concepts. While the great theologians of the past knew this, many popular preachers and writers fell into the temptation of representing God as a being among beings—the highest and best among many. Uneducated people, of course, believed that God was somewhere up in the sky, and that eternity was simply a time that never ended.

Today we know that we can only lisp about divine things.

Whatever glimpses of God can be gained through the Bible, through philosophy, and through the experience of the spiritual life leave our thirst unquenched. The believer does not, in the ordinary sense of the word, know God; he affirms God in a kind of darkness which rules out any positive and direct concepts of Him. As St. Thomas Aquinas used to say, the only thing we can say about God with complete accuracy is what God is not.

Undoubtedly it is easier to be an atheist today than it has been for centuries. This is due to all the reasons we have mentioned, and especially to the fact that there are less social pressures in favor of religious faith. If we set great store by church statistics, we shall regard this as a symptom of decline, but we should not forget that the freedom not to believe is one of the most precious results of Christian influence. Christianity insists so much on personal integrity that it protects the unbeliever's right to follow his conscience. Where unbelief is a real possibility, faith can achieve its full power. A man who believes in God where there is no social pressure urging him to do so can be sure that in believing he acts with full authenticity; and his faith becomes a sign to others that God truly lives.

The reflective believer sometimes feels closer to the serious atheist than to some of his fellow believers. He feels embarrassed by those who imagine that they know exactly what God is like and what he wants, and irritated by all the loose God-talk he hears about him. He loathes the vulgarity of those who turn the name of God into a shibboleth. Since he worships the "hidden God" he knows that the best form of discourse about Him is often a reverent silence.[11]

The reflective believer and the conscientious atheist are bound together by a deep brotherhood.[12] Both are aware that faith is faith. God's existence is not obvious, nor can it be demonstrated with geometrical cogency. To affirm God is a free act depending on a highly personal interpretation of life and the universe. In this sense, it is a risk. The serious believer cannot join with the bigoted Christian in a witch hunt against atheism for he knows that conscientious atheism contains precious values and is sometimes nearer the truth than certain crude and unexamined forms of theism. To affirm the true God, one has to deny all the gods produced by that "busy factory of idols" (as Calvin called it), the mind of man.

Serious theology will always be open to a dialogue with atheism, because the witness of atheism is needed to prevent Christians from oversimplifying, and thus falsifying, their idea of God. When God is taken too much for granted, we begin to think of Him in the wrong way, and thus involve ourselves in all sorts of false and insoluble problems. Atheistic criticism can help us to see that these problems often have their root in a false and untenable notion of God, and thus helps the theist to purify his own faith.

When we speak of God's inaccessibility in our time it is worth remembering that if some of the traditional channels by which men have found God seem to have run dry, others are perhaps opening up. The struggle for truth and human values which is of such concern to conscientious men of our day, including many who call themselves atheists, is very possibly a new locus of God's self-manifestation in history. A passionate concern for civil rights and peace, for example, can easily be a disguised form of the love of God. By rigorous analysis it can, I think, be shown that wherever there is a truly authentic human love, the love of God is in some sort present, even though it is not recognized as such.

FAITH IN GOD: HELP OR HINDRANCE?

So much by way of reply to the first of the three arguments against theism presented above. The second and third charges—namely that God is not helpful and that He is positively detrimental to human progress—can be evaluated together. There is merit in the objections to the extent that they make it clear that our relationship to God must not be passive or servile. Men have always had a measure of responsibility to engage in building a better world, but until recently they have not had the power to reshape it decisively. Many evils had to be tolerated patiently because men could not eliminate them.

If some early Christian preachers seemed to counsel resignation and even to condone institutions such as slavery, this is no reason why a Christian today should do likewise. God demands that we should actively set about organizing social structures consonant with the dignity of man.

The images which depict men as God's puppets or slaves are misleading. Already the New Testament was able to proclaim that we are no longer slaves but freemen, friends, and sons. Even more is this true today, now that, as Bonhoeffer put it, "the world has come of age." We must cease to look on God as a kind of authority figure standing over against man. Our dominant God-image should be that of one who loves and gives himself to man. Love does not enslave the other or impede his development. It brings out his highest potentialities, his freedom and creativity. Love is the key to freedom without selfishness, service without enslavement.

If we are seeking optimum conditions for human freedom we shall easily see that they are not obtained by eliminating all reference to God. Unless a man finds his ultimate concern and final good beyond all that this world can give or take from him, he will not have the strength to stand up under adversity or the courage to give himself completely. He will be tossed about by his own passions and manipulated by his fellow men. The love of God is the most liberating of all experiences. So free were the Christian martyrs that not even the threat of death could make them submit to tyranny.

Bonhoeffer himself, in the very letters in which he describes how God is "teaching us to get along without him," remarks that his fellow prisoners who lack faith in God often succumb to panic during the air raids. Theirs, he says, is a fragmented existence. "By contrast, Christianity plunges us into the many dimensions of life simultaneously." "We assimilate these dangers into the wholeness of life."[13]

Langdon Gilkey, in a recent book about the Europeans and Americans with whom he was interned in China during the war, makes much the same point. In the last paragraph he sums up the fruits of his experiences:

Men need God because their precarious and contingent lives can find final significance only in His almighty and eternal purposes, and because their fragmentary selves must find their ultimate center in His transcendent love. If the meaning of men's lives is centered solely in their own achievements, these too are vulnerable to the twists and turns of history, and their lives will always teeter on the abyss of pointlessness and inertia. And if men's ultimate loyalty is centered in themselves, then the effect of their lives on others around them will be destructive of that community upon which all depend. Only in God is there an ultimate loyalty that does not breed injustice and cruelty, and a meaning from which nothing in heaven or on earth can separate us.[14]

If the experience of Bonhoeffer, Gilkey, and a host of others is any criterion, a consciously affirmed relationship to God is, in the long run, essential to sustain man's efforts to create a fully human world order.

Of course it remains the task of believers in every generation to prove by their example that their faith has this dynamic power. Those who have never appropriated their faith by a true personal decision often fail to reflect it in their lives. Nietzsche was able to protest with some plausibility that Christians could not possibly believe the gospel they professed, because they went around with such long faces. Recently I heard Altizer say that his entire theory would be proved false if he were to meet a single contemporary man who really derived joy and creativity from his faith in God. In my own experience I seem to have met hundreds of such persons, but I would still admit that the average Christian does not act as if Christ had released him from subjection to every alien power and had established him in a peace and joy which the world can never destroy.

CAN JESUS REPLACE GOD?

There remains our last question, whether Christ the man can take the place of God for the Christians of our day. As I have mentioned, van Buren, Hamilton, and Altizer all maintain that He can.

To some degree this position is in continuity with that of other modern Protestant theologians (e.g. Barth and Bonhoeffer), who have held that Christ is the only self-disclosure of God. If we can know nothing about God except what we find in Christ, why can we not say that Christ the man is enough and that there is no real need to refer to God?

One major difficulty in this approach is that when one begins to say, as the radical theologians do, that Jesus is the focus of our ultimate commitment, the universal norm and the supreme inspiration for our idealism, one begins to make Him something more that a man. If He were just one particular realization of our common humanity, it would be senseless to exalt Him to a position of unique and definitive preeminence. As some critics have pointed out, van Buren, after saying that God-language is meaningless, inconsistently uses the language of transcendence in speaking about Jesus. Altizer, as we have seen, goes so far as to say, God is Jesus.

It seems to be clear that Christians have always meant something very definite in using the name God in connection with Jesus Christ. For some, Jesus has been the original revelation of God. More commonly men have come to Him, as the first Christians did, with a previous conviction that there is a God; but He has transformed their ideas about what God is. As we have seen, the question of God is raised not only by the life of Jesus, but by an analysis of the human situation in any age, including our own. Through reflection on the problems of life many of our contemporaries have come to believe in God as the transcendent, personal source of value and meaning.

Christian atheism cannot really solve the objection that the life and teaching of Jesus, as we know them from the New Testament, were totally centered about God. He laid down the love of God as His first commandment, and His own service of men was totally motivated by fidelity to His Father's will. If anyone wishes to get along without God, it may legitimately be objected that he is no longer making Jesus his norm in any significant way.

TOWARD A LIVING FAITH

The new atheistic Christianity is largely inspired by dissatisfaction with the philosophical theism which has grown up in
the West under the influence of Greek speculation. Whatever
satisfaction with the philosophical theism which has grown up
in the West under the influence of Greek speculation. Whatever
be the value of such metaphysical thinking, we must, I think,
agree that much of the popular literature on God has been too
rationalistic and abstract to do justice to the Christian sources.
The God of "popular metaphysics," if I may coin such a term,
is a remote and frigid figure who seems unconcerned with man
and uninvolved in human history. But the great theologians
have never forgotten that the God of the Bible is essentially
mysterious, not least so because of the surprising ways in which
He makes himself immediately present in man's history.

In the early years Christianity did not appear to be first of all
a system of doctrine, still less a philosophy about God. It was
a preaching of the good news of man's redemption through
Christ. The new religion was originally called, very fittingly,
"the way" (see Acts 9.2). As a way of life, Christianity must
continually prove itself by its fruits. The Gospel lays down the
norm, "By their fruits you will know them" (Mt 7.20). Radical
theology is in part a protest against a Christianity which has
become too doctrinaire, too remote from life, too isolated from
the needs of men.

If we are convinced that God lives, it is easy to become
impatient with the extravagances of the Christian atheists. We
are tempted to strike back in a spirit of revenge or to stop up
our ears and cry, "they have blasphemed." But I have tried to
indicate that we should do far better to study the motivation
behind this movement, and if we do so we shall find that the
defects of historical Christianity have given some occasion for
this revolt. We shall see that the radical theologians are sensitive
to the needs of our times, and are anxious to emphasize certain
aspects of Christianity which have been too little noticed.

There are two ways in which the challenge of Christian

atheism can be met. One is by showing, through logical analysis, that the reasoning is faulty. But this method by itself will never succeed because it makes no effort to cope with the religious situation of which the new movement is symptomatic. The other way is for believers to show, in their lives, that faith in God is still possible, necessary, and productive of good results. Christianity in the first centuries was a practical demonstration of this: the love and courage of Christians, derived from their faith, astounded the world.

God in himself remains what He is, and nothing we can do adds to, or detracts from, His reality, but so far as men are concerned, God can be alive or dead in the world. If Christians are servile conformists, timid, selfish, and gloomy, they fail to make God live, but if they are open and courageous, free and generous, God lives in them. If God is to live in the world He needs witnesses whose lives are radiant with a dynamism and devotion which are not of this world. Perhaps the best answer to the "death of God" theologians was given by the second century Jewish rabbi, Simon Bar-Yochai, who summed up much of what I have tried to say in a challenging sentence which he placed in the mouth of God: "If you are my witnesses, I am God, and if you are not my witnesses I am, so to speak, no longer God."[15]

NOTES

1. Myth, Symbol, and the Biblical Revelation

1. See K. Rahner, S.J., "What is a Dogmatic Statement?" *Theological Investigations* 5 (Baltimore, 1966) 58–60. I. T. Ramsey has shown the inadequacy of observational language in the territory of faith; see his *Religious Language* (London, 1957).

2. For a full treatment with extensive bibliography, see S. Wisse, *Das religiöse Symbol* (Essen, 1963). In English, valuable contributions by Tillich and others may be found in F. E. Johnson ed., *Religious Symbolism* (New York, 1955).

3. See the famous words of Augustine concerning the miracles of Christ: "Interrogemus ipsa miracula, quid nobis loquantur de Christo; habent enim, si intelligantur, linguam suam. Nam quia ipse Christus Verbum Dei est, etiam factum Verbi verbum nobis est" [In *evan. Ioh.* 24, 1 (Corpus christianorum, series latina 36, 244)].

4. Susanne K. Langer, *Philosophy in a New Key* (Cambridge, Mass., 1942) 284f.

5. Austin Farrer, *The Glass of Vision* (Westminster, Eng., 1948) esp. chap. 8.

6. C. H. Dodd, *The Interpretation of the Fourth Gospel* (Cambridge, Eng., 1958) p. 137.

7. Austin Farrer, *A Rebirth of Images* (Westminster, Eng., 1949) 17.

8. Pius XII taught that Scripture, as well as tradition, "tot tantosque continet thesauros veritatis, ut numquam reapse exhauriatur" [*Humani generis* (1950); see Denzinger-Schönmetzer, *Enchiridion symbolorum* (32nd ed., Freiburg, 1963) 3886].

9. John Knox, *Myth and Truth: An Essay on the Language of Faith* (Charlottesville, 1964) 28. For a similar view, see B. H. Throckmorton, Jr., *The New Testament and Mythology* (Philadelphia, 1959) 94–105.

10. Brevard S. Childs, *Myth and Reality in the Old Testament* (Naperville, 1960) 13–16.

11. John L. McKenzie, "Myth and the Old Testament," *Myths and Realities: Studies in Biblical Theology* (Milwaukee, 1963) 182–200, 266–68.

12. R. Wellek and A. Warren, *Theory of Literature* (New York, 1942) 196; a similar point is made by J. Knox, *op. cit.*, p. 24.

13. P. Tillich, "Mythus," *Die Religion in Geschichte und Gegenwart* 4 (2nd ed. 1930) 370; J. Sløk, "Mythus," *ibid.*, 4 (3rd ed. 1960) 1264.

14. In his polemic against Bultmann, Barth insists on the permanence of myth in the modern world—a point he proceeds to exemplify by referring to "the myth of the twentieth century, the Marxist myth, the myth of the Christian West, etc." But are these properly myths? See H. W. Bartsch ed., *Kerygma and Myth* 2 (London, 1962) 109.

15. McKenzie, *art. cit.*, p. 190.

16. M. Eliade, *Images and Symbols* (New York, 1961) 57–58.

17. *Id.*, "Methodological Remarks on the Study of Religious Symbolism." *The History of Religions: Essays in Methodology* (Chicago, 1959) 103.

18. P. Tillich, *art. cit.*, col. 366.

19. Cassirer's philosophy of myth is found in several works, most importantly in *The Philosophy of Symbolic Form* 2; *Mythical Thought* (New Haven, 1955).

20. For an exposition and critique, see R. Hostie, *Religion and the Psychology of Jung* (New York, 1957).

21. M. Eliade, *Patterns in Comparative Religion* (New York, 1958) 416–26.

22. P. Tillich, *The Dynamics of Faith* (New York, 1957) 49. Tillich's doctrine of myth has been fully analyzed in P. Barthel, *Interprétation du langage mythique et théologie biblique* (Leiden, 1963) 152–98.

23. So, for example, G. Miegge, *Gospel and Myth in the Thought of Rudolph Bultmann* (London, 1960) 118–19.

24. J. Knox, *op. cit.*, p. 78.

25. L. Billot, S.J., *De inspiratione sacrae Scripturae* (4th ed.; Rome, 1929) 155.

26. "Il y a toutefois un genre qu'on doit exclure *a priori* de la Bible comme 'indigne' de Dieu: c'est le 'mythe,' parce qu'il introduit l'erreur et la fiction dans l'essence même des spéculations religieuses sur la Divinité" [in P. Synave, O.P., and P. Benoit, O.P., *La prophétie: Somme théologique, 2a–2ae, qq. 171–78* (Tournai, 1947) p. 369 n.1]. But note that in the English translation [*Prophecy and Inspiration* New York, 1961)], made with some additions and corrections by the author, this is modified to read (p. 161): "... any kind of 'myth' which would introduce error or fiction into the very essence of religious speculations about the Deity." Among the manualists, J. M. Vosté and C. Pesch, like Billot, flatly assert that myths are excluded from the inspired books. M. Nicolau, *Sacrae theologiae summa* 1 (2nd. ed. Madrid, 1952) p. 1055 (part 4, no. 188), holds that myth as such cannot be present in the Bible, but that myths may be cited or used as literary ornaments by the biblical authors. A. Bea, *De Scripturae sacrae inspiratione* (2nd. ed. Rome, 1935, no.89) says that it may not be affirmed a priori that God cannot teach men even by myth, "dummodo curet ut haec genera ut talia cognosci possint et verbis non necessario ascribatur veritas proprio sensu historica."

27. Pius IX, *Syllabus Errorum* (Denzinger-Schönmetzer 2907) and Decree of the Biblical Commission of 1909 (*Enchiridion Biblicum* [4th ed.] 325).

28. The phrases quoted are from B. S. Childs (*op. cit.*, p. 102), who is criticizing certain Protestant views of *Heilsgeschichte*.

29. For a convenient summary, cf. H. Cazelles, "Mythe et l'A. T.," *Dict de la Bible, Supplément* 6, 246–61. Also, more briefly. T. H. Gaster in *Interpreter's Dictionary of the Bible* 3, 481–87.

30. John L. McKenzie, *art. cit.*, p. 291.

31. H. Gunkel, "Mythus and Mythologie im A.T.," *Die Religion in Geschichte und Gegenwart* 4 (2nd ed. 1930) 381. Also, G. Stählin, "Mythos," in G. Kittel, *Theologisches Wörterbuch zum Neuen Testament* 4, 787.

32. Karl Barth, *Church Dogmatics*, III/I (Edinburgh, 1938) 83.

33. *Ibid.*, I/1 (Edinburgh, 1963) 376.

34. *Ibid.*, III/1 84–90.

35. This point is made by H. Fries, "Mythos und Offenbarung," in J. Feiner *et al.* ed., *Fragen der Theologie heute* (Einsiedeln, 1957) 39.

36. J. L. McKenzie has assembled a collection of OT passages of this type in *Theological Studies* 11 (1950) 275–82. For his present judgment on their mythical character, see *art. cit.* (n. 11 above) 193.

37. B. S. Childs, *op. cit.*, chap. 3.

38. C. H. Dodd, *The Bible Today* (paperback ed.; Cambridge, Eng., 1961) 112. O. Cullmann, who likewise labels the biblical descriptions of the prehistory and posthistory as myth, draws a very sharp opposition between myth and history; see *Christ and Time* (Philadelphia, 1950) 94–96.

39. H. Cazelles, *art. cit.*, col. 260–61.

40. 1 Tim 1.4; 4.6f.; 2 Tim 4.3f.; Tit 1.14. The two references to myth in the Old Testament "deuterocanonicals" are no more complimentary: Sir 20.19, Bar 3.23.

41. Strauss's conception of myth has been studied by C. Hartlich and W. Sachs, *Der Ursprung des Mythosbegriffes in der modernen Bibelwissenschaft* (Tübingen, 1952) chap. 5, and by P. Barthel, *op. cit*, (note 22, above) pp. 36–42.

42. On the views of R. Reitzenstein and W. Bousset, see S. Neill, *The Interpretation of the New Testament, 1861–1961* (Oxford, 1964) 160–65.

43. R. Bultmann, "New Testament and Mythology," in *Kerygma and Myth* (London, 1953) 1–44 This essay does little more than restate, in more programmatic form, the essential content of his article in *RGG* 4 (2nd ed., 1930) 380–94, reprinted without change in the 3rd ed.: 4, 1278–82.

44. Heinrich Schlier, "Das N. T. und der Mythus," *Hochland* 48 (1956) 201–12. For a concurring view, see H. Fries, " Entmytholologisierung and theologische Wahrheit," in H. Vorgrimler, ed., *Gott in Welt* (Freiburg, 1964) 366–91, esp. pp. 380–91.

45. H. Schlier, *art. cit.*, p. 212.

46. A. von Harnack, *Die Entstehung der Christlichen Theologie und des Christlichen Dogmas* (1927) 16; quoted by G. Miegge, (note 23, above) 106.

47. *Protrepticus* 12, 119, 1 (*GCS* 1, 84), H. Rahner, in his *Greek Myths and Christian Mystery* (London, 1963), splendidly develops this theme from patristic sources.

48. M. Eliade, *Images and Symbols*, 168f.

2. The Theology of Revelation

1. René Latourelle, S. J., *Theology of Revelation* (Staten Island, N. Y., 1966). This is a slightly revised translation of his French work of 1963, to which he has added a brief section on the Epistle to the Hebrews, and a rather full commentary on the first two chapters of the Vatican II Constitution, *Dei Verbum*.

2. In a number of important articles, chiefly published in the *Catholic Biblical Quarterly*, David M. Stanley, S. J., has skillfully developed this insight. See, also, his *The Apostolic Church in the New Testament* (Westminster, Md., 1965), *passim*.

3. Romano Guardini, *Die Offenbarung: Ihr Wesen und ihre Formen* (Würzburg, 1940) 47–48.

4. See Maurice Eminyan, S. J., *The Theology of Salvation* (Boston, 1960) 56–59; K. Rahner, S. J., "Observations on the Concept of Revelation," in K. Rahner and J. Ratzinger, *Revelation and Tradition* (New York, 1966) 16.

5. Frederick E. Crowe, S. J., "The Development of Doctrine and the Ecumenical Problem," *Theological Studies* 23 (1962) 27–46, concludes: "... one might say, therefore, that the material element of this phase of revelation will not be completed till the last day, but the formal element was completed nineteen centuries ago in the center of time in the Holy Land" (p. 40).

6. Maurice Blondel, *History and Dogma* (New York, 1965) 279.

7. Jean Mouroux, *I Believe*, tr. M. Turner (London, 1959) 73–74. More recently Karl Rahner has developed a theory of the transcendental and predicamental aspects of revelation which enables one to see "why a materially false act of faith can be a genuine act of faith," *art. cit.* (note 4 above), p. 24.

8. Latourelle, p. 198, quotes Newman's statement: "When you knew nothing of the revealed light, you knew not the revealed darkness" (*Plain and Parochial Sermons* 1 [London, 1834] 211).

9. Max Lackmann, *The Augsburg Confession and Catholic Unity*, tr. W. R. Bouman (New York, 1963) x.

10. K. Rahner, "Was ist eine dogmatische Aussage?" *Schriften zur Theologie* 5 (Einsiedeln, 1962) 74; see Eng. trans., "What is a Dogmatic Statement?" *Theological Investigations* 5 (Baltimore, 1966) 60.

11. See J. S. Bruner. *On Knowing: Essays for the Left Hand* (Cambridge, Mass., 1962) 74.

12. *The Glass of Vision* (Westminster, Eng., 1948) 110.

13. *Ibid.*, p. 61.

14. "Gnòsis and Revelation in the Bilble," *Scottish Journal of Theology* 9(1956) 44.

3. Reflections on "Sola Scriptura"

1. See T. G. Tappert, ed., *The Book of Concord* (Philadelphia, 1959) 464–65.

2. William Chillingworth, *The Religion of Protestants, A Safe Way to Salvation* in *The Works of W. Chillingworth* (Philadelphia, 1844), 480–81.

3. Denzinger-Schönmetzer, n. 1501.

4. Melchior Cano, *Loci theologici*, III, De Traditionibus apostolicis, cap. 3, *in Opera* (Venice, 1759) 79.

5. Robert Bellarmine, *De controversiis christianae fidei*, I, bk. IV, ch. 12 (Naples, 1856). p. 140.

6. Joachim Salaverri, S.J., *De Ecclesia Christi*, Thesis 19, in *Sacrae theologiae summa* 1 (Madrid, 2nd ed., 1952) 740.

7. *Ibid.*, p. 751.

8. P. C. Rodger and L. Vischer (ed.), *The Fourth World Conference on Faith and Order* (New York, 1964) 51–52.

9. D. M. Paton, "Montreal Diary," in Rodger and Vischer, *op. cit.*, p. 24.

10. Carl F. H. Henry, "Montreal Jamboree: Theological Stalemate," *Christianity Today* 7 (Aug. 30, 1963) 1123.

11. Oscar Cullmann, "Les récentes études sur la formation de la tradition évangélique," *Revue d'Histoire et de Philosophie religieuses* 5 (1925) 460.

12. The Council of Trent, sess. 4, Denzinger-Schönmetzer, n. 1507.

13. Jaroslav Pelikan, *The Riddle of Roman Catholicism* (New York, 1959), 193.

14. Jaroslav Pelikan, *Luther the Expositor* (St. Louis, 1959) 88.

15. Paul Tillich, *Systematic Theology* 1 (Chicago, 1951) 36–37.

16. See Karl Rahner, S. J., art. "Biblische Theologie," *Lexikon für Theologie and Kirche* 2 (rev. ed., 1958), col. 449–51; also G. H. Tavard, "The Holy Tradition," in L. Swidler (ed.), *Dialogue for Reunion* (New York, 1962), 66.

4. The Constitution on Divine Revelation

1. For excerpts from this speech see X. Rynne, *Letters from Vatican City* (New York, 1963) 161–63, and R. B. Kaiser, *The Pope, the Council, and the World* (New York, 1963) 176–79.

2. Already on Oct. 29, 1965, the Fathers had approved the final schema and requested its promulgation by a vote of 2,081 to 27 with seven votes null.

3. R. Latourelle, S.J., *Theology of Revelation* (Staten Island, 1966) 16. The statement that, for Protestants, "man is alone before

the word of God" is a generalization that would have to be nuanced for various groups of Protestants, especially in our own generation, when the ecclesial and sacramental dimensions of Christianity are more widely recognized than previously.

4. See Y. Congar, O.P., *Report from Rome II* (London, 1964) 164.

5. The words here quoted are from the first of the three amendments presented by the Pope, and represent an insertion into the *textus emendatus* of 1964.

6. Faith and Order Paper no. 40, pp. 20–21, published in *Faith and Order Findings* (London, 1963).

7. See *Herder Correspondence* 2.1 (Jan. 1965), 19.

8. The words here quoted reflect the second amendment proposed by Paul VI. The previous drafts had declared that "one must profess that all the books of Scripture, with all their parts, teach salutary truth firmly, faithfully, completely, and without error." This phrasing evidently seemed too definite in restricting the effects of inspiration to salutary truths alone. The final formula leaves open the question of whether God has not guaranteed other truths by the privilege of inerrancy. See R. Rouquette, "La quatrième session du Concile," *Études* 323 (Dec. 1965), 682–83.

9. The first sentence of art. 19 presently reads: "Holy Mother Church has firmly and with absolute constancy held, and continues to hold, that the four Gospels just named, *whose historical character the Church unhesitatingly asserts*, faithfully hand on what Jesus Christ, while living among men, really did and taught for their eternal salvation *until the day he was taken up into heaven* (see Acts 1.1)." The italicized words were added to the textus emendatus in response to the third of the Pope's *modi*, as a precaution against interpretations which would unduly minimize the connection between the Gospels and Jesus' actual doctrine and conduct.

10. Quoted by X. Rynne, *The Third Session* (New York, 1965), 47.

11. O. Cullmann, "The Bible in the Council" in *Dialogue on the Way* (Minneapolis, 1965) 136.

5. The Church and the Faith of Catholics

1. *Summa Theol.* 2–2, q. 174, a. 6 c.

2. Gal 3.26 f. etc. See on this point M. Fraeyman, "Het kerkelijk social aspect van het geloof," *Collat. Brugenses et Gandavenses* 3 (1957) 32.

3. *Summa Theol.* 3, q. 68, a. 9, ad 2. Cf. ad 3: "puer, cum baptizatur, non per seipsum sed per alios credit."

4. *The Spirit of Catholicism* (New York, 1929), 129. On this subject see also P.A. Liégé, O.P., "L'Eglise, milieu de la foi chrétienne," *Lumière et Vie* 23 (1955) 597–620.

5. *Summa Theol.* 2–2, q. 1, a. 10, ad 3.

6. J. Ternus, S.J., "Von Gemeinschaftsglauben der Kirche," *Scholastik* 10 (1935) 24, brings out the function of the ancient Creeds as "contesseratio."

7. H. de Lubac, S.J., *The Splendour of the Church* (New York, 1956) 22–23. See de Lubac, "Credo Ecclesiam" in *Sentire Ecclesiam* (Freiburg, 1961) 13–16.

8. R. Garrigou-Lagrange, O.P., *De Revelatione* (Rome, 1945) I, 514.

9. Eph 3.13. See the use made of this text in J. Mouroux, *I Believe* (London, 1959), p. 105.

10. See G. Marcel, *The Mystery of Being* 2 (Chicago, 1951) 135. A. Brunner, S.J., has some apposite reflections in "Glauben und Gemeinschaft," *Stimmen der Zeit* 163 (1959) 450f.

11. See G. Marcel, *Philosophy of Existence* (London, 1948), chap. 3.

12. St. Cyprian, *De catholicae ecclesiae unitate* 6; in Rouët de Journel, *Enchiridion Patristicum*, n. 557.

13. The relationship of the authority of the Church to divine faith is well treated by the following: H. Vignon, S.J., *De virtutibus infusis* (Rome, 1943) 149–60, 216–18; G. de Broglie, S.J., *Pour une théorie rationnelle de l'acte de foi* (Paris, n.d.) II, 28–32; F. Malmberg, S.J., *Ein Leib – Ein Geist* (Freiburg, 1960) 13 f., 118. G. H. Tavard, in his *Holy Writ or Holy Church* (London, 1959) p. 69, quotes the quite orthodox statement of Wessel Gansfort: "I believe with the Holy Church; I believe in accordance with the Holy Church. But I do not believe in the Church, because believing is an act of *latria*, a sacrifice of theological virtue to be offered to God alone."

14. Vatican Council I, sess. III, cap. 3; Denzinger-Schönmetzer n. 3013.

15. Karl Rahner, in his "Dogmatic Notes on 'Ecclesiological Piety,'" *Theological Investigations* 5 (Baltimore, 1966) 336–65, calls attention to the polar tension between the Church as evident sign of credibility and as hidden mystery of faith. He asks (pp. 342 f.): "But might we not perhaps venture the paradox that, the more the Church is the community of those who *believe* 'contra spem in spem' that God has done great things in them (i.e., of those who believe precisely because they accept the servant-form of the Church, and help to endure

it patiently to the end), the more (and really only thus) the Church will also become—precisely in this way—that 'signum elevatum in nationes' of which the first Vatican Council speaks so triumphantly?"

16. On the sustenance given to the life of faith by the Church's ministry of intercession, and her dispensation of the sacraments, see A. de Bovis, S.J., "Ecclesia Mater Fidei," *Revue d'Ascétique et de Mystique* 30 (1954) 97–116, and his article "Foi" in *Dictionnaire de Spiritualité* 5 (Paris, 1962) col. 529–603.

6. The Church and the Faith of Protestants

1. *Summa Theol.* 2–2, q. 5, a. 3 c.

2. John of St. Thomas, in 2–2ae. *de Fide*, disp. I, a. 1, no. 27; Laval Univ. ed. (Quebec, 1948), p. 37.

3. *Cursus theol.* (Paris, 1879) XI, disp. VIII, dub. 3, no. 41, p. 406.

4. Orestes Brownson, *Works* (Detroit 1882–87), V, 423–62.

5. John Henry Newman, *Discourses to Mixed Congregations*, especially in Discourses X and XI, seventh ed. (London, 1886) 192–237.

6. See, for example, the views of O. Cullmann in his "Reply to Roman Catholic Critics," *Scottish Journal of Theology* 15 (1962) 36–43. From a basically Calvinist point of view see Max Thurian, *Visible Unity and Tradition* (Baltimore, 1962) 22–23.

7. See the remarks on this point by J. Daniélou, S.J. in J. Bosc, et al., *The Catholic-Protestant Dialogue* (Baltimore, 1960), 106.

8. See S. Kutz, "The Inner Testimony of the Spirit," *The Ecumenist* 1, no. 3 (Feb.–Mar., 1963) 38–40.

9. Augustine, *Contra epistolam fundamenti*, cap. 5, no. 6; *P. L.* 42:176.

10. Augustine, "Extra Ecclesiam catholicam . . . potest . . . fidem habere et praedicare, sed nusquam nisi in Ecclesia catholica salutem poterit invenire," *Sermo ad Caesareensis ecclesiae plebem*. no. 6; *P.L.* 43:695.

11. This point is made by K. Rahner, "Dogmatic Notes on Ecclesiological Piety,'" *Theological Investigations* 5 (Baltimore, 1966) 352, who declares: "Hence it cannot be said either in theory or in practice (at least in most cases) that one believes in the Gospel simply because the Church is the object of one's faith. Rather (in spite of what St. Augustine says) the Church is an object of one's faith because one believes the Gospel."

12. C. Journet, *The Church of the Word Incarnate* 1 (New York, 1955) 510. See L. Billot, S.J., *De Ecclesia Christi*, ed. ˉ5a (Rome, 1927) I, 397.

13. M. Lackmann, *The Augsburg Confession and Catholic Unity* (New York, 1963) 22.

14. A schematic contrast has been made by G. Weigel, S. J., *Faith and Understanding in America* (New York, 1959), chap. 1. For an excellent phenomenological analysis of the faith of Catholics and Protestants from a slightly different point of view, see W. H. van de Pol, *The Christian Dilemma* (New York, 1952) 33–49.

15. See E. Kinder, "Evangelische Katholizität," *Kerygma und Dogma* 6 (1960) 69ff.

7. The Protestant Preacher and the Prophetic Mission

1. "Est enim praedicare quoddam prophetare vel prophetias exponere"; *In Lucam* 9.2, quoted by A. Rock, O.P., *Unless They Be Sent* (Dubuque, Iowa, 1953) 167, n. 92.

2. "Ad presbyterum pertinet interpretari et exhortari, quod est quasi prophetare," *In 4 sent.*, d.5, q.2, a.l, q.2, ad 2m. See *In Matt.*, c. 7, where he writes: "Dicendum quod prophetae sunt doctores in ecclesia et praelati."

3. C. Moeller, "Théologie de la parole et oecuménisme," *Irénikon* 24 (1951) 313, 332.

4. C. Rauch, "Qu'est ce qu'une homélie?," *Maison-Dieu* 16 (1948) 36.

5. See V. Schnurr, C.SS.R., "Situation und Aufgabe der Predigt heute," in T. Filthaut and J. A. Jungmann, S.J., eds., *Verkündigung und Glaube* (Freiburg, 1958), 200.

6. E. Przywara, S.J., "Christian Root-Terms: *Kerygma, Mysterion, Kairos, Oikonomia*," in W. Leibrecht, ed., *Religion and Culture: Essays in Honor of Paul Tillich* (New York, 1959) 115.

7. *Ibid.* It should be observed, however, that in Mk 1.44 par and Mk 7.36 par *këryssein* is used to describe unauthorized proclamation. Cf. the comment of G. Friedrich on this text in his article in G. Kittel, ed., *Theological Dictionary of the New Testament* 3 (Grand Rapids, 1965) 708.

8. *In epist. ad Rom.*, c. 10, lect. 2.

9. Martin Luther, *Scholia* on Rom 10.14 (*WA* 56, 422–23). That Luther never abandoned his doctrine regarding the necessity of a

proved mission is clear from his writings against the Anabaptists, whom he accused of prophesying without being divinely sent. To distinguish himself from the "false prophets" of Zwickau, Luther invoked his own title of "doctor," thus claiming a certain recognized authority to teach. See Y. Congar, O.P., *Vraie et fausse réforme* (Paris, 1950) 509–20.

10. G. Friedrich, *art. cit.*, p. 712f. In the same sense see the Protestant F. J. Leenhardt, *The Epistle to the Romans* (London, 1961), 273. For the Catholic exegesis of the same text, see R. Cornely, S.J., *Commentarius in s. Pauli apostoli epistolas* 1 (2nd ed., Paris, 1895; reprinted 1927) 561; K. H. Schelkle, *Discipleship and Priesthood* (New York, 1965) 69f.; L. Cerfaux, *Recueil* 3 (Gembloux, 1962), 186f.

11. Rock, *op. cit.*, p. 157 (italics supplied).

12. "Praedicator autem se habet sicut disponens exterius ad fidem"; *De verit.*, q. 27, a.3, and 12m. See *Sum. Theol.*, 2–2, q. 6, a.1.

13. This point is convincingly made, for example, by E. Haensli, "Verkündigung heute aus lebendigen theologischen Einsichten," in J. Feiner *et al.*, eds., *Fragen der Theologie heute* (2nd ed., Einsiedeln, 1958) 478.

14. *Sum. Theol.* 2–2, q. 177, a.2 c, "Gratia sermonis" is a short expression used by St. Thomas to designate two of the *gratiae gratis datae* mentioned by Paul in 1 Cor 12; *scil.*, "sermo sapientiae" and "sermo scientiae".

15. *Ibid.*, a.1 c.

16. Thomas Aquinas, *Contra Gentiles*, 3, 154: "Ea vero quae homo cognoscit . . . "

17. *Sum. Theol.* 2–2, q.177, a.1, ad 4m.

18. E. Mersch, S.J., *The Theology of the Mystical Body* (St Louis, 1951) 543.

19. E. Mura, *Le corps mystique du Christ* 2 (Paris, 1934), 380.

20. Leo XIII, *Satis cognitum*, *ASS* 28 (1895–96) 718. Cf. Vatican II, *Dei Verbum*, n. 7; *Lumen gentium*, n. 20.

21. St. Thomas says that bishops alone are qualified to give "instruction in the deep mysteries of faith and in the perfection of the Christian life"; *Sum. Theol.* 3, q. 71, a.4, ad 3m.

22. Rock, *op. cit.*, pp. 135–37. For the doctrine of St. Thomas on this point, see *Sum. Theol.* 3, q. 67, a.2, ad 1m. The Council of Trent affirmed: "Praedicationis munus, quod episcoporum praecipuum est. . . .", Sess. 24 de Ref., cap. 4. Vatican II in *Lumen gentium* n. 25 repeats this and in *Presbyterorum ordinis* n. 4. gives a similar primacy to proclamation of the gospel among the duties of priests.

23. "Concionari in ecclesia"; *CIC*, c. 1342, 2.

24. M. Scheeben, *Handbuch der kath. Dogmatik* 1 (Freiburg, 1927) no. 167, p. 91.

25. Benedict XV, Encyclical *Humani generis*, *AAS* 9 (1917) 307.

26. Lateran Council IV, cap. 3 (Denzinger-Schönmetzer n. 809).

27. Bull *Inter cunctas*, Feb. 22, 1418, art. 37–38 (*DS* 1278–79).

28. Sess. 7, can. 10 (*DS* 1610); Sess. 23, cap. 4 (*DS* 1767), can. 7 (*DS* 1777).

29. *CIC*, c. 1328.

30. J. McVann, *The Canon Law on Sermon Preaching* (New York, 1940) 60.

31. St. Thomas, *Quodlibetales*, 12, q. 18, art. 17 (Parma ed. 9, 628).

32. *Contra impugnantes Dei cultum et religionem*, cap. 4 (Parma ed. 15, 17). See *Sum. Theol.* 2–2, q. 187, a. 1 c.

33. D. M. Stanley, S.J., "The Concept of Biblical Inspiration," *Proc. Cath. Theol. Society of America*, Thirteenth Annual Convention, 1958, pp. 88–89.

34. "Réflexions sur la théologie du sermon," in *Prédication et prédicateurs* (Cahiers de la *NRT* 3; Tournai, 1947) 25–48.

35. *Ibid.*, p. 47.

36. K. Barth, *The Word of God and the Word of Man* (New York, 1957), 125f. (Italics in original).

37. Charles, *art. cit.*, p. 34.

38. Moeller, *art. cit.*, pp. 320–21. Moeller uses the term "preaching" in a somewhat peculiar sense, restricting it to what other authors prefer to call "evangelization." This fact affects the meaning of the statement here quoted.

39. H. Asmussen, "Fünf Fragen an die Katholische Kirche" in Asmussen and W. Stählin eds., *Die Katholizität der Kirche* (Stuttgart, 1957) 386–89.

40. *Ibid.*, p. 387.

41. P. Althaus, *Die christliche Wahrheit* (3rd ed., Gütersloh, 1952) 111–12.

42. A. Bea, S.J., "Valeur pastorale de la parole de Dieu dans la liturgie", *Maison-Dieu* 47–48 (1956) 138.

43. L. Billot makes the point that the preaching of the Catholic magisterium continues to have a profound influence on all churches that call themselves Christian; see *De Ecclesia Christi* 1 (5th ed.; Rome, 1927) 397, and the comment of C. Journet quoted above, p. 122.

44. *Sum. Theol.* 2–2, q. 177, a. 2 c and ad 1m, ad 3m.

45. St. Thomas interprets this text as affirming the necessity of external confession for salvation: *Sum. theol.* 2–2, q.3, a.2, *sed contra.*

46. *Enarr. in psalm.* 116:10 (*PL* 37, 1243). For a full treatment of St. Augustine's doctrine on this point, see. E. J. Hughes, *The Participation of the Faithful in the Regal and Prophetic Mission of Christ according to St. Augustine* (Mundelein, Ill., 1956).

47. *Sum. Theol.* 2–2, q.3, a.2.

48. *Sum. Theol.* 3, q. 71, a.4, ad 3m.

49. *Sum. Theol.* 2–2, q.33, a.3.c.

50. *Ibid.*, a.4, ad 2m.

51. Y. Congar, O.P., *Lay People in the Church* (Westminster, Md., 1957) 359.

52. Quoted *ibid.*, p. 289. Cf. Vatican Council II, *Lumen gentium*, n. 11; *Ad gentes*, n. 21.

53. E. Mersch beautifully analyzes the implications for Christian unity of the testimony given by German Protestants "who, during the Second World War, remained faithful to Christ even at the cost of life"; *Theology of the Mystical Body*, 504.

54. Prospero Lambertini (the future Pope Benedict XIV) laid down the principle, "uno verbo, sicut materialis haereticus martyr esse potest, ita et materialis schismaticus"; *De servorum Dei beatificatione* 3, 20, 6 and 7. Pius XII alluded to the existence of martyrs among dissident Christians in *Sempiternus rex, AAS* 43 (1951) 642–43, and in *Orientales ecclesias, AAS* 45 (1953) 5. The question of Protestant martyrs has been discussed by C. Journet, "L'Argument du martyr: A propos du martyrologe protestant de Jean Crespin," *Nova et vetera* 6 (1931) 285–300; 7 (1932) 200–204.

55. G. Philips, *Le rôle du laïcat dans l'église* (Paris and London, 1947) 233.

56. R. Lombardi, S.J., *The Salvation of the Unbeliever* (London, 1956) 300. See E. du Mont, *La situation du protestant baptisé et de bonne foi* (St.-Maurice, Switz., 1959) 194.

57. *Epist.* 98, 5 (*PL* 33, 362).

58. *Sum. Theol.* 3, q. 72, a.5, ad 2m.

59. W. A. Visser 't Hooft, ed., *The Evanston Report* (New York, 1955): Report of the Faith and Order Section, p. 91.

60. *Die Katholizität der Kirche*, p. 386.

61. P. Tillich, *The Protestant Era* (Chicago, 1948) 174.

62. Luther assails the Catholic con eption of the sacrament of order most virulently in his *De captivitate babylonica* (*WA* 6, 560–64). On p. 564 he states: "sacramentum ordinis aliud esse non potest quam ritus quidam eligendi concionatoris in Ecclesia."

63. For a High Church view see Stählin, *Symbolon* (Stuttgart, 1958) 275.

64. A. E. Garvie, *Towards Reunion*, p. 158, as quoted by E. J. Palmer, writing in H. N. Bate, ed., *Faith and Order: Proceedings of the World Conference, Lausanne* (New York, 1927) 236.

65. M. G. G. Scherer, in Bate, *op. cit.*, pp. 248–57.

66. This is a favorite theme of Congar, who develops it rather brilliantly in his *The Mystery of the Church* (London, 1960) 174–86. Elsewhere he points out the tendency of some Catholics to identify the work of the Holy Spirit too exclusively with the operation of ecclesiastical apparatus partly justified some of the reactions of the Protestant Reformers. But as Congar himself wisely cautions, we should not approve of the Protestant practice of making a law out of God's freedom in order to dissolve the very structure of His work; see *Vraie et fausse réforme*, p. 482.

67. H. Schlier, *Die Verkündigung im Gottesdienst der Kirche* (Cologne, 1953) 50–68.

68. *AAS* 35 (1943) 200; America Press transl. (New York, n.d.) n. 21.

69. J. B. Franzelin, S.J., *De ecclesia Christi* (Rome, 1887) 427. Cf. the condemned propositions of Quesnel, nos. 26–29 (*DS* 2426–29), and of the Synod of Pistoia, no. 22 (*DS* 2622).

70. T. A. Sartory, O.S.B., "Kirche und Kirchen," *Fragen der Theologie heute* (op. cit., note 13, above), 370.

71. Clement of Alexandria, for example, wrote: "Quoniam quemadmodum Judaeos Deus salvos esse voluit, dans eis prophetas, ita etiam Graecorum spectatissimo in propria sua lingua prophetas excitatos ... a vulgo secrevit"; *Stromata* 6, 5 (*PG* 9, 261B). St. Augustine likewise affirms: "Dubitandum non est, et gentes suos habere prophetas"; *Contra Faustum* 19, 2 (*PL* 42, 348).

72. Newman, *Discourses to Mixed Congregations* (London, 1897), 158.

73. Congar, "Some Reflections on the Schism of Israel in the Perspective of Christian Divisions." *Dialogue Between Christians* (Westminster, Md., 1966), 179. See Gregory Baum, O.S.A., *Progress and Perspectives* (New York, 1962), chap. 2.

74. K. Rahner, *The Dynamic Element in the Church* (New York, 1964) 63.

75. "Iam vero in pluribus Orbis partibus, quum ex variis externis eventibus et animarum mutationibus, tum maxime ex communibus fidelium orationibus, afflante quidem Spiritus Sancti gratia, in multorum animis ab Ecclesia Catholica dissidentium desiderium in dies excrevit ut ad unitatem omnium redeatur, qui in Christum Dominum credunt"; *AAS* 43 (1950) 142. Eng. transl. in B. Leeming, S.J., *The Churches and the Church* (Westminster, Md., 1960) 282.

76. As J. Colson puts it, such a prophet implicitly sins against the dogma of the Trinity, for he seeks to choose the Third Person in preference to the Second; see *Les fonctions ecclésiales aux deux premiers siècles* (Paris, 1956) 364. Ronald Knox's *Enthusiasm* (New York, 1950) gives a fascinating, but pitiful chronicle of deluded charismatics.

77. R. Villain, S.M. and J. de Baciocchi, S.M., *La vocation de l'église* (Paris, 1954), 222.

78. Bouyer, *The Spirit and Forms of Protestantism* (Westminster, Md., 1956), *passim*.

79. Congar, "Reflections on the Schism of Israel," p. 180.

80. *Op. cit.*, pp. 188–89. He mentions that Y. Brilioth, the Lutheran Archbishop of Uppsala, has himself noted this.

81. "De ordine ecclesiastico docent, quod nemo debeat in ecclesia publice docere aut sacramenta administrare nisi rite vocatus," Augsburg Confession, art. 14.

82. H. Kraemer, *A Theology of the Laity* (Philadelphia, 1958) 73.

83. *ASS* 29 (1896–97) 202 (*DS* 3319).

84. T. A. Sartory, O.S.B., *The Ecumenical Movement and the Unity of the Church* (Westminster, Md., 1963) 195.

85. *Ibid.*, pp. 196–98.

86. J. Gribomont, O.S.B., "Christenstand und Kirchlichkeit," *Una Sancta* 13 (1958) 176.

87. Scheeben makes an important distinction among three kinds of religious teaching: official, authentic, and authoritative. The Protestants, he points out, admit the first, but deny the second and third. See *op. cit.* note 24, above, 1, 44, nos. 68–69.

88. Melanchthon in his Apology for the Augsburg Confession states clearly "... Ministri funguntur vice Christi, non repraesentant suam personam, iuxta illud: Qui vos audit, me audit (Lc 10.16)"; art. 8 [*Die Bekenntnisschriften der Evangelisch-Lutherischen Kirche* (Göttingen, 1952) 246].

89. See C. Antoine, "Etats de vie," *DTC* 1, 905; also G. Jacquemet, "Etat de vie," *Catholicisme* 4, 538.

90. G. Jacquemet, "Grâces d'état," *Catholicisme* 5, 175.

91. *Sum. Theol.* 3, q.62, a.6 c. Significantly, St. Thomas does not confine this type of value to the Sacraments of the Old Law. He accords a similar value to ceremonies introduced prior to the Law by the private authority of individuals moved by a prophetic instinct; see *Sum. Theol.* 1–2, q.103, a.1 c.

92. J. Hastings, ed., *Encycl. of Religion and Ethics* (Edinburgh, 1917) 7, 545, *s.v.* "Ordination."

93. On the manna as a figure of the Eucharist, see *Sum. Theol.* 3, q.80, a. 1, ad. 3m.

94. For St. Thomas' doctrine on *votum sacramenti*, see *Sum. Theol.* 3. q.68, a. 2; q.73, a. 3; and q.80, a. 1. The Catechism of the Council of Trent spelled out the Catholic doctrine of Eucharistic communion in desire.

95. *Mystici corporis, AAS* 35 (1943) 243; *DS* 3822; *Suprema haec sacra, AER* 127 (1952) 307–15; *DS* 3869.

96. *Sum. theol.* 3, q.64, a.8, ad 2m.

97. Leo XIII declared that what constitutes the priesthood is "above all else, the power to consecrate and offer the true body and blood of the Lord in that sacrifice which is no mere commemoration of the sacrifice accomplished on the cross"; *Apostolicae curae, AAS* 29 (1896–97) 201 (*DS* 3316).

98. F. Thijssen, "Bezinning op Hans Asmussens vragen," *Het Schild* 36 (1959) 68.

99. The term "quasi-sacramental" was used by Newman in his discussion of the value of the Anglican Eucharist, *Difficulties of Anglicans* 1 (London, 1888) lect. 3, p. 88. In the same connection Fr. Rickaby pointed out that many Anglicans made "spiritual Confessions and spiritual Communions, Confessions and Communions of desire, but not sacramental. The Anglican gets more, because he desires more; and he desires more, because he believes more of the mystery"; J. Rickaby, S.J., "Dr. Pusey's Letters," *Month* 93 (1899) 170. By the same principle we may assert that the Protestant who believes more of the mystery of the apostolic ministry normally receives greater graces on the occasion of his ordination, even though his faith be accompanied by an error about the capacity of the ordaining prelate to confer that ministry.

100. Along these lines see the original and stimulating approach to Protestant ministries in F. J. van Beeck, S.J., "Towards an

Ecumenical Understanding of the Sacraments," *Journal of Ecumenical Studies* 3.1 (Winter 1966) 57–112.

101. Asmussen, "Das Kirchliche Amt in unserer Generation," in *Die Katholizität der Kirche*, p. 283.

102. Thijssen, *art. cit.*, p. 67.

103. Newman's handling of this question as an Anglican may be found in his sermon "The Fellowship of the Apostles," *Parochial and Plain Sermons* 6 (London, 1882), 190–205. In Lecture 3 of *Difficulties of Anglicans* 1, 80–95, he returns to this question from a Catholic point of view. As if replying to Asmussen, he admonishes the Anglicans (p. 95): " . . . you have presumed to pronounce it blasphemy against the Holy Ghost to doubt that they [scil., your pious thoughts, etc.] came into your hearts by means of your Church and by virtue of its ordinances. Learn, my dear brethren, a more sober, a more cautious line of thought. . . ."

8. The Orthodox Churches and the Ecumenical Movement

1. See G. Baum, O.S.A., "The Catholic Church and the W.C.C." in G. Baum, ed., *Ecumenical Theology Today* (New York, 1964), 121–30; E. Lamirande, O.M.I., "Could the Roman Catholic Church Become a Member of the World Council of Churches?" *Revue de L'Univérsité d'Ottawa* 35 (1965) 209*–236*.

2. These two schools are contrasted by G. Florovsky, "The Doctrine of the Church and the Ecumenical Problem," *Ecumenical Review* 2 (1949–50) 152–61.

3. Cited in the collection of documents, "Les Eglises Orthodoxes et le Mouvement Oecuménique," *Istina* 2 (1955) 78–83, 180–214; quotation from p. 81.

4. Text in *Istina, art. cit.* pp. 83–91; quotation from p. 86.

5. G. Florovsky, "The Orthodox Churches and the Ecumenical Movement Prior to 1910," chapter IV of Ruth Rouse and S. C. Neill, *A History of the Ecumenical Movement* (Philadelphia, 1954) 214.

6. These circumstances are detailed by M.-J. Le Guillou, O.P., "L'Église Orthodoxe et le Mouvement Oecuménique," *Istina* 2 (1955) 57, note 14.

7. Quoted by L. Zander, "The Ecumenical Movement and the Orthodox Church," *Ecumenical Review* 1 (1948–49) 270.

8. See text given in *Istina* 2 (1955) 97–98.

9. T. Tatlow, "The World Conference on Faith and Order," Rouse and Neill, *op. cit.*, p. 418.

10. Text in *Istina* 2 (1955) 97–98.

11. Tatlow, *loc. cit.*

12. Le Guillou, *art. cit.*, pp. 58–59.

13. Text in H. N. Bate, ed., *Faith and Order*: Proceedings of the World Conference, Lausanne, Aug. 3–21, 1927 (Garden City, 1928) 18–23.

14. On the work of Velimirovic and Bulgakov at this Conference, see N. Zernov, "The Eastern Churches and the Ecumenical Movement in the Twentieth Century," Rouse and Neill, *op. cit.*, pp. 654–57.

15. Text in H. N. Bate, *Faith and Order* (cited note 13 above), 382–86; quotation is from pp. 383–85.

16. Text in L. Hodgson, ed., *The Second World Conference on Faith and Order* (New York, 1938), 154–58.

17. Le Guillou, *art. cit.*, p. 60.

18. *Ibid.*, p. 61.

19. Zernov, *op. cit.*, p. 658.

20. Text in *Istina* 2 (1955) 184f.

21. Le Guillou, *art. cit.*, p. 72.

22. From the Resolution on the question, "The Ecumenical Movement and the Orthodox Church" at the Moscow Conference of July 8–18, 1948, as quoted in the *Istina* collection of documents (note 3 above), p. 186.

23. L. Zander, *art. cit.*, p. 268.

24. *Ibid.*, p. 267.

25. *Ibid.*, pp. 267–68.

26. Orthodox reactions to Amsterdam are described by P. Dumont, "L'Assemblée d'Amsterdam et l'Orthodoxie grecque," *Irénikon* 23 (1950) 88–96.

27. Text in W. A. Visser 't Hooft, ed., *The First Assembly of the World Council of Churches* (New York, 1949) 220 (the official report).

28. Dumont, *loc. cit.*

29. Text in *Ecumenical Review* 5 (1953) 167–69.

30. Le Guillou, *art. cit.*, p. 67.

31. Text in O. S. Tomkins, ed., *The Third World Conference on Faith and Order* (London, 1953) 123–26; quotation from p. 125.

32. For statistics see *St. Vladimir's Seminary Quarterly* 3 (1954–55), 22f.

33. Text in *St. Vladimir's Seminary Quarterly* 3 (1954–55), 31-36.

34. Texts in *The Evanston Report* (New York, 1955), 92–95, 329–31.

35. Issue of Sept. 22, 1954, as quoted in *St. Vladimir's Seminary Quarterly* 3 (1954–55), 31–36.

36. *Ibid.*, p. 54.

37. *Ibid.*, pp. 58–60.

38. Article in *Anaplassis* (Feb. 1955) as quoted in *Istina* collection of documents (note 3 supra), p. 202.

39. Texts in *Ecumenical Review* 14 (1962) 232–34.

40. Printed in *Ecumenical Review* 14 (1962) 192–202.

41. See W. A. Visser 't Hooft, ed., *The New Delhi Report* (London, 1962) 152.

42. *Ibid.*, p. 37.

43. *Ibid.*, p. 67.

44. "Report on New Delhi," *Christianity Today* 6 (Dec. 22, 1961), 269.

45. *Oekumenische Probleme in der Neugriechischen Theologie* (Leiden, 1964) 91. Chapters 4 and 5 of this work give an excellent brief survey of the developments since Evanston.

9. The Ecumenical Perspection of Popes John and Paul

1. "Ecclesia Catholica," *AAS* 42 (1950) 142–47. Eng. trans. in B. Leeming, S.J., *The Churches and the Church* (Westminster, Md., 1960), 282–87.

2. Christmas message, 1958; *AAS* 51 (1959) 10; Eng. trans., *The Pope Speaks* 5 (1958–59) 131.

3. Pope John XXIII, Address to officials of Pontifical Missionary Societies, *Osservatore Romano*, May 11, 1960, p. 1.

4. Encyclical *Ad Petri Cathedram*, June 29, 1959; *AAS* 51 (1959) 515–16; Eng. trans. in T. Cranny, S.A., ed., *Pope John and Christian Unity* (Garrison, N.Y. 1963) 45. The reference is to St. Augustine on Psalm 32, *Enarr.* II, 29; Migne, *P. L.* 36:229.

5. *Ad Petri Cathedram, loc. cit.*

6. As quoted in *Herder-Korrespondenz* 13 (1958–59) 274–75.

7. Eng. trans. in T. Cranny, *op. cit.*, p. 50.

8. See *Herder-Korrespondenz* 14 (1959–60) 8–9; quoted in H. Küng, *The Council, Reform, and Reunion* (New York, 1961) 6–7.

9. Quoted by B. Leeming, S.J., article, "Interchurch Relations," *America* 104 (Jan. 14, 1961) 465.

10. J.-B. Montini, Eulogy of John XXIII, *Documentation Catholique* 60 (1963) col. 849.

11. See *The Pope Speaks* 9 (1963–64), 9.

12. *Loc. cit.*

13. Address to Council of Sept. 29, 1963; Eng. trans. in T. Cranny, S.A., ed., *Pope Paul and Christian Unity* 1 (Garrison, N.Y. 1964), p. 27.

14. Original French text in *Osservatore Romano*, Oct. 19, 1963; Eng. trans. in T. Cranny, *Pope Paul* (*op. cit.*), pp. 32–35.

15. Address of Sept. 29, 1963; see Cranny, *op. cit.*, p. 19.

16. Address to Observers of Oct. 17, 1963; *ibid.*, p. 32.

17. Address at Bethlehem, Jan. 6, 1964; *ibid.*, p. 60.

18. Address of Sept. 29, 1963; *ibid.*, p. 26.

19. Address of Jan. 6, 1964; *ibid.*, p. 62.

20. Address of Sept. 29, 1963; *ibid.*, p. 21.

21. *Ibid.*, p. 22

22. *Ibid.*, p. 19.

23. *Ibid.*, p. 78.

24. L. J. Suenens, *The Gospel to Every Creature* (Westminster, Md., 1963), preface, p. vii.

25. Athenagoras, *Documentation Catholique* 61 (1964) col. 193f., note 4.

26. Pope Paul VI, *Osservatore Romano*, Jan. 18, 1964; Eng. trans., *The Pope Speaks* 9 (1963–64) 289.

27. See T. Cranny, *op. cit.*, p. 21.

28. A. Wenger, A. A., in *La Croix*, Jan. 16, 1964; quoted in *Documentation Catholique* 61 (1964), col. 193.

10. Ecumenical Dialogue and Apostolic Renewal

1. The Dogmatic Constitution on the Church, *Lumen gentium*, n. 17.

2. *Loc. cit.*

3. *Ibid.*, n. 15.

4. Reuel Howe, *The Miracle of Dialogue* (New York, 1963) 50.

5. *Ibid.*, pp. 49 f.

6. Yves Congar, O.P., "Progress of the Ecumenical Dialogue," *Theology Digest* 11 (1963) 68; condensed from his article, "Les étapes du dialogue oecuménique," *Evangéliser* 16 (1962) 345–61. My own analysis of the varieties of dialogue has been strongly influenced by this article.

7. Gregory Baum, O.S.A., *Progress and Perspectives* (New York, 1962) 182.

8. In Lukas Vischer, ed., *A Documentary History of the Faith and Order Movement* (St. Louis, 1963) 27.

9. See Gustave Thils, *La théologie oecuménique* (Louvain, 1960), 20.

10. Vischer, *op. cit.*, p. 85.

11. *Ibid.*, p. 77.

12. *The Evanston Report* (New York, 1955) 32.

13. Quotations will be from the translation in W. M. Abbott, *op. cit.*, with minor modifications.

14. Decree on Ecumenism, n. 10.

15. *Ibid.*, n. 4.

16. *Loc. cit.*

17. *Ibid.*, n. 9.

18. *Ibid.*, n. 4, n. 9.

19. *Ibid.*, n. 11.

20. *Ibid.*, n.3, n. 4.

21. *Ibid.*, n. 11.

22. *Ibid.*, n. 4.

23. *Ibid.*, n. 11.

24. *Ibid.*, n. 9.

25. *Ibid.*, n. 6.

26. *Constitution on the Church, op. cit.*, n. 8.

27. *Decree on Ecumenism*, n. 6.

28. *Loc. cit.*

29. *Ibid.*, n. 15.

30. *Ibid.*, n. 17.

31. *Loc. cit.*

32. *Ibid.*, n. 4.

33. *Ibid.*, n. 3.
34. *Ibid.*, n. 4.
35. *Loc. cit.*
36. *Ibid.*, n. 7.
37. *Ibid.*, n. 6.
38. *Ibid.*, n. 8.
39. *Ibid.*, n. 4.
40. *Constitution on the Church, op. cit.*, n. 14.
41. *Decree on Ecumenism, op. cit.*, n. 18.
42. *Ibid.*, n. 24.
43. *Loc. cit.*
44. *Ibid.*, n. 4.
45. George Tavard, *The Church Tomorrow* (New York, 1965) 190.
46. *Decree on Ecumenism, op. cit.*, n. 7.
47. *Ibid.*, n. 4.
48. *Loc. cit.*
49. *Ibid.*, n. 1.
50. *Ibid.*, n. 4.
51. *Ibid.*, n. 12.
52. *Constitution on the Church, op. cit.*, n. 17.
53. *Decree on Ecumenism, op. cit.*, n. 3.
54. Howe, *op. cit.*, p. 79.
55. Yves Congar in R. C. Mackie and C. C. West, eds., *The Sufficiency of God* (London, 1963) 83.

11. Paul Tillich and the Bible.

1. A. T. Mollegen, "Christology and Biblical Criticism in Tillich," C. W. Kegley and R. W. Bretall, eds., *The Theology of Paul Tillich* (New York, 1952) 230.

2. See notably G. *H. Tavard, *Paul Tillich and the Christian Message* (New York, 1962) and the articles collected in T. A. O'Meara, O.P., and C. D. Weisser, O.P., *Paul Tillich in Catholic Thought* (Dubuque, 1964), C. J. Armbruster, S.J., *The Vision of Paul Tillich* (New York, 1967) appeared too late for use in this essay.

3. See the chapter on "The Meaning of Revelation" in Tillich's *Systematic Theology* 1 (Chicago, 1951) 106–31.

4. *Ibid.*, p. 110.

5. See the chapter on "Actual Revelation," *ibid.*, pp. 132–47.

6. *Ibid.*, p. 35; see pp. 114–15.

7. *Ibid.*, pp. 124–29, 145.

8. On the question of symbolic assertions about God, see *ibid.*, esp. pp. 238–44.

9. See Tillich's article, "The Present Theological Situation," *Theology Today* 6 (1949–50), 306.

10. See Tillich's *Biblical Religion and the Search for Ultimate Reality* (Chicago, 1955), 1–5.

11. Tillich, *Systematic Theology* 1, 240.

12. Quoted by R. Niebuhr, "Biblical Thought and Ontological Speculation in Tillich's Theology," Kegley and Bretall, *op. cit.*, p. 221.

13. Tillich, *Systematic Theology* 1, 259.

14. Niebuhr, *art. cit.*, p. 218.

15. *Ibid.*, p. 220.

16. *Ibid.*, pp. 225–26.

17. Tillich, "The Present Theological Situation," p. 307.

18. Tillich, "A Reinterpretation of the Doctrine of the Incarnation," *Church Quarterly Review* 147 (1948–49) 145.

19. Tillich, *Systematic Theology* 1, 130.

20. T. A. Mollegen, "Christology and Biblical Criticism in Tillich," in Kegley and Bretall, *op. cit.*, p. 233.

21. Tillich, "A Reinterpretation," pp. 145–46.

22. Tillich, *Systematic Theology* 1, 136–37.

23. Tillich, "The Present Theological Situation," pp. 306–07.

24. Tillich, *Systematic Theology* 1, 36.

25. *Ibid.*, p. 158.

26. *Ibid.*, p. 130; see pp. 3,36.

27. *Ibid.*, p. 117.

28. Mollegen, *op. cit.*, p. 237.

29. Tillich, *Biblical Religion*, pp. 21–22.

30. Tillich, "A Reinterpretation," p. 135. Cf. Phil 2:5ff.

31. Tillich, *Systematic Theology* 1, 136. Cf. Jn 12:44.

32. *Ibid.*, p. 115. See p. 15.

33. *Ibid.*, p. 37.

34. *Ibid.*, p. 52.

35. *Ibid.*, pp. 3, 52.

36. *Ibid.*, pp. 34–35.

37. *Ibid.*, p. 47.

38. *Ibid.*, p. 50.

39. *Ibid.*, p. 48.

40. *Ibid.*, p. 37.

41. *Ibid.*, pp. 50–52.

42. *Ibid.*, pp. 48–50.

43. *Ibid.*, p. 36.

44. *Ibid.*, p. 49.

45. A. T. Mollegen, *art. cit.*, p. 237.

46. Tillich, *Biblical Religion*, p. 60.

47. Tillich, *Systematic Theology* 1, p. 21.

48. Tillich, *Biblical Religion*, p. 85.

49. Nels F. S. Ferré, review of *Biblical Religion*, in *Christian Century* 72 (1955) 1273.

50. "The Ontology of Paul Tillich," Kegley and Bretall, *op. cit.*, p. 149.

51. *Ibid.*, p. 341.

52. In letter to G. Weigel, S.J., *Gregorianum* 37 (1956) 53–54; reprinted in *Paul Tillich in Catholic Theology* (*op. cit.*), p. 23.

53. Tillich, *Systematic Theology* 1, p. 115.

54. G. Ernest Wright, "The Faith of Israel," *The Interpreter's Bible* 1 (Nashville, 1952) 366.

55. This point of view is well expressed by H. Bouillard, S.J., "The Christian Idea of the Miraculous," in P. Flood, O.S.B. ed., *New Problems in Medical Ethics* 1 (Westminster, Md., 1953), pp. 247–59. See also L. Monden, S.J., *Signs and Wonders* (New York, 1966), pp. 54–57, 347.

56. *Summa Theol.*, 2–2, q. 174, a. 2, ad 3m. The Thomistic doctrine of scriptural inspiration is admirably expounded in P. Synave, O.P. and P. Benoit, O.P., *Prophecy and Inspiration* (New York, 1961).

57. Tillich, *Systematic Theology* 1, p. 130. See supra, p. 229.

58. "Epistemology and the Idea of Revelation," Kegley and Bretall, *op. cit.*, p. 213. Tillich's fuller treatment of the problem of the "historical Jesus," in Volume 2 of *Systematic Theology* written since these remarks were first published, shows no real change or clarification of his basic position, and is justly criticized by B. J. R. Cameron, "The Historical Problem in Paul Tillich's Christology," *Scottish Journal of Theology* 18 (1965) 257–72. See below, chapter 12, p. 252.

59. O. Cullmann, *Christ and Time* (Philadelphia, 1950) 27, n. 10.

60. See G. Tavard, *Paul Tillich and the Christian Message* (*op. cit.*) p. 25.

61. The Councils, in their authoritative interpretations of sacred texts, frequently invoke the witness of Catholic tradition, using expressions such as, "quemadmodum Ecclesia catholica ubique diffusa semper intellexit," or some equivalent. For examples, see Denzinger-Schönmetzer, nn. 223, 1514, 1740, 3054. On the role of tradition as a hermeneutical principle see the Vatican II Constitution on Divine Revelation, nn. 9–10.

62. G. Weigel, "The Theological Significance of Paul Tillich," *Gregorianum* 37 (1956) 50; reprinted in *Paul Tillich in Catholic Thought* (*op. cit.*), p. 19.

63. The transfiguration of Platonic and Aristotelian philosophy under the impact of the Judaeo-Christian revelation has been brilliantly sketched by E. Gilson in *The Spirit of Mediaeval Philosophy* (New York, 1936), especially the last two chapters. I have indicated my own views on the relationship between biblical and systematic theology in a contribution to J. P. Hyatt, ed., *The Bible in Modern Scholarship* (Nashville, 1966) 210–16.

64. See Kenneth Hamilton, *The System and the Gospel* (London, 1963).

12. Jesus as the Christ

1. A full and discerning treatment of current German and Anglo-American positions may be found in Hugh Anderson, *Jesus and Christian Origins* (New York, 1964). The history of the discussion is ably surveyed in Alan Richardson, *History Sacred and Profane* (Philadelphia, 1964) and Stephen Neill, *The Interpretation of the New Testament* (*1861–1961*) (London, 1964). For recent Catholic points of view one may consult the articles by B. Rigaux and F. Mussner summarized in *Theology Digest 9* (Winter, 1961), 26–32 and *Theology Digest 12* (Spring, 1964) 21–26. See also J. Burke, O.P., "The Historical Jesus and the Kerygmatic Christ," *Concilium* 11 (Glen Rock, N.J., 1966), 27–46.

2. H. Ristow and K. Matthiae, eds., *Der historiche Jesus und der kerygmatische Christus* (Berlin, 2d ed., 1961).

3. English text with commentary by J. A. Fitzmyer, S.J. in Paulist Press pamphlet (Glen Rock, N.J., 1965). The Vatican II Constitution on Revelation, n. 19, does little more than summarize this historic document.

4. S. V. McCasland, "Christ Jesus," *Journal of Biblical Literature* 65 (1946) 377–83, holds that the two formulas have virtually the same meaning. L. Cerfaux, however, finds a difference of emphasis: see *Christ in the Theology of St. Paul* (New York, 1959) 508.

5. H. J. Holtzmann, *Die svnoptischen Fvangelien, ihr Ursprung und geschichtlicher Charakter* (Leipzig, 1863), p. 1, quoted by Heinz Zahrnt, *The Historical Jesus* (London, 1963) 44.

6. George Tyrrell, *Christianity at the Crossroads*; reset edition with a foreword by A. R. Vidler (London, 1963) 49.

7. *The Quest of the Historical Jesus* (New York, paperback ed., 1961), 4.

8. *Ibid.*, p. 3.

9. *Der sogenannte historische Jesus und der geschichtliche, biblische Christus* (Munich, 1956). Eng. trans. by Carl E. Braaten, *The So-called Historical Jesus and the Historic, Biblical Christ* (Philadelphia, 1964).

10. R. Bultmann, *Jesus and the Word* (New York, 1934). For a salutary caution against exaggerating the negative import of the words just quoted see James M. Robinson, *A New Quest of the Historical Jesus* (London, and Naperville, Ill., 1959) 65, note 4.

11. Bultmann applies this principle to the historical question of Jesus' messianic consciousness in his *Theology of the New Testament* 1 (New York, 1951), 26.

12. See "The Primitive Christian Kerygma and the Historical Jesus" in C. E. Braaten and R. A. Harrisville, eds., *The Historical Jesus and the Kerygmatic Christ: Essays on the New Quest of the Historical Jesus* (Nashville, 1964), 15–42.

13. See Tillich, *Systematic Theology* 1 (Chicago, 1951) 130. A fuller discussion of the whole problem of Jesus and history is given *ibid.*, II (Chicago 1957) 97–117.

14. Joachim Jeremias, "The Present Position in the Controversy Concerning the Problem of the Historical Jesus," *Expository Times* 69 (1958) 333–39. See Jeremias' *The Problem of the Historical Jesus* (Philadelphia, 1964).

15. *Art. cit.*, p. 338.

16. Ethelbert Stauffer, *Jesus and His Story* (London, 1960) 12.

17. See R.. Schnackenburg's review in *Biblische Zeitschrift*, n. F. 1 (1957) 313–15.

18. T. W. Manson, "The Life of Jesus: Some Tendencies in Present-Day Research," in *The Background of the New Testament and its Eschatology* (Cambridge, 1956) 211–21.

19. V. Taylor, *The Life and Ministry of Jesus* (London, 1954) p. 33.

20. *Ibid.*, p. 183.

21. *Ibid.*, p. 37.

22. K. Barth, *Church Dogmatics III/2* (Edinburgh, 1960) p. 446. For Bultmann's reply see his *Essays: Philosophical and Theological* (New York, 1955) 260 f.

23. O. Cullmann, *Christ and Time* (Philadelphia, 1950) 31f. Bultmann's review is reprinted in his *Existence and Faith* (New York, 1960), pp. 226–40. Cullmann continues his polemic against Bultmann in *Salvation in History* (New York, 1967).

24. C. H. Dodd, *The Apostolic Preaching and its Developments* (London, 1936), chapter 1.

25. C. H. Dodd, *History and the Gospel* (London, 1938) 37.

26. Gregory Dix, *Jew and Greek* (Westminster, Eng, 1953) 5.

27. Ernst Kinder, "Historical Criticism and Demythologizing," in C. E. Braaten and R. A. Harrisville, (eds.), *Kerygma and History* (Nashville 1962) 119.

28. Althaus, *The So-Called Kerygma and the Historical Jesus* (London 1959), esp. pp. 46–9. The American edition of this book is entitled *Fact and Faith in the Kerygma of Today* (Philadelphia, 1960).

29. Harald Riesenfeld, *The Gospel Tradition and Its Beginnings* (London, 1957) 27f.

30. Birger Gerhardsson, *Memory and Manuscript: Oral Tradition and Written Transmission in Rabbinic Judaism and Early Christianity* (Lund, 1961). For a careful summary and evaluation by J. A. Fitzmyer, S.J., see *Theological Studies* 23 (1962), 442–57. Some "difficulties and obscurities" in the Riesenfeld–Gerhardsson thesis are pointed out by W. D. Davies in "Reflections on a Scandinavian Approach to 'The Gospel Tradition'" in *Neo-Testamentica et Patristica* (Suppl. to *Novum Testamentum, 6*) (Leiden, 1962) 14–34.

31. See above, note 9. The post-Bultmannian approach is enthusiastically presented by H. Zahrnt (*op. cit.*, note 4 above) and critically appraised by H. Anderson (*op. cit.*, note 1 above). Balanced appraisals of this school, by R. E. Brown and P. J. Cahill respectively, may be found in *The Catholic Biblical Quarterly* 26 (1964), 1–30 and 153–78.

32. Bornkamm, *Jesus of Nazareth* (New York, 1961) 169f.

33. *Ibid.*, p. 26.

34. *Op. cit.*, p. 92.

35. See Bultmann, "The Primitive Christian Kerygma and the Historical Jesus" cited *supra*, note 12.

36. Bultmann, in *Der historische Jesus....* (cited above, note 2), p. 235.

37. In the light of this broader concept of history our conclusion harmonizes with that of Barth, who speaks of the "simple exegetico-dogmatic fact that the real historical Christ is no other than the biblical Christ attested by the New Testament passages, i.e. the incarnate Word, the risen and exalted One, God manifest in His redeeming action as He is the object of His disciples' faith." *Church Dogmatics* I/2 (Edinburgh, 1956), pp. 64f.

13. The Death of God Theologies

1. Paul M. van Buren, *The Secular Meaning of the Gospel* (New York, paperback, 1966) 141.

2. William Hamilton, *The New Essence of Christianity* (New York, 1961) 65.

3. Among the many useful guides to the movement published so far, special mention may be made of T. W. Ogletree, *The Death of God Controversy* (Nashville, 1966). Further references, with evaluations, are given in my review article, "Some Recent Death-of-God Literature," *Theological Studies* 28 (1967) 111–18.

4. D. Bonhoeffer, *Letters and Papers from Prison* (New York, paperback, 1962) 218 f.

5. See J. A. T. Robinson, "Can a Truly Contemporary Person *Not* Be an Atheist?", an appendix in his *The New Reformation?* (Philadelphia, 1965) 112.

6. *Op. cit.*, p. 147.

7. W. Hamilton, "The Death of God," *Playboy* (August 1966), 139.

8. J. J. Altizer, *The Gospel of Christian Atheism* (Philadelphia, 1966) p. 69.

9. This passage, used with Hamilton's permission, is taken from his personal correspondence with the author and repeats, in substance, what he previously wrote in reply to Dean Pike.in the correspondence columns of *Playboy* (November 1966) 12.

10. For an excellent development of this thought see Karl Rahner, S.J., "Science as a 'Confession'?" in *Theological Investigations* 3 (Baltimore, 1967) 385–400.

11. See the remarks to this effect with which Leslie Dewart concludes his stimulating work, *The Future of Belief* (New York, 1966) 214–15.

12. In addition to Rahner's article already cited, one may read on this point Michael Novak, *Belief and Unbelief* (New York, 1966).

13. *Op. cit.*, p. 189.

14. Langdon Gilkey, *Shantung Compound* (New York, 1966), 242.

15. Quoted by Gabriel Vahanian, *No Other God* (New York, 1966) 29. The same quotation provided the title for the valuable little book of Y. Congar, O.P., *Si vous êtes mes témoins* (Paris, 1959).

INDEX

Adam, K., on communal character of faith, 105

Adrian VI, Pope, 111

Albert the Great, St., 129

Alivisatos, H. S., Athens Conference, 174–175; Orthodox program at Faith and Order Conference, 170

Althaus, P., on biblical accounts of Jesus, 138; Bultmann, criticism of, 257–258

Altizer, T. J. J., Christian atheism, 272–273, 274; death of God theology, 267–268; on joyous Christians, 280

Amsterdam Meeting (1948), see World Council of Churches— Amsterdam meeting (1948)

Analogy of being, 62

Anastasius, Metropolitan of Russian Church in Emigration, 175

Anglican Church, episcopal collegiality and reunion, 199; "Ordination of desire," 160; reunion efforts, 167; validity of orders, 155; validity of preaching in, 136

Anglicans, rule of faith, 118; share in Catholicity, 124

Apostles, graces for preaching task, 131; recipients of revelation, 52

Apostolate, types of Catholic, 215–216; see also Laity, Apostolate of, Non-Catholic Christianity; Witness bearing (Christianity)

Apostolic succession, 133

Apostolicae Curae (bull, Leo XIII), on Anglican orders, 155

Asmussen, H., on Protestant ministry, 147, 162; on Protestant preaching, 137–138

Atheism, positive aspects of, 277–278; scientific progress and, 272

Atheism, Christian, background of the phenomenon, 268–269; explanation, 273; objection to, 274; validity of, 281

Athenagoras, Metropolitan of Thyateira, Lund Conference, 178–179; New Delhi W.C.C. Assembly, 184

Athenagoras I, Patriarch of Constantinople, New Delhi Assembly, 182; Paul VI at Jerusalem with, 200–201

Athens Conference (1936) of Pan-Orthodox Theologians, see Pan-Orthodox Conferences

313